THE TOWER PRINCESS

THE TOWER PRINCESS

A FAIRY TALE LIVED

Michelle Tocher

Illustrations by Richard Row

The Tower Princess: A Fairy Tale Lived

Copyright © 2005, 2021 by Michelle Tocher

All rights reserved. No part of this book may be reproduced in any form without permission in writing from the author.

ISBN 978-0-9738776-0-1

WonderLit Press, 2021, Toronto, Canada

Michelle Tocher
www.wonderlit.com
www.michelletocher.com

Design by Jennifer Stimson with original cover design by Sabrina Gardiner-Michaud

"I understood from my own experiences that they (dreams) were not escapes from reality at all but deeper voyages into the heart of life. Paradoxically, dreams and folktales pointed me towards waking up rather than staying asleep."

Kay Stone, The Golden Woman

"Far from being escapist ... folk and fairy tales are means of coming to terms with the world as it is—of confronting reality, not running away from it ..."

Donald Baker, Functions of Folk and Fairy Tales

INTRODUCTION

No doubt you have heard it said that an overly wishful, dreamy sort of person is "living in a fairy tale." In the western world, fairy tales have become confused with wishful thinking and fantasizing, and that is what I thought about them too until, in my mid-twenties, I heard my first fairy tale told by an Irish bard named Alice Kane.

I had come to an event in Toronto called 1,001 Friday Nights of Storytelling, and the year was 1981. I was 25 and I had set out to write a freelance article for *The Globe and Mail* on the renaissance of oral storytelling.

As I listened to Alice's melodious voice I had the impression that she was a water woman, bringing water to the desert of the world. The cadence of her spoken words and the images they invoked, gave me an entry into a bright world just on the other side of this one. From that place inspirations flow. Comfort flows. Understanding flows. She was greening the wasteland.

The Tower Princess records a time when, nearly two decades later, I turned to fairy tales for help. It was the year 2000. I had been living with chronic pain for seven years and could find no diagnosis or treatment. I had started to slip into a dangerous depression and all the griefs of the past were roaring up from underground.

By then, I had run a communications company for ten years. I had learned how to tell stories and had been an active performer on the Friday Nights and in festivals. I had read most of Joseph Campbell's books and I had been deeply nourished by the writings of P.L. Travers, Marie Louise-von Franz, and many Jungians and psychologists with an interest in myth and fairy tales. I had developed a great love for fairy tales. I was fascinated by the way they expressed the human struggle with loss, pain, family violence and exile. They spoke in pictures, in "the forgotten language of myth," as Erich Fromm called it.

I felt privileged to take my listeners to a land where spells are made and broken, where animals speak, and nature is intelligently involved in one's destiny.

My chronic pain began in 1993 when I injured my back, and over the decade it engulfed me like the thorn hedge in *Sleeping Beauty*. I couldn't sit or stand for more than a few minutes without needing to lie down. I had to shutter my communications business, and cancel my travel plans and speaking engagements. I struggled mightily against the forces of pain, while at the same time I felt an inward pull into the depths. Intuitively I felt drawn to the wisdom of the fairy tales I'd been telling, but I didn't know how to access that wisdom.

Then one day I came upon a passage by P.L. Travers, author of *Mary Poppins*. She had written a collection of essays under the title, *What the Bee Knows*, and in one of those essays she wrote:

"We go to the myths not so much for what they can mean as for our own meaning. Who am I? Why am I here? How can I live in accordance with reality? The myths never have a single meaning, once and for all finished. They have something greater; they have meaning itself. If you hang a crystal sphere in the window it will give off light from all parts of itself. That is how the myths are; they have meaning for me, for you and for everyone else. A true symbol always has this multisidedness. It has something to say to all who approach it."

By suggesting that we look for our *own* meaning in the fairy tale, Travers gave me a key to unlocking the meaning of the stories. I didn't have to come up with a universal interpretation of the fairy tale in order to appreciate its wisdom. All I had to do was to go into a single story, think of it as a country, and head for the scenes that were meaningful to *me*.

One of the most important things I have learned from the wise teachers in the Toronto storytelling community (Alice Kane, Lynda Howes, Joan Bodger, Celia Lottridge and Marylyn Peringer) was to respect traditional stories. Those who teach through Storytelling Toronto share a reverence for the old narratives that had been passed down orally for generations. They advise young storytellers not to change the lines of the tales but to embrace them, warts and all.

I decided that I would practice that respect and, at the same time, I would move in between the lines and look around with my own eyes. I would trust my imagination to give me pictures that were meaningful, just as my dreams did.

I had to get myself oriented, of course. Fairyland is a large country, filling volumes with tales from all over the world. I decided to confine my explorations to the Grimms' collection. I had told many of the stories and felt powerfully connected to certain characters, especially women and girls who had been exiled or were trapped in prison towers. By some combination of love and magic, these servants, orphans, goose girls, and lonely princesses were able to make beauty out of the raw materials of their fate. Maybe they could show me how to spin some gold of my own.

I was interested most of all in the figure of the princess. It seemed to me that of all the characters in the fairy tale, she had been the most misunderstood in our culture. All we need to do is think of what we imagine when we call someone "a princess." Like the fairy tale itself, the princess has been maligned and misapprehended. We think a princess is an indulged, whiny girl-child, but in these symbolic stories she spoke to me of the noble feminine heart.

I wanted to know what it meant to be a "true princess" and, to do so, I soon realized that I would need to meet her on her own ground. I felt her stories would have something precious to show us about a noble feminine part of ourselves that had been banished or lost. On a personal level, I wanted to contact her character as a source of strength in meeting the real possibility that I might be confined and in pain for the rest of my life.

I had kept a dream journal for years and I had always recorded my dreams side by side with my daily experiences. I decided to treat my interior venture in the same way. I would faithfully report my important encounters in the land of faerie, while also reporting the concurrent events of my outer life.

I had many strange experiences when I stepped into the country of the fairy tale. Things happened that I did not expect, and at times they dramatically challenged me to separate reality from fantasy. I eventually found my way into the story of Rapunzel, and received from her some profound insights that made it possible for me to meet my reality on its own terms.

I also learned how to navigate the fairy tale, and my experiences laid the foundation for a life's work with mythic stories. I discovered a way to use imagination intentionally as an instrument of knowing. A fairy tale that holds your fascination can become a stunning mirror for the soul and a source of collective revelation. We all know what it's like to be shelved like the steadfast tin soldier, abandoned in the woods like Hansel and Gretel, or robbed of our identity like Cinderella. The characters in the stories are aspects of our own selves, and if we go and meet them on their own ground, they can show us something important. I know this to be true because I have since worked with many groups and individuals who have stepped into fairy tales and found their own revelations. As they wend their way to a happy or hopeful outcome, the stories give us a thread to follow when we're lost in the woods. I was certainly lost when I came to the edge of the forest and, to this day, the light that I received from the fairy tale shimmers in the atmosphere. It gives me a universal kind of faith, a belief in the magic and purpose that are knit into every ordinary day.

CONTENTS

Introduction vii

Chapter One—The Fall of the Princess 11

Chapter Two—The Dark Side of the Moon 23

Chapter Three—The Big Shock 41

Chapter Four—Breaking Spells 53

Chapter Five—Nowhere 63

Chapter Six—The Tower Princess 77

Chapter Seven—Help from the Fairies 87

Chapter Eight—The Fishwife 99

Chapter Nine—Gothel's Garden 113

Chapter Ten—Raising Rapunzel 125

Chapter Eleven—The Tower 145

Chapter Twelve—The Window 159

Chapter Thirteen—Gothel's Problem 171

Chapter Fourteen—Deliverance 183

Chapter Fifteen—In Hiding 199

Chapter Sixteen—Lightning Strikes 211

Chapter Seventeen—At the World's End 223

Chapter Eighteen—The Dark Gift 241

Chapter Nineteen—The Rise of the Princess 265

Chapter Twenty—Settlement 287

Epilogue 299

Acknowledgments 302

About the Author 303

CHAPTER ONE

THE FALL OF THE PRINCESS

It All Began with Fairy Tales

I can't imagine a world without fairy tales. They have always been a source of warmth and light. They invoke a time when the pleasures of life were simple, when the wind howled outside, but it was warm by the fire and a great old aunt sat in the rocking chair, knitting and spinning a tale that had the whole room spellbound. I am attracted to the people who can go into other worlds; they seem to be so much more able to live in this one. Every time I have ventured into a fairy tale, I have come back with a new perspective on life.

During the winter of 1999, I spent hours reading fairy tales. I had been unwell for a few years, and I had looked to the tales as a source of wisdom and comfort. I wandered through enchanted forests, sat by magic springs, explored castles and met the figures that inhabited them. In particular, I became interested in the princess. To my surprise, she wasn't the two-dimensional character I had imagined—locked in a tower and crying for help, or stuck by a spindle and waiting to be woken by a prince. I read story after story, and rarely found a princess who was weak, passive, and fainting.

Take Cinderella, for instance. It would seem at first glance to be the most superficial of all fairy tales. The Disney adaptation is rooted in a version of the story that was written by Charles Perrault in the late 1600s. It contains the signature fairy godmother, along with a lot of seemingly frivolous fashion and flounce. However, if you look a little deeper into the Perrault story you will find a Cinderella who is suffering from a lack of self-worth, and her spirituality is perhaps a wee bit too high-minded for her own good. When she is dressing her sisters for the ball, they ask her if she would like to go, and she says, "Oh, you jeer me, for it is not for such as I to go to such a place." Why not, you might wonder? Does she never allow herself to have a little fun?

When she does finally succumb to the frivolity (thanks to the fairy godmother) she brings her generous spirit to the ball and makes sure that her sisters are treated to oranges and citrons. When they get home, her sisters are positively gushing about the mysterious princess who clearly stood out in the crowd by showing them "a thousand civilities."

Like Cinderella, many "princesses" in fairy tales are just ordinary peasant or servant girls. Their princess nature is revealed in the noble way they meet misfortune and injustice. I combed through story and after story, retelling them from the vantage point of the "true princess." The more I studied her character, the more I came to see that without her, humanity would be a cold race, driven by sex, survival, and power. She gets thrown into every possible predicament—she is ridiculed, imprisoned, abandoned, abducted, forced into hard labor, and exiled. Whether she starts out rich or poor, she is a sensitive soul who is deeply affected by cruelty and injustice. She meets her hard experiences with compassion and generosity, attracting kindred spirits everywhere.

She is the heart of the world.

I spent so much time with the princess that my own heart ached, and I had to put her stories down. Then one morning, on Valentine's Day, I went outside and walked up the hill to church. I had started going to the Unitarian church on Sundays, just to see if I could find a spiritual community somewhere and perhaps make some new friends.

My mind was on getting up the hill. It was a cold, sunny day with a few large flakes of snow flying around in the air.

All of a sudden, I *saw* her.

She had staggered into a clearing and had fallen under the weight of her heart. She lay on her belly on a bed of moss, her golden hair rolling down her body like a wave of sunlight. She wore a blue riding coat and an ivory skirt, and her boots were made of soft white leather. Her heart had burst through her coat, and her veins and arteries ran back into the earth like the roots of a tree. She was unconscious, but even if she had awoken, she would not have been able to move because she was inextricably attached to the earth.

I could not imagine what surgery might release her. I had never seen anything more beautiful or upsetting. The vision was no daydream, no idle fantasy. It was a realization more real and true than the hill I was climbing, the bright day, and the snow flitting around in the air. Yet how could I tell anyone what I had seen? I wouldn't be able to explain the vision, not even to my closest friend. What would I say? "I have

seen the heart of the world, and she has fallen and I don't know how to save her!" What was I to do? Go to the newspapers and say, "You're missing the big story—the crime of the century. I have seen the heart of the world, and she is on the ground. Listen to me!"

For more than two weeks, my own physical heart ached and contracted, and I found it difficult to breathe. It woke me up at night, throbbing. Finally, I shared my vision with an aboriginal counselor and friend who had been providing support to me by phone. I figured if anyone could understand what I had seen, she could. After I told her the story, she said that I had seen a vision of Mother Earth.

"She is often portrayed by our people as a woman lying on the ground, with her face to the sun and her heart attached to the earth," she said. She thought it was a beautiful image and couldn't understand why I was so affected by it.

"But her face wasn't turned up," I said. "She was turned facedown. She had staggered into that forest under a weight that had become unbearable. She could no longer carry her *burden of grief*."

My counselor fell silent and then she said: "When the heart of the woman is on the ground, the people are finished, no matter how brave the warrior or straight the lance."

After some time, I decided that I would not flee from the terrible vision. I would dwell there. I would come back again and again. I would draw the finest cloak over her, and I would call upon all the good fairies to watch over her. I couldn't wake her or rescue her. But I could believe in her. I could be a presence of hope.

In the Here and Now

At the time I saw the princess, I was living in the center of Toronto with my husband, Ian. We had no children, just a little canary named Sam, who, at the ripe old age of 11, was still singing at the top of his lungs and greeting us every day with a voice so piercing and exuberant that even with the windows closed he could be heard out on the street.

We lived in a rented apartment on the second and third floors of a renovated old house, overlooking a little island of green across the street around which the cars churned. The city was very noisy, and on our street a continual river of traffic and nearby trains roared by.

By the year 2000, I had been out of work for five years due to my health. I had run a communications business that served the nonprofit sector, and I had worked hard at creating big awareness programs for small organizations. In 1993, while exercising, I experienced an earthquake in my body. Something in my spine and hips shifted. The muscles in my back and neck seized. For days I couldn't get out of bed and when I recovered, I couldn't walk without limping, nor lift my right leg to go up the stairs. Then the pain began. I couldn't sit up for more than ten minutes without intolerable suffering. I couldn't meet deadlines or get through a workday. I tried everything to fix the problem. I went to physiotherapists, doctors, orthopedic surgeons, osteopaths, chiropractors, and spiritual counselors. Finally, the disorder was named *fibromyalgia*—meaning chronic pain in the muscles and fascia. There is no known cause or treatment for this condition, which mostly affects women, and the diagnosis is really just a description of a set of symptoms which include extreme muscle tenderness, insomnia, anxiety, fatigue, and depression.

Meanwhile, Ian sold his company, and we bought three hundred acres of rolling green farmland east of the city. An old farmhouse on the property had fallen into ruin, and Ian decided to renovate it. He and a carpenter friend spent their weekdays out in the country. They stripped the house down to its wooden frame, redesigned the rooms, and built it back up again. It took a couple of years to finish, but now the house was completed, and Ian and I had been going back and forth every other week from the city to the country.

I was deeply grateful to have access to the country, to be enveloped night and day by stars, birdsong, fragrant grasses, and gentle winds. It was a great luxury to have space to walk in and pure air to breathe. I had spent many years struggling to create programs that would meet the needs of others, and it had all been such an enormous effort and sacrifice. But as I walked through the country fields and forests, I marveled at the easy abundance of nature. It relaxed me just to be in a meadow, amid grasses and wildflowers growing at their own pace and seeding in their own time. The earth produced life with a generosity that was beyond my grasp.

At 44, I had come to the middle of my life, and my career path, as I knew it, had disappeared. The only work I had to do in the here and now was to find a way to ease the pain, calm my nervous system, and bring my soul to some sort of peace. My business life was a disappearing shore. I could never go back there. I couldn't see the future either. Perhaps I would live the rest of my life in pain. I was trying to find a way to be okay with that, but deep down I feared that I had seen the princess because I *was* the princess, and I had almost, but not quite, lost heart.

The Missing Heart

For weeks the vision of the princess stayed with me. My heart throbbed. Tears flowed unbidden. My doctor suspected that I was suffering from depression, but I resisted antidepressants. I had seen something in myself and in the world that was valid and real. I looked for the heart in everything—in every conversation, every book I read, and every television program I watched. Everywhere I looked, it seemed the heart was missing. How different would the world be if the heart of the woman were not on the ground?

I felt a call to write more about the princess, and my mind went scurrying around to outline the work. I could compare princesses from fairy tales around the world, and look at their shared and unique predicaments. But even as I put pen to paper, I could see the princess turning to stone and becoming a figure of intellectual scrutiny rather than a living presence. I wondered how to get close to her, how to bring her to life.

The fairy tales suggested that to know the true princess, one must be prepared to take on the burden of the heart. That person is no "lightweight," as we discover in the Grimms' story, *The Goose Girl at the Well*.

The story begins when a great king decides to divide his land between his three daughters. To figure out who should get what, he proposes a little game. Each of his daughters must tell him how much she loves him.

The two elder sisters think up things that they know will flatter him. One says, "I love you as much as the sweetest sugar." The other says, "I love you as much as my prettiest dress." The youngest daughter doesn't want to play the game. When her father insists, she says, "The best food does not please me without salt, therefore I love you like salt."

The king is outraged. If she likes salt so much, she can have it. He orders a huge sack of salt to be strapped to her back and banishes her without a penny to her name. Weeping, she goes into the night and trudges up the mountain, weighed down by her burden. The tears of the princess turn into pearls and roll down the path.

Eventually, the princess comes to the hut of a little old crone who tends a flock of geese. People think she's a witch, especially the young men who bully her. She's kind to the princess and takes her in. She gives her work. She can do the spinning and the household chores. While she is with the old goose woman, the princess disguises her face by wearing a mask, pretending to be the old woman's aging daughter.

Every night the princess goes down to the well in the valley, peels off the wrinkled skin, and washes it in the water. She lays the mask out on the grass to dry under the light of the moon. Her sorrows flood back, and she weeps so many pearls that the grass is strewn with them.

One day a young nobleman comes walking along the mountain path. Unlike the boys who run away from the old witch, he's amazed at the strength of the elderly woman with her burden of kindling, wild apples, and pears. He asks her, "How can such a tiny, frail, old woman like yourself carry such a load?"

The crone replies, "Oh, you have no idea of the weight of the burdens that are carried by the poor."

Well, he may not know, but he is willing to help her carry her burden. She puts her load on his back, and hangs a basket of apples on one arm and pears on the other. He's nearly brought to his knees by the crushing burden. He stumbles up the mountain, sweating. Stones roll under his feet, and the weight of the load seems to increase with every step. Then, to make it worse, the old woman herself jumps on his back and beats him with her whip, driving him to move faster. The poor fellow is practically crippled by the time he gets to her hut.

The old woman's aging daughter comes out into the yard and he doesn't pay much attention to her. Meanwhile, the old woman tells him to rest outside. She goes into the hut, and a few minutes later, she comes out with a gift. It's an exquisite emerald box containing a single pearl.

The young man thanks the old woman and heads down the mountain. After three days, he comes to the castle of the king and the queen who have banished their daughter. He introduces himself to the royal couple, kneels before the queen, and honors her by giving her the emerald box. When she opens it, she's shocked to see the pearl that is one of her daughter's tears.

"Where in the world did you get this box?" she asks.

He explains that it came from an old woman living up on the mountain with her elderly daughter. The queen asks the count to lead her and her husband to the hut. At this point, they're desperate to reconcile with their daughter, whose absence has created great sorrow and regret.

The old woman knows they're coming, and she tells the princess to go into her room, take off the old skin, and put on the dress she wore the night she came to the hut. "Stay hidden until I call you," she says, and the girl does as she is told.

The king, queen, and count arrive at the hut, and the old woman calls "her daughter" out of her room.

When the king sees her, he drops his head on her shoulder and weeps. "My daughter, I have given away my kingdom. What can I give you?"

The old woman says, "Your daughter needs nothing from you. I give her the tears she has wept on your account, for they are precious pearls and worth more than your whole kingdom."

No sooner has she spoken than the walls of the little hut waver and melt, and the house transforms into a beautiful castle. The geese become handmaidens, and the old woman dissolves into thin air. Her identity is never known, but those who tell the story suspect that the witch was the godmother who gave the princess the gift of weeping pearls in the first place.

I thought about that story for weeks. A good fairy tale wants to be read over and over. It wants to walk down the street with you, burrow into your dreams, attach itself to your memories and nestle within your heart.

I kept seeing the princess stumbling up the mountain in the night, weighed down by her sack of salt. She didn't want to lie to her father, and for that, she lost everything. Exile would be hard enough to bear. But the truly crushing burden of her sorrow was her father's denial. He failed to recognize the love and the courage it took to be honest, when everybody else was lying. She had to live with the "old skin" of appearing wrong when, in fact, she was the one who had *been* wronged.

In a world where appearances count so much, it's easy to think that our only reality is what we see on the surface. The strange predicament of fibromyalgia is that you can look perfectly normal on the outside, while inside you feel like an aged person, sore all over, sleep deprived, and tired. I couldn't carry around heavy things or bend to reach for pots and pans. I had to sit with pillows behind my back, and it wasn't possible to last more than a few minutes walking or standing without having to lie down. People didn't understand. One day when Ian and I were walking home from the grocery store and he was carrying the bags as usual, a young man on a bicycle came flying by and shouted at me: "Why don't you carry your own weight?"

Some medical professionals I had met didn't even believe in fibromyalgia. They implied it was a figment of the imagination, an excuse for not carrying groceries, going to work, doing household chores, and getting in line with the rest of the population.

No wonder I identified so deeply with the princess. Like her, my suffering was invisible. I appeared to the world as Cinderella did to her stepsisters—at best, irrelevant and, at worst, shamefully passive and weak.

We all come to a time in our lives that is defining. Depression was defining. How did I want to carry the weight of pain and invisibility? Like it or not, it was my reality. The predicament could be said, from one point of view, to be interesting. Curious. Strange. What had life given me here?

I found strength in the idea that I was in this situation for a reason. Not a reason of my own making, resulting from wrongdoings or bad karma. I was here to know something, see something. There was a big story at work, and *her* story was *my* story. Where was it leading me?

CHAPTER TWO

THE DARK SIDE OF THE MOON

The Godmothers' Arrival

One afternoon in April, I had a sudden urge to go and get my pen. It was the urge of a reporter who is called to cover an important event. The moment I set pen to paper, I was transported to a dark place that I immediately named "the dark side of the moon." I stood there alone, amid stars that were so bright I felt as if I could reach up and pull them out of the sky.

A thrill of anticipation ran through me, as if I were about to witness some extraordinary, celebratory event. I decided to trust that my imagination was preparing to show me things that I wouldn't be able to see any other way. So, in keeping with the perspective that seemed appropriate, I assumed the attitude of a quaint old reporter scribbling away.

The first thing I wrote down was the headline:

"Fairy Godmothers Meet on the Dark Side of the Moon"

It is quiet here on the dark side of the moon, but not for long. The fairy godmothers have begun to arrive. They come from here, there, and everywhere, shooting in like stars, exploding like fireworks, and landing like snow. They are coming in for their regular monthly meeting, which concerns the role of fairy godmothers in the third millennium. Alas, they are wrestling with a problem which has not yet found a solution.

They are landing now, so I must go straight on to tell you what they look like. They are all females, and there the similarity ends. They come in all shapes and sizes. They are fat and thin, old and young, and many are so wizened you can hardly see them. Some carry wands; others hold sticks, scepters, or crystals; and some have pets that sit on their shoulders or follow them around. I don't mean to suggest ordinary domestic pets or even wild animals that have been tamed. The godmothers make pets of stars and trees, walking sticks, rolling stones, and other oddities. They are also surprisingly luminous, lit from within like Tiffany lamps, providing the only source of light here on the dark side of the moon.

Now they are settling, more or less, in the shape of a crescent moon, and awaiting the arrival of the speaker. They are all talking at once, so the atmosphere is buzzing, and very few are looking up to greet the visitor.

Today's specially appointed speaker is Lucy Light Featherwaite, who has been chosen, evidently, not for her eloquence, but because she has been absent for the last half-dozen meetings and the ladies want to know what's up. Ah, but now she is arriving, floating down like a feather, swinging this way and that and taking so much time to descend that all the yakkers stop and gawk, wondering what for heaven's sake is holding up the show.

Now that she has lit on the ground, her features are vividly apparent. She is wearing a bright purple wig; an emerald satin cloak with a stiff, queenly collar; a pink tutu (with leggings to match); and a huge pair of black patent leather shoes. Her silver crown has been cut out of cardboard and covered in tinfoil, and she bears a star-tipped wand. She has painted dots on her

face that resemble freckles (only they are green), and her eyes are round and marine blue. She carries a well-worn carpet bag, into which she has stitched the name of every place she has ever visited over three thousand years.

Now, I won't tell you that she's getting a warm welcome. The mood is generally disgruntled here on the dark side of the moon. For one thing, she is late. An earlier arrival would not have made any difference. The gals would still be annoyed. They can be heard grouching about being unemployed—laid off by humans, as a result of disbelief. Oh, they might have some influence when a child is younger than four, but when they get into school and learn to read, the fairy godmother, along with all her gifts, is sent packing.

Fairy godmothers appear to have given up on human beings. They've stalked off to distant planets and moons around the solar system. The only thing keeping them together is this monthly ritual meeting on the dark side of the moon. The rest of the time they're out doing mischief or sulking in caves, or perhaps trying some remote form of communication in the hope that one day they'll be received. They are all experiencing the grief of going unrecognized, and lest we think that this has no consequence for human beings, we need only to look into any set of wonderless eyes.

Many of the fairy godmothers have taken to gnawing on bones, something they do when they're irritated. They carry them in a bag and take them out whenever they need a bit of comfort. They don't mind sharing them either, and the size of her bag of bones may be said to be in equal proportion to a godmother's discontent. Sorry to say, there are many large bags of bones here in our midst.

Presently, the godmothers have resumed their yakking and are giving Lucy Light Featherwaite no airtime at all. She opens her bag and releases a huge white crow which flies squawking over the crowd, growing in size and volume until the ladies stop talking because they can't hear their own voices. Lucy snaps her fingers and the crow disappears in a puff of white smoke, leaving nothing but a single falling feather. All eyes are fixed on Lucy.

She begins to speak, and for someone who is wearing a tutu, her voice is surprisingly commanding—a strong contralto delivered through a vessel that bears the cracks of many thousand years.

"It's all very well for fairy godmothers to get together every month and commiserate about being laid off," she begins, going straight to the point. "But humans at every age are still living with the better part of themselves—that is to say, *us*—flying around in space. And because they don't know we are out here, it's not likely that they are going to come looking for us anytime soon.

"What I'm saying is, it's not enough to just meet here monthly on the dark side of the moon, and moan about the loss of fairy influence in the world. We are going to have to become more creative. No, I am not talking about sorcery here for those of you who are itching to wave your sticks around. I am talking about the approach. We need to figure out how to approach our orphaned godchildren in ways that they can understand, without frightening them. I daresay they won't remember us. They are bound to find us looney, so to say … but look here, we've had enough mooning around."

She waves her silver wand as if to shoo away an invisible advisor, and she swims forward to speak more directly to the crowd of odd women.

"It's no use, Lucy dear." A little crooked figure has spoken. She stands no higher than Lucy's knees. She wears a red kerchief on her head and is accompanied by a little white elephant who is lending his trunk for support. "The children shut us out long ago, and those two world wars didn't help either. They pretty much blew out our fairy wattage. It's no wonder that most of us have given up. We haven't got enough substance left to survive another indignity. It's a surprise to me, quite frankly, that we even continue to hold these meetings."

"Hear-yeeee!" the godmothers shout, and the elephant, too, raises his trunk to screech in agreement.

"People don't even write books about us anymore," says a cloudy godmother who wavers in the crowd like a white reed in the water of the night. She blinks her two wide ghostly eyes.

"Maybe we should move to another solar system," barks a middle-aged dame who stands very solid and square, wearing a kilt and several dozen layers of animal skins. She sweeps a caber-sized staff in front of her, scattering the surrounding godmothers who have forgotten to give her a wide berth.

Once again, there is a great flurry of conversation and consternation, and Lucy listens, cocking her head this way and that. She stands firm with slightly turned out arms and turned out feet, like some insect ballerina about to take flight.

After they have aired their grievances, Lucy resumes her speech.

"For a moment, if you will, let us look at the problem from the human point of view. They have sent us packing, so to say. But the question is, why? Why have we lost our influence among human beings? I ask each and every one of you to consider that question. Why do they not acknowledge us? Why have they refused the gifts that are rightfully theirs? What has happened to humanity?

"What I'm coming to here is the need to be assertive in a creative way—a loving way. Let's throw out the bones, girls! We need to come up with a plan."

With that, all the fairy godmothers begin talking at once about the loss of their influence and how to go about regaining it. Oh, there are a few naysayers who go flying off in disgust, but by and large there is such a flurry of interest that an observer might be tempted to say that Lucy Light Featherwaite has rekindled their hope.

Ballet Dancer

I'm not sure how I got to the meeting of the fairy godmothers. I simply arrived here to report an event. I feel as though I have been recruited by these ladies, and I won't say that I'm not delighted to be in their midst. After Lucy's presentation, I don't return to the here and now, to my office on the third floor and the sunny April morning that has woken up outside. The meeting hasn't finished.

I hang around on the sidelines and try to pick up bits of information. I can't see much clearly, just a gabble of color—chiefly pink, white, and green—flecked with things like stars, pieces of clothing, and flowers that are being thrown up into the air. They are all tightly gathered around Lucy, like children at a party might crowd around a magical trunk or a tiny clown or some such thing. Everybody is speaking at once, and I can't figure out what they are saying. Oh, I could make it up (and I am sorely tempted to do so), but I want to be as true as I can to what I'm actually seeing.

Suddenly, out of the crowd of pink and white, out of the starry black of the night, Lucy Light Featherwaite appears. She comes waltzing toward me, waving her little witching stick. As she approaches, I see (and hear) music coming from seven little stars and a pair of drumsticks that bounce above her head. She smiles widely. Her chin is tilted heavenward and her eyes are half-closed in bliss. She doesn't have to carry her carpet bag. It dances alongside her, suspended in space. Her hips are swaying, her arms are swinging, and on every fourth beat, she kicks a big foot. Then, in an eyeblink, it's over. The little stars and the drumsticks disappear.

Lucy opens her popping blue eyes, extends her hand, and says, "Hello, dear. You must be the writer. So pleased you could come."

I am flabbergasted. I do not—I repeat, do not—want this story to involve *me*. If I get all wrapped up in it, I will lose my quaint, comfy perspective. But apparently, it doesn't matter what I think. Lucy is getting ready to have a little chat. With a flourish, she waves her wand, and a park bench appears. She waves it again and produces a gas lamplight, firmly affixed to the moon rock.

"Don't want to alter the decor too much," she remarks. "Just enough to get a bit of a sit-down." She lifts her green cape up over her shoulders, squats in a most unladylike manner, and plops down on the bench. "I was very pleased to finally get through to you. As you can see, we've got a bit of a communication problem here. Have a seat!"

She arranges her tutu around her, smoothing it out. "I was going to wear my blue freckles, but I thought I'd try the green—give you a bit of a surprise."

I gape at her. I can't believe my eyes. It does me no good to close them. I just see Lucy. I open them. I see Lucy.

"Well, now don't tell me you don't recognize me," she says. "The tap shoes. The tutu. Remember?"

Suddenly, a scene from way back in childhood flashes across my memory. I was about four years old, and my mother had enrolled me in a ballet and tap dancing class. I wore a pink leotard and tights, a tutu, and black tap shoes. I hated the shoes, but I *loved* my tutu.

One day the teacher called my mother aside, and she said, "I think you're going to have to take Michelle out of the class."

"Why?" my mother asked.

"Because she won't do anything!" said the teacher. "She just stands in front of the mirror and stares at her tutu!"

Lucy is blinking at me with her googly eyes. "Remember what you saw in the mirror? You were far too advanced for that class. Dance teachers. Bah, humbug!"

I am dumbfounded. Why *did* I stand frozen in front of that mirror? What was I seeing? Lucy? What was Lucy doing in the mirror? I am trying to summon the answers when I notice that Lucy has started to squirm. She rocks her bum back and forth as if she has an itch, as though something is biting her butt.

"Look here," she says. "I enjoy a stroll down Memory Lane as much as the next person, but this isn't the time. We've got work to do. You're part of the *plan*."

What plan is she talking about? The plan to reinstate the godmothers in this world? What kind of crazy plan is that?

"Actually, I'm sort of busy right now," I say. "I need to find real work."

"Well, you just found it." Lucy leaps to her feet. "Let's go make some introductions!"

The Introduction

"Hear-YEE, HEAR-YEE!" Lucy shrieks, sending a moon-rock-shattering note through the crowd. We're standing on a bandstand that Lucy has conjured up for the purpose of introducing me. We are bathed in two pools of light that shine happily at our feet. They are lime green and cherry red, and they smell like sherbet.

Silence falls over the group. Lucy continues. "LadEES, I have a special surprise for you today. Believe it or not, we have the honor of *a human* here in our midst."

A human, where? The godmothers scatter, holding out their arms and looking up into the sky as if they expect to catch something from above.

"Here, right here," shouts Lucy. "Beside me. Look here."

"I can't see a human being," states the gruff aforementioned figure in the tartan skirt.

Someone shouts, "We need a person with spectacles!"

"All present, stand by," pipes a little voice at the rear.

The godmothers swarm into two groups to make an aisle for a petite dark-skinned woman wearing a starry indigo cape. She comes rolling through the crowd like a wave coming to shore. Her feet are not apparent under her rippling cloak. Perhaps she has no feet at all.

She glides up the steps of the bandstand and stops about three feet away from me. Steadying herself, she places a monocle over one eye, and rocking upward and downward, she gets a good look-see.

"Oh, yes. She is human all right," she declares. Then she rolls back into the crowd like a bowling ball into a den of pins, sending the godmothers flying in all directions.

As the news is absorbed, the crowd takes a deep breath, and when they exhale, the godmothers let out the most extraordinary golden fairy dust. It streams out of their mouths, and lands on everyone and everything in our midst, including me.

Then I hear many little voices piping, "Now I can see her! I can too! There she is. Over there, see? She's taking form. Oh dearie, look over there, oh my, my, my...."

The love of a thousand mysteriously wise and ancient souls envelops me, gathering sweetness until it becomes intoxicating. It smells and tastes like maple sap and carries a potent nostalgia. I feel their yearning for a lost world, the confusion of being scattered like ashes from the hearth, the grief of searching everywhere but never finding a lost child. I am that child to them, and they are my lost mothers, and we are all swept up in the homecoming.

"I am proud to introduce to you our writer, who has been summoned here for the purpose of helping us reestablish contact with humanity. She isn't here for her own reasons, you understand. We haven't been linked up properly. But I do believe she has consented to lend us her skills. You have consented, haven't you?" Lucy asks me as an aside.

I nod, agreeing, because, well, what else am I going to do?

"Whether or not you can see her is neither there nor here. What's important is that she has a degree in communications. You do have a degree in communications, don't you, dear?"

"Um, well, yes...."

"And for that reason, I have recruited her!"

She turns to me. "You see, my child, we need to get ourselves organized. You know a great deal about the fairy world already, and you have spent your lifetime helping organizations to get their messages out—messages relevant to human and planetary well-being and such. Well, now we're giving you the challenge of a lifetime. We, the godmothers of the fairy realm, equipped as we are with the knowledge of the mirror worlds, are trying to reach humanity. You do understand that we have been banished for well over a hundred years and that our language has perhaps become too archaic. We may have to make some changes, perhaps throw out some old baggage. But we have no idea what baggage to part with, you see, for we have lost contact with you dear humans...."

Back to Earth

At that point, the transmission broke up. I tried to reconstitute the image in my mind, but it was no use. There was nothing on my inner TV screen but snow.

For several days, I walked around in a fog. Every so often I would pick up a transmission, but then I would lose it. After a week had passed, I began to think that the excursion to the dark side of the moon was simply an imaginative romp and not, as I had supposed, a significant event on the inner planes requiring input from me.

Still, it was such an unusual experience! I was left thinking, *What was that all about?* And: *What have I just signed up for?* I couldn't get the godmothers out of my mind. What did they mean when they said they were disconnected from the human race? What were the magical gifts they wished to give us? I had never imagined anything like these characters. My aboriginal counselor told me that she could travel to other worlds and commune with spirits, but she didn't know anything about fairies. Whatever was happening, I had to sort it out on my own.

Several weeks went by, and the magic aperture to that other world closed. I started to doubt my sanity and chastised myself for spending too much time with fairy tales and princesses. I needed to resume my search for a real-world project—write a brochure or an article for someone, or read the news and dose up on realism.

But I felt deadened by realism. The mythic world had always been my natural habitat. Ever since childhood, I had been attracted to fairy tales and mythic stories. The attraction was more than sentimental. Fairy tales reminded me that we are more than we appear. More in what way, I didn't know, but throughout my life I had glimpsed something on that other shore—a golden world that had not faded through time. It had not departed. It had only become somewhat, somehow removed.

The truth was, no project had ever come my way that was more fascinating than the problem of the fairy godmothers, and so I began to do a little research. There were all sorts of stories emerging at the end of the nineteenth century depicting the departure of the fairies from the world. The event was even reported in the news, as people caught sight of fairies leaving in troops, driven out by noisy cities, pollution, rationalism, and disbelief. In her book, *Strange and Secret Peoples*, Carole G. Silver quoted Fiona Macleod suggesting that fairies were departing, not because they were changing, but because humanity was changing. We were losing our fairy sight—the sensitivity that allowed us to see them in the first place. Macleod wrote:

> [T]he Gentle People have no longer a life [in] common with our own. They have gone beyond gray unvisited hills. They dwell in far islands perhaps where the rains of Heaven and the foam of the sea guard their fading secrecies.

One speaker in Silver's book announced that the displaced Scottish elves had flown to the "shadowy side" of the moon to find a home away from mortals! Had I really found them?

I started to become more serious about Lucy and her idea to conduct a communications campaign. Her purpose was not that different from the clients I had served in the past. They had a message, and they wanted to reach the world with it. I had done hundreds of similar projects in my communications business. So, *if*—just say *if*—I were to create a communications program for the fairy godmothers, what sort of program would it be? No doubt an awareness campaign of some kind. But the godmothers wanted more than awareness. They wanted real connection with human beings. Apparently, they possessed a whole store of gifts that humans were either unable or unwilling to receive. What sort of gifts? I went back to the fairy tales that I knew and scoured them for fairy godmothers. It wasn't possible to conduct a straightforward search. Fairy godmothers—if you take them to mean feminine gift givers—appear as fairies, wise women, godmothers, crones, birds, frogs, and toads. They bestow gifts on the unborn, the newly born, and grown-ups who are lost and without direction.

THE TOWER PRINCESS

I found twelve of them gathered together in the Grimms' fairy tale, *The Briar Rose*. They were invited to the palace for the christening of the king and queen's newborn baby girl. There were thirteen wise fairy women in the kingdom, but the thirteenth hadn't been invited to the feast. The king made the rather lame excuse that he only had twelve golden plates for them to eat upon, so one of them had to be left at home. I suspected that the king wasn't too keen on receiving the gift of the thirteenth wise woman. Fairies are not only bringers of welcome gifts. They bring unwelcome ones too—ugly features, deformities, and disabilities that will hobble the child. The king was an extremely protective father, and I don't think he wanted his baby girl to receive what the thirteenth had in mind. In any case, the christening got underway ...

... and right in the middle of the ceremony, the thirteenth fairy woman bursts into the hall. She is enraged and hurt that she hasn't been invited. She marches through the room and points a long finger at the baby in the cradle. "The king's daughter shall, in her fifteenth year, prick her finger on a spindle and fall down dead!" she cries.

The crowd is shocked. But then the twelfth fairy, who has not yet given her gift, steps forward. She doesn't have the power to eliminate the curse, but she can amend it. "It shall not be death," she says, "but a deep sleep into which the princess shall fall—a sleep of a hundred years."

Shaken, the king orders that all the spindles in the kingdom be gathered up and burnt. He doesn't want a single spindle or pointy object to be allowed into the castle.

The king's daughter, who might otherwise be raised with the awareness of her fate, has absolutely no idea that she has been cursed. She grows up in a very protected environment and perhaps only senses that people are keeping secrets from her.

Then, on her fifteenth birthday, her parents are called away for mysterious reasons, and the princess finds herself unguarded in the castle. She dashes out of her room and goes poking around. She looks into rooms and bedchambers, and peers behind curtains and under stairs. Eventually she finds her way to an old, ruined tower. She climbs the narrow, winding staircase and opens a little door to a room where an old woman sits by the window, spinning. The princess greets the strange woman and she is instantly fascinated by the spindle.

"What is it that thing that is rattling round so merrily?" she asks, reaching for the pointy object.

The spinning woman hands it to her and she pricks her finger on it. All at once she is overwhelmed by a profound fatigue. She falls backward onto the bed behind her and sinks into a deep sleep.

The sleep spreads through the whole castle. The king and queen, who have just come into the hall, wither to the floor where they were standing. The courtiers, the cook, the fire in the hearth, the doves on the roof, the horses in the stable, the dogs in the yard, the spiders on the wall—all stop moving and do not stir again.

As I reflected on the story, I wondered if the fairy godmothers were speaking of the same kind of gifts that the fairies gave to the princess at the christening. Did they possess the gifts that we all need to fulfill our unique destinies? Do we reject our own fairy godmothers for the same reason the king rejected the thirteenth? He wouldn't want his child to receive a dark gift. He would want her to have a perfect life with no suffering. No sharp objects, no injuries—no point.

It's not an archaic notion. In the developed urban world, most of us can quite easily wall ourselves off from the existence of pain, loss, aging, disability, disease, and death. The Buddha began in the same way. Enclosed in a beautiful castle, he was fenced off from the reality of life on the streets of Benares. It was only when he went beyond the castle walls and saw people aging, suffering, and dying that he understood his calling in life.

It occurred to me that if the magical gifts of the godmothers were both light and dark—that is, roses with thorns—they would not be an easy *sell*. Who wants to know the losses we will face in this lifetime or the struggles that will define us? Yet if we aren't willing to accept our dark gift, then maybe other gifts go unused.

That's about as far as I could go on my own. I would need more input from the godmothers. My mind kept wandering back to Lucy in her ridiculous tutu and big, shiny patent leather shoes. She was a mirror reflection of me at the age of four. Maybe she was trying to give me my dancing gift. If so, she didn't succeed. Dancing ended for me on the day I was removed from the class. No more tutus for me. I went back to wearing jeans and plaid shirts. I grew up a goofy, leggy, clumsy tomboy, and the dancing dream receded into that distant realm that holds all fantasies that will never, in a billion years, be realized.

The Well

One morning I was standing in front of the mirror in my usual groggy state. I had just put my contacts in, and my face had come into view. I didn't look like somebody who felt ninety in her bones. At forty-something, I only had a few wires of gray sprouting from my curly brown hair. My eyes were still brightly blue. I still had that big, wide smile, albeit clouded by two vertical frown lines between my eyes. What would win—the critical frown or the mouth so eager to laugh?

I reached for my toothbrush and felt a tickle in my right ear, as if a bug had gotten in. Then I heard Lucy's voice coming through, surprisingly loud and clear.

"Go to the well," she said. "That's how to make the link-up. Ordinary mirrors make poor transmitters—too superficial. See you anytime."

In the center of the imagined place where my counsellor had taught me to go, there was a well. Fed by tiny underground springs, it was now overflowing. Every time I went to it in my imagination, it became more present and vivid. Even when I forgot to think about it, the well was there, embedded in the depths of an ancient forest where enormous softwoods grew—redwood, spruce, cedar, and pine. Their exposed roots mingled with the stones, and wove in and out through a network of crisscrossing streams. The forest floor was carpeted with green moss, ferns and flowers scattered here and there, creating shelter for a thousand tiny worlds.

It was not difficult to go to the well in my imagination, but it was extremely hard to stay there, especially when pain interfered and yanked me back to the physical world.

I put my toothbrush down and went to sit in my reading chair. I could hear cars honking and brakes screeching outside my window. By nine o'clock, people were late for work, and their anxiety could be felt seeping in through the walls. The drivers had to navigate a confusing set of stop signs at the intersection across the street, and so we were used to hearing these early morning outbursts of anger.

I closed my eyes and tried to concentrate. As usual, I saw nothing at first, but as I settled into the emptiness, trusting the possibility that the well would come into view, I became aware of standing on a smooth, cool stone at midday. A large, flat-topped slab of granite jutted out over the sparkling pool. I gazed down into the water and wondered if I might see my reflection. The pool was the color of sapphire with a luminous emerald center that reflected the sun at the top of the sky. I couldn't get a fix on my image because the water was moving, stirred by some sort of merry commotion going on beneath.

After a few moments it occurred to me that the pool had no intention of becoming still. It was waiting for me to unstiffen, relax; become more like the water lapping at the edge of the basin and curling around the reeds. Who knew what secret activity was going on underneath? The pool teemed with mischief, reminding me of children playing under a covered Sunday dinner table. I became so caught up in the play of the water that I hardly noticed the flame of the sun being turned down slowly. One by one, stars appeared, glimmering on the surface of the well. My own reflection disappeared, leaving only a shimmering outline, created from the fairy dust that remained on me from the dark side of the moon. I saw myself as the fairies had seen me, glittering in the night—a golden sketch on a dark velvet pool....

"She's *here*," an old woman shrilled.

CHAPTER THREE

THE BIG SHOCK

The Working Group

"In*deed*," says Lucy with a satisfied emphasis on the word *deed*. She sits to my left at a table, wearing reading glasses and a leather airplane cap, circa World War II. Several other godmothers are perched around the elliptical slab. It is made of a milky pink stone with purple veins running through it. A golden glow emanates from within the stone, conveying a feeling that it is a living organism. We're in some kind of cave illuminated by walls that shine with a pearly interior light.

Several passageways lead into the recesses of the cave, and I can hear water dripping and gurgling over stones. The sound is soothing. There must be a river in the cave, maybe the river that carried me here. Perhaps I have a boat somewhere that is waiting to take me back when the meeting is over. I'm comforted by the thought because I have no idea where imagination has taken me.

The cave also has an entrance at about one o'clock, leading outside—wherever that is. No light comes in from the opening, and I have the impression that the mouth of the cave opens straight out into space. Stalactites resembling clear, pink icicles hang from the ceiling above the table, and catch the hues of light that emanate from the walls of the room. Every now and then water drips from the ice. It occurs to me that they are the original chandeliers, and everything else, no matter how fine the crystal, is derivative.

"Hello, dear," says the godmother sitting opposite me at the table.

She is perched on a high chair so that her eyes will be level with the others present here. I recognize her glittering indigo cloak instantly, and the thick monocle that enables her to get a fix on me. Her milk chocolate skin is soft as chewed leather, and she has no teeth. Her lips have retired into her mouth, but her eyes are as black as buttons, and the stars on her cloak swim merrily around, orbiting one another in what strikes me as a continual, joyful dance.

"It is such a relief to be in the presence of a human," she creaks. "You are brave souls to go down into such heavy matter. It takes almost all your light. I don't know how you do it, but bless you, child." She squeezes her little black eyes shut, and for a moment, all the stars on her cloak become still. "Bless you," she repeats after a few moments have passed.

Lucy clears her throat and puts her pencil down. She has been busily writing notes on a large stack of withering paper. "Lad*ies*, let us come to order." She turns and scrutinizes me over the bifocals perched on her rather round, small nose. Does she ever look like a bug!

"We haven't found a way to address you, dear," she says.

I am suddenly aware of the others who are present. The large, square woman clad in skins and a kilt is standing several feet away, with her staff firmly planted beside her. She stares straight ahead with unblinking eyes, and I notice that an eagle is carved into the stone at the top of her staff. She remains expressionless, but I am quite sure the eagle winks at me.

The thin, white godmother is also here, moving through the room like a sinuous ribbon of cloud. She has a sensitive air about her, as if she could easily disintegrate or be blown away. I sense that if she comes any closer she will be able to read my thoughts.

Lucy pulls her glasses off her nose and smiles. She has a tiny, sweet I-adore-you smile that emits the smell of strawberries. "So, dear, how shall we address you?"

It doesn't seem appropriate to use my human name. I am in a different universe—a place where things are turned inside out—and what is familiar to me is foreign to them. Who am I to them? Who am I here? I have no words. I say, "I'm, ah ..." And then I pause to marvel because the *ah* sound swells into the atmosphere and resonates through the chamber. It's a beautiful note.

"She's a singer!" The reedy girl flies straight to me and hovers, looking at me with her astonished emerald eyes.

"What is her song?" Lucy asks.

"It is a song of hope," creaks the crone in the starry cloak.

"Very well," says Lucy. "Ladies, I am pleased to welcome our dearest Hope." She licks the tip of her index finger and starts to flip through some papers. "Now, Hope, we have taken the liberty of composing a working group. In your absence, I've gone over some old cases of yours, and I see that when you're working with a large group of people, you encourage them to form a smaller advisory group. I've selected this group based on certain criteria." She picks up a piece of paper and bobs her head up and down, as though reading words written in columns. "Where are we now? Oh, yes."

Where did Lucy get this file? I try to imagine her rifling through the storage unit where all my old business files are stashed.

"First, as you say in your paper here, 'The client must have a high level of motivation to get their message out to the world.' Well, we all have that.

"Second, 'they must have a clear objective.' I believe we do. We want to reconnect with our human counterparts and give them the gifts that are their birthright. We all share this objective, do we not?"

"Oh yes, Lucy dear," says the godmother across the table, swimming in her sea of stars.

"Third, we must develop a strategic plan. And in order to do so, we must first get in touch with our audience, or public, as you put it, and find out what twenty-first-century humans know about us so we get a measure on the distance between us. Hmm. That won't be easy. We don't know much about humans, and they seem to have lost sight of us altogether. But anything is possible now that you're here, dear."

I'm starting to feel uncomfortable. Lucy has taken control over a method she knows nothing about, and I'm worried that we've started off on the wrong foot. Already, she's got expectations of me that I know darn well I can't fulfill. I have no intention of doing audience research for the fairy godmothers. It's hard enough to be unemployed and have a condition that people suspect is all in my head. But if I start asking my friends what they think about fairy godmothers and what might be their resistors to the idea of receiving their magical gifts, I might as well just check myself into the looney bin!

"Now, would you like something to drink? Perhaps our host can bring us one of those coconut concoctions."

Everyone turns to look over into the recesses of the cave. There in the corner, near the entrance, sits a dragon. At least, he looks like a dragon. He isn't very large, about the size of a medium-sized dog. He has greenish skin with orange, red, and yellow hues and a very wide, orange mouth. He has crammed himself into a hollow near the entrance, and he smiles shyly with his arms wrapped around his chest. It would not be possible to imagine a more nonthreatening dragon! He wiggles some long fingers at us by way of saying hello. His nails are long and look to be painted orange.

"Our host for this meeting is a gnonomous, and we are grateful to him for providing such comfortable headquarters. I'm afraid I can't give him much of an introduction. All we know about him is that he is a gnonomous, which is to say, unknown to us all. What I can tell you is that, like all dragons, he has a tendency to become very attached to humans. Extremely attached." Lucy puts her eyeglasses back on her nose and looks at me rather sharply as if to say, "So mind your p's and q's."

The dragon disappears and then, only a second later, reappears with a tray of very tall glasses filled with a greenish milky fluid that is topped with slices of lime. He has extraordinarily long arms for such a thin body, able to reach to all ends of the table from one place. Having set the glasses down, he grins like a child who has just done a very good deed and pads back to his corner of the room on big, smacking feet. The sound echoes through the hall.

"So now, let us continue with introductions." Lucy presents the indigo-clad woman sitting across from me. "Gangee is with us. She is the keeper of the harmonious worlds. Gangee is the mother of many stars—that is to say, bright souls who go into dark places. She has a line on many things, so to speak, and she is also an accomplished spinner. She can make fine yarn out of practically anything.

"Now over there, is my cousin, Greta Greatwaite. You may find her a bit brusque, but I assure you that you could not find a better, more knowledgeable friend. She holds within her cavities a great volume of fairy lore, although her ability to access that information has been diminished as of late." Lucy loudly clears her throat.

"And now over there—come in, dear—here is Willow."

The white, reedy figure wafts closer and hovers around Gangee like a halo. I can detect the vague form of a face with long green eyes and a hollow for a mouth.

"Willow is very versatile and can take on many shapes. She can travel into the dreams of human beings—only if she is permitted, of course, and it goes without saying that she rarely receives an invitation because she has not been known for some time. In her loss of contact, she has developed a sensitivity that might be said to be equal to that of a gnomomous.

"Now where is Tatatee? Her report is due." Lucy turns to me. "You will remember Tatatee—she travels with her elephant. She has been off polling the godmothers, with regard to the question I posed at our meeting: 'Why did we lose our influence?'"

Right on cue, Tatatee appears at the entryway perched atop her white elephant. She bears a large and rather yellowed, dog-eared scroll. I recognize the red kerchief and notice that she is also wearing blue jeans and a white western shirt with red lapels and silver buttons.

All heads bow to Tatatee, like flowers in the rain. I am aware that she is the oldest of them all—the wisest of the wise, the tenderest, the sweetest, the bravest, and, like the others in the room, I feel humbled to be in the presence of her tininess.

With knobby fingers that are like the roots of a gnarled tree, she begins to uncurl the scroll. "We have completed our study," she announces in a thin, wavering voice.

"And your findings?" Lucy asks.

"We, the godmothers of the planet Earth, having assessed the matter of our lost influence, have come to the conclusion that the problem is ... serious."

I burst out laughing. "After all your research, that's what you've found? That the problem is *serious*?"

Gangee nods soberly and says, "That doggone star."

A Big Noise

I'm laughing at the word *serious* when all of a sudden, the image of a huge blue-white star explodes in my mind. I'm blinded by its light and deafened by its noise. Over the clamor, I can hear Tatatee calling me to come and investigate it.

"No!" There's no way I'm getting closer to that star, but Tatatee and her elephant are headed out into space, and I'm connected to them like a dog on a leash. I fight the connection, pulling back. I can hear her talking about the "Sirius effect." The closer she gets to the star, the more racket there is in my head—in my whole nervous system.

Finally, I give in. "Okay, okay, I'll *see* it!"

Suddenly I'm with Tatatee, standing on a platform connected to the arm of some sort of multi-armed spaceship that looks like the octopus ride in a fairground. We're being swung through space in graceful arcs, flying through billions of shards of light that are exploding from the star and whirling around us like snowflakes. They look like broken pieces of a mirror, and glint in the distant sunlight as they stream down to Earth, where they form a flashing, circular cloud. It rings the globe.

"I can't get this close!" I yell. "Take me out of here!" I can't tolerate the brilliant light of the star; its cruel, cutting edges; and the head-splitting noise. It's like a thousand heavy metal rock bands playing simultaneously. It feels like power, pure and simple—power without light, warmth, compassion, softness; power without *love*. It's a superstar, driven by the unstoppable, senseless drive for stardom.

"*Stop it! Stop it!* Get this star out of my head!"

At last, Tatatee understands. She grabs me, and with supreme force, throws me out of her world, back to the ground.

Grounded

I threw my notebook onto the floor and ran around my studio, holding my head. I didn't know what had just happened, but I was frightened out of my wits. I couldn't get the star out of my head. It was seared into my brain. My heart banged in my chest. I felt like I had been electrocuted.

Every single doubt I had about consorting with godmothers crashed in on me. What on earth had I been thinking? What had started out as a lark had gone *way* too far. I had pushed beyond the limits of my own mind, and now what? I had a star in my head, and I seemed unable to expel it. I couldn't turn it off, and I couldn't hide from its hard, cold, shattering light. It was like being in an MRI machine, blasted by noise that sounded like the repeated words, "Bad, bad, bad, bad," only there was no technician to turn off the machine because it was in my *brain*.

"*Shut up!*" I cried, holding my head. I had to stop thinking. I ran downstairs and out onto the back porch. "Breathe the air, Michelle. It's okay. It's okay." But it wasn't okay. What had I done to myself? Why couldn't I just leave well enough alone?

Needless to say, I didn't go back to the godmothers in the days that followed the big shock. The pain in my body had intensified, and the nerve fibers down my arms and legs felt hot and wound up. I struggled to sleep, and when I did, I had nightmares of being tortured by scientists who were using my body for experimentation. I feared that I had gotten into the eye of some cruel power that was driving me (and all human beings) to the precipice of destruction. It didn't want to be seen, and now that I had seen it, I had been tagged. I would be destroyed.

I have never felt at home in my own skin, but now I wanted out of my skin. I was a tangle of nerves gone berserk—a field of static electricity, unable to ground myself or tell anyone what I had seen.

What had I done?

As for Sirius ... What did I know about Sirius? I tentatively approached the subject. Sirius. The Dog Star—the brightest star in the sky. In Egypt, Sirius rises at the time when the Nile floods, heralding a new year, a fertile new cycle. The Egyptians calibrated their calendar with the motions of Sirius and they saw the Nile River as the star's gift. Sirius is also connected with the Dogon, an ancient tribe of people who have lived in the Republic of Mali for thousands of years. Long before the telescope was invented, the Dogon knew about a tiny, heavy, invisible star orbiting Sirius, which they believed governed the rest of the stars, and caused them to stay in place. For the Dogon, that invisible star was the seed of creation. According to Robert K. G. Temple, author of *The Sirius Mystery*, the Dogon people say that their knowledge of Sirius came straight from the Sirians' own mouths, ancient visitors who passed their knowledge to the Dogon way back somewhere in antiquity. Modern scientists have confirmed that Sirius B does exist. It is a tiny, heavy, imploded star known as a white dwarf.

If my inner experience had something to do with the real Sirius, then the subject was way too big for me. I wasn't about to go up against a *star*.

Confrontation

Several days passed, and during that time, I listened to every soothing meditation tape I possessed, went for walks, and sought refuge at the farm. I blamed myself for letting my imagination run wild. If I wanted a project so badly, why didn't I go after something concrete? Why did I have to venture into the fairy world? There are reasons for not going into that realm. People go mad ... or disappear. What had I gotten into? What had gotten into me?

I was also angry with those godmothers, whoever they were. They had seemed so loving and kind. Why would they betray me? I kept thinking about Lucy in her tutu. Very funny. But the get-up was a setup. On some level, though, the tutu was meaningful. Lucy reminded me of the teachers I had when I started taking modern and ballet dance classes in my twenties. They were drill sergeants. The object was to completely control your body and make it do exactly what you willed it to do. I was an avid student. I have often thought to myself, *I didn't get bulimia. I got ballet.* From adolescence, I had felt constantly watched and assessed by others. Dance enabled me to control the way I stood, the way I sat, the way I raised my arms, the way I walked and ran. I stretched and strengthened and pushed my body until, at thirty-seven, it broke. Now Lucy was attempting to control my psyche the way I had controlled my body. No way would I let that happen. But maybe it already had. I could not get that chaotic, clanging star out of my system.

Noise invaded me from inside and out. I was overwhelmed by inner voices of anger, fear, and self-recrimination, and driven round the bend by honking cars, rumbling trains, construction crews, and motorcycles. I couldn't walk around the block without wearing earplugs. I had to make it stop. I would confront those godmothers, whoever they were.

Soon after I made the decision, I found myself right back in that warm, golden-lit room, sitting adjacent to Lucy at the oval table.

Lucy is leafing through pages of the file and yakking. "Now that we have identified the source of our disconnection, we need to look at the problem from a human point of view. That's where you come in, dear," she says, smiling sweetly.

"*No!*" I shout, standing up. "I am *not* proceeding this way, Lucy. I don't care how important your campaign is. I won't be manipulated. Don't you see what you've done to me? My nerves have been shattered by the noise of that star. I will not allow you to hurt me! Look, I don't know who you are. Maybe you're fairy godmothers; maybe you're even trying to save the world. I don't know. But I won't be controlled or used like some kind of tool! I don't care how important your campaign is. I quit."

Throughout my speech, Lucy has been gazing at me with frank, wide-eyed admiration, which is disconcerting to say the least. When I'm done, she bolts to her feet and says, "Well then, we must do exactly as you wish."

"Quite right," says Tatatee, nodding and puffing out her little chest.

"What do you wish?" Lucy asks.

"I wish you to give me peace."

"Well now," says Lucy. "It just so happens that we're pretty good at granting wishes. Please, try not to be surprised."

Ping! Her fighter's cap disappears, revealing a bald head with pink skin speckled with green dots, and a pair of bobbing antennae.

Ping! Her cloak vanishes and is replaced by gauzy wings that resemble new leaves, transparent and delicately veined in the light.

Ping! Her pen becomes a wand with a smidgen of blue-white light crackling on the tip.

"So much for dressing to impress," she remarks.

"Who are you?"

"We're your fairy godmothers, to be sure," says Tatatee. "And your wish for peace is a good one. Let us not forget that the ultimate frontier is a settlement."

"Yes, and now we will leave you in peace," says Lucy. "Your wish is granted." She taps me on the shoulder with her wand and all the godmothers vanish at once.

Sitting at my desk, I felt a peculiar lightness of being. A memory from childhood sailed in. I was ten years old, and I had taken my first air flight. The stewardess came along and gave me a little badge to wear—a pair of golden wings. Then she tapped me on the shoulder and said, "Fasten your seat belt, dear. We will be landing soon."

CHAPTER FOUR

BREAKING SPELLS

Mother Love

As the days passed, I spent time in the country, gardening and getting as close to the earth as I could. It seemed to be the best remedy for calming my nervous system. Spring had arrived, and the bluebirds were nesting in the boxes that Ian and I had made the year before. Every time I saw a little patch of blue fluttering over the green lawn, my heart would leap with joy. I marveled at the brave beauty of the spring flowers—the luminous blue scilla, the shy snowdrops, and the bold crocuses who defied the winter snow.

As I planted seeds in my little round vegetable garden, I felt a surge of new vitality. I had made a declaration to Lucy and all those other spirit mothers. Sure, who wouldn't want to be part of some big world-saving mission? But I had another job to do, even more important. I had to save myself. It seemed like such a humble, mundane thing to have to do, to care for myself and abandon the clamor to be a *star*.

I hated the whole business of self-care. It would be much easier to care for someone else than to deal with my own health problems. It felt like a colossal waste of time running around to doctors and looking for ways to ease the pain, when there were so many more important things to do. I could be investing my energies in building a business or working for a charitable organization. I had wanted to make a difference in the world. But no. All I had to do was to look after myself and find a route to wellness. Ugh!

Yet my resignation from Lucy's campaign had sent a powerful message from my mind to my body: "I will look after you." My body had not trusted my busy, ever-occupied mind to do anything but push, but now I was experiencing a regime change. Some happy bluebird, some vivid crocus, some new seed in the earth had burst into being.

Although I was still quite raw and didn't want Lucy around me, that wrinkled old godmother, Gangee, moved in closer. She wrapped me in her cloak of swimming stars, whispered into my ear at night, and rocked me to sleep with soothing words. It isn't easy to formulate what Gangee said. She gave me the impression that each one of us is absolutely central and deserving of love. Everything else orbits around our capacity to cherish ourselves and raise ourselves up under the love of a good mother. Gangee conveyed to me that a good mother does not turn away from herself. She includes herself in the ring of love.

Unspelling

One morning, when I went to make an entry in my journal, I heard the high, thin voice of Tatatee in my head. She was writing me a letter!

> I am privileged to be able to touch down for a moment. I would like to address my words to Hope.
>
> We have so much grief in the invisible worlds because our children are orphaned. We know how much you need to be comforted and cared for on your own ground. We do not know how external powers have employed you, but we are aware that you are terribly driven by the shattered mirrors to spend all your remaining beauty on becoming visible.

What I want to say, my dearest child, before I go, is to claim your own ground. Do not get caught between the mirrors. You cannot be one person on the inside and another on the outside. Are you the inside person or the outside person? If you think you are only what appears, you are under a spell.

Let us take, for instance, the king who was turned into a frog. It happened, as you know, because some witch spelled him frog.

F-R-O-G.

"Well, that must be me," he said, looking at his image in the pond. He looked like a frog. He leapt like a frog. He believed he was the frog he saw in the mirror. But was he a frog? Oh no. He was a king who had forgotten his true nature. It took a princess to bring him to his senses. She did not want to eat or sleep with a frog, and at last she hurled him against the wall in disgust. Then they were able to live happily, forever. Oh, yes, and I do mean forever. Never again, at any time, would that beautiful soul let himself be spelled by any other name but K-I-N-G.

You all have a noble destiny, and we earnestly wish to serve you. But you must come into your own. If you do not feel love or recognition from the visible world, then look inside. Nature has given you another pair of eyes.

I will see you again, my daughter, my blessed one. The worlds of your heart are opening as you find the ground to grow in. We are caring for you, and for all the little seeds.

With love from your fairy godmother,

Tatatee

Tatatee's letter caused me to wonder. Do I see myself as a frog? My self-conception was formed way back by my schooling in the Catholic Church. I learned early on to view myself as a sinner, stained by original sin. Through the Roman Catholic Church, I had absorbed a foundational myth about myself and humans in general. We had disobeyed

God by eating the fruit of knowledge, and God showed no signs of getting over it. He had driven us from the Garden of Eden, and for the rest of time, we would have to toil to make ourselves lovable and regain some position of worth. In church we would thump our chests and repeat, "Lord I am not worthy to receive you. Only say the word, and my soul shall be healed."

I figured I would never win God's approval. For one thing, I was no saint, but more importantly, I was a girl. There were no altar girls at church, no women priests giving the mass. If you were born a girl, there was no way to get into The Club. I assumed that I would always be on the outside looking in, and consequently, I put a huge effort into getting accepted at school and winning approval in every form: marks, merits, degrees, promotions, awards, applause ... you name it.

But now, prompted by Tatatee, I started to seriously ask myself, *Do I believe in God? Do I believe in what God says about who I am? Who is God to me?* It all came down to my image of God. What was it?

I permitted myself to see the most basic and primitive picture, a picture that I might have drawn in fourth grade. A bearded man in the sky with angry eyebrows. Maybe there was a little sun in the background, but this was a temperamental God whose mind you could not know or trust. He expected blind obedience from humans, and it didn't matter if his demands were unreasonable. You did what you were told, and if you disobeyed or questioned his authority, you could expect dire consequences. This God offered happiness to a chosen few but the rest of us would suffer in purgatory until we'd done our time. Or, we'd burn in hell and be damned forever.

My dad got the dubious privilege of acting out the role of the Old Testament God in the household. At six-foot four with piercing blue eyes and a brilliant, decisive mind, he made a convincing God, and we six kids clamored for his approval. When my mother became frustrated with us, she often said, "Wait till your father comes home!" We feared his end-of-day-time judgements, not to mention the punishments.

I stopped going to church when I was eighteen, but that did nothing to dispel my image of God. Any mention of the word *God* would summon that wrathful figure with his thunderbolt. I couldn't get past that image to know my own spiritual beliefs. And I couldn't see myself as anything but a sinner, marked at birth by original sin. Like the oval-shaped birthmark on my right thigh, it could not be washed out.

But something had changed. In spite of the fact that the godmothers had terrified me, they had reaffirmed what I knew in my heart—namely, that we are all deserving of love. We are not unworthy little frogs.

Still, to shake myself free of the bonds, I had to take another step. I had to directly confront my image of God. So one day, I closed my eyes and allowed myself to see God, just the way I had pictured him as a little girl. I looked into his intimidating face, his bearded chin jutting out of ominous black clouds, lightning flashing around his head, and I said, "I don't believe in you, God. You are not my god. I don't know who my god is, but you're not *it*." Then I marched back into the world.

Well. The terror! The guilt! I felt sure that God would strike me down for my heresy. I was amazed at the fear that had lodged in my cells, and the crushing weight of guilt.

Two days later, the phone rang. My dad was on the other end. He and my mother were headed to Vancouver for my youngest brother's wedding. I couldn't go because I was in too much pain to travel, which was a whole other department of grief. In any case, my father was mad. It had nothing to do with me—it had to do with the government of Canada and his fury with liberal policies. But every time he vented his anger, I would go into a state of shock. I would become Dorothy trembling before the Great Oz, and no amount of self-admonishment could change my response. He was my *father*, and not only that, but God's stand-in. This time, however, I interrupted him. I told him I couldn't listen to his anger, and I hung up.

Ian and I went out to the farm that weekend, but I could find no peace. Guilt is not only a weight but a pressure—and the pressure to call my father and beg for forgiveness became so intolerable that one afternoon, when I was bending over a row of sunflowers, my back went out. I limped into the house and collapsed on the bed. For days I lay flat on my back, unable to move. My old mind said, *See? God struck you down!* But my spirit said, *I'm not defeated. I'm here. Love is in charge, now. I'm not going to let others control me with fear, not even God.*

Then, strangely enough, there was another test. I had an appointment to go to the hospital for an interview with a doctor, who was going to assess my needs and enroll me in a pain management program. I had waited nearly a year for the appointment.

The ward was on the fourth floor of the hospital, and I found it empty—no patients, no doctors, no nurses anywhere in sight. A lone woman behind a desk gave me a form to fill out. Before long, a dark-haired man in a white coat appeared. We shook hands. I followed him to an office that didn't belong to anybody. There were only two things on the desk: his briefcase, which was closed, and my file, which was open.

The doctor sat down and flipped through the papers in my file. "So you've been in pain for a long time," he said.

He asked about my history. I told him the now familiar and somewhat thread-worn story about my pain. It started when I hurt my back while exercising in 1993. Soon after, I couldn't lift my right leg. Then I began to limp. Then the pain increased in volume, then it became intolerable, then came the nerve blockers, the physiotherapy, the massage therapy, and finally, the visit to the Mayo Clinic (at a cost of nearly USD$10,000) where the problem was finally named *chronic myofascial pain syndrome*, a type of fibromyalgia.

"But nothing is treating the pain," he said. "You've had all kinds of examinations."

"Yes, two CAT scans and an MRI."

"And they've found nothing unusual."

"No."

"What religion are you?" he asked.

"I was raised as a Roman Catholic," I said, confused by the question.

"Are you practicing now?"

"No. I left the church when I was eighteen."

He closed my file. "Religion is important," he said.

I was confused. "I believe spirituality is important," I stammered.

He leaned over the desk. "*Humility* is important," he said.

I shrank into something very small while he proceeded to outline the three aspects of wellness—mind, body, and spirit—as if I had never encountered the concept of holistic health.

Then he said, "Since I find no physical evidence of a problem, I can only conclude that you have a *broken spirit*."

I reeled. My spirit couldn't be broken. It was the only thing I had that was strong. But here was a doctor, a specialist in pain management, whose authority was backed up by years of medical training and experience. He had to be right. But wait a minute. How could he diagnose my *spirit*? Did he have some kind of special X-ray for that? No, this was a *spell*—the very thing Tatatee had warned me about!

In the end, he gave me no treatment plan—no referral to a pain management class or a swim program, or any other option. All he gave me was a tiny piece of yellow sticky paper, on which he had scrawled the telephone number of a Jesuit priest who would take me "back to the scene of the crime" in childhood, and restore me to the Catholic faith.

I drove home in a state of shock, and as soon as I got to my office, I wrote down the whole experience so that I wouldn't disbelieve myself. Reason has a way of invalidating a bizarre experience on the basis that it cannot possibly have happened.

I wrote a letter to the director of the program to tell her what had transpired, and then I showed the letter to my family doctor, who was flabbergasted.

"You've got to copy this to the president of the hospital," she said.

So I did, and then all hell broke loose. The director of the program called my family doctor and reamed her out. She accused me of breaching the "sacred trust" between doctor and patient, and to punish me, she denied me access to her program's care.

The whole thing was unbelievable, but I refused to see myself as an unworthy outcast. I simply signed up for another program and slept a little better, knowing that the gaslighting doctor would think twice the next time he tried to break a person's spirit. Maybe there would be one less person in this world who spelled her name F-R-O-G.

CHAPTER FIVE

NOWHERE

The Train Station

One night, just as I'm reaching over to turn out the light, I find myself back in inner space. Big stars twinkle in the sky, emitting the light of rubies, sapphires, diamonds and emeralds. They have a soft, comforting presence, like the loving eyes of ancestors who have seen everything and now see everything as beauty.

I appear to be standing on the platform of a train station. The tracks before me gleam in the starlight, and disappear into black space to my left and right. It is not clear where the trains come from or whither they are bound. I turn around and see a pink neon sign flashing over the station platform. "SOMEWHERE," it reads. Very funny.

Then I notice Lucy coming toward me out of the night. She half skips, half walks, brimming with delight. There are musical notes bouncing in the air all around her, and the song sounds strikingly like "Chattanooga Choo Choo." She wears white gloves, a green wig, and a camel-colored trench coat that balloons out over her tutu. Behind her, a train with blinding white headlights comes galloping in. Lucy is yakking at me. I can't hear what she's saying in the steam of the train until it has come to a gusting, screeching stop.

She gives me a big hug and a wet, smacking kiss. "Well now," she says, "we've come to the end of the line." She pats her coat, releasing a puff of gold dust.

"*Porter*!" she shrills. She pulls off one of her gloves, sticks two fingers between her teeth, and lets out a whistle that would shatter glass.

A monkey in a royal blue uniform and a pillbox hat appears down the platform and galumphs toward us, pushing a cartful of bags. Behind him, an unruly crowd of godmothers is boarding the train.

"Where are you headed?" I ask Lucy.

"Nowhere!" she exclaims.

The monkey begins loading her bags onto the train. There are about half a dozen of them. They look like Santa's gift bags and are stuffed to bursting, but they must not be very heavy because the porter easily tosses them into the cabin. They practically float to the top of the steps.

I am happy to hear that the godmothers are leaving—a little sorry to see them go, but clearly, they're cooperating with my request.

"What's in the bags?" I inquire.

"No bones, I can tell you that!" Lucy grins, and jabs an elbow into my rib. "A little theatrical paraphernalia. A few magic tricks. My wand, of course." She rubs her hands together, distracted by the porter. When he's finished loading her bags, she digs into her coat pocket and pulls out a wad of cash. She peels off a few bills, and the porter doffs his cap. He heads down the platform, tail swinging happily.

"We've decided to travel light," says Lucy. "No point in taking a lot of baggage Nowhere! We had a big clean out, and now we're all sweetness and light. Too sweet for my liking but

..." She brushes off those distracting invisible things that buzz around her head like bees.

"Let me get this right," I say. "You're leaving here, which is Somewhere, and you're going someplace called Nowhere, along with all the rest of the godmothers."

"Yes, that's right." A ripple of delight shivers through her. "Isn't it exciting?"

I don't know what to think. "What will happen to your campaign?"

She looks at me as if I am dull. "It's going Nowhere, of course."

Oh.

"Right. Well, best be off. Bye-bye dear." She claps her hands together, and they make a soft, satisfied pop. In a puff of smoke, she is gone.

Nowhere

After the godmothers departed, I felt strangely at peace. I had no plans. I had no image of God to replace the God I had refused. The land within cleared, and lay as open and available to possibility as the land without. Summer arrived at the farm. As the little seeds in the earth woke and broke their husks, I could practically hear them pushing up through the earth. Each little seed came to life in its own time and bloomed according to a plan that was embedded within it. To grow, it had to leave the dark womb of Earth and journey to the world above ground, where, if it withstood the conditions of the climate, it could open and release seeds just like itself.

Every summer, the meadow changed. This year, the hawkweed thrived. The hills were covered with its tiny orange and yellow sun blossoms. Hawkweed is a flower that ventures everywhere and often grows alone and solitary among the other blooms, bravely waving in the breeze on thin, straight stalks. Last year was the year of Queen Anne's lace—its tall, elegant blossoms dominated the landscape, growing together in white clouds that floated above purple bugloss, pinks, and yellow campion.

Every morning after doing my physiotherapy, I hiked up the big hill behind the farmhouse. Sometimes it was hardly possible to get to the top, and on other occasions, I felt stronger. There were good days and bad days, sun days and rain days. I accepted them equally. I stopped trying to fix the pain or get rid of it or past it or out of it. I stopped struggling to defeat it. I wished only to come to peace, to live in equanimity with what one suffering friend called her "dark sister pain." It was an experience of settling into my body, like a bird settling into its nest. Pain and sleepless nights no longer pushed me out of my body. Now when the pain became intense, I became especially gentle, kind, and calm. I was starting to see that pain could be an ally in the fulfillment of my wish for peace. One of the things that Gangee had whispered to me was, "Pain is driving you like a cow, to the pasture of peace."

All my life I had struggled to settle, to come home, but I never knew where home was. My family had moved so many times when I was a child that I couldn't find my roots anywhere. I went to ten schools in twelve years, and as an adult, I had lived in practically every major city in Canada (and a few small towns besides). I felt like Dorothy in *The Wizard of Oz*, with malfunctioning ruby shoes. I clicked them, but they never took me home. Even at the farm, I had no feeling of belonging. Ian and I were not farmers (far from it!). We were city folk at best, newcomers with no stomach for raising farm animals and killing things. While our neighbor shot his chipmunks to get them out of his garden, we fed ours and carried the mice and spiders out of our house!

The person who was helping me to become grounded, and find peace in pain, was my aboriginal friend and counselor. Her work centered on helping people to use their imaginations to create a sacred inner space. She taught them to orient themselves according to the medicine wheel, in seven directions (east, south, west, north, above, below, and within). Once you established your sacred place, it became the heart of your world—the place for meeting spirit allies, asking questions, receiving guidance, making offerings to the earth, and giving thanks.

That was the theory, at any rate. I loved my counselor's work, but so far, I had failed to anchor myself. I did have that *well* in my inner world, but whenever I went inside, it would never be the same. It kept morphing. I couldn't fix it or make it real. I couldn't depend on it. Allies would appear and then disappear. I found it strange that with all my imaginative powers, I couldn't believe what I saw in those visualizations. It was agony not to be able to find the ground of my being.

Every time my counselor phoned, she would begin by asking me, "Where are you now?" and I would tell her a different place. When the godmothers arrived on the scene, I began shooting all over the cosmos. I am sure she wondered, *Where in the world is Michelle?* I felt like a neurotic, lost, *white* woman—rootless, with no deep tradition, unable to find myself in time or space, inside or out.

One day, she called for a session, and she began in her usual way. She guided me down into the depths and then asked me, "Where are you?"

"I'm Nowhere," I said.

The word rang out like a bell, ringing through all the worlds. It was the truest thing I had ever said to her—an admission that was at first alarming and then embarrassing.

"Can you tell me whether that is a general state or a specific place?" she ventured.

"It's just Nowhere," I said. That was all I could say. I tried to describe it, but there was really no point. I had nothing to say.

My counsellor understood, and though I think she was concerned about me, she respected what Nowhere meant. It meant no images, no allies, no directions; and it meant no more working together, at least for a while. We had come to the end of the line.

As I put the phone down, I felt relieved. Being Nowhere meant that

I had no responsibility to get anywhere at all. I started to laugh. It had never occurred to me that when the godmothers went Nowhere, they would take me too. But here I was. And Nowhere, I came to see, is a pretty active place.

For one thing, it is teeming with people. They are all people who have failed to get Somewhere. They have been rejected, or they have lost their way, or like me, they have abandoned all hope of ever getting Somewhere. Somewhere is a high mountain that the whole world seems to be climbing. The higher you go, the more focused you become. Nowhere is an ever-greening ground with room for everyone. In Somewhere, the price of admission is expensive—you need degrees and medals, awards and titles to enter. But Nowhere is a place for everybody. Here, the admission is free. It is the admission itself: "I'm Nowhere!"

In Nowhere, the inns are never full. There are always more seats in the auditorium than people to fill them, and there is more than enough food for one and all. Everyone is included, and no one is without friends. There is no lack here: no loneliness, no longing, and no judgment.

The inhabitants of Nowhere are little people. Little people are what the folks in Somewhere would consider to be nobodies. They have no status whatsoever. They include all the fallen—humans, angels, and fairies, of course. My best and wisest friends were little people, I noticed. They didn't need to be big. Ian was a little person. He had a certain gnomish view of the world. One day, when I was headed out to an important meeting with my new publisher, he stood at the base of the stairs and declared, "Don't forget the little people. You'll meet us on the way up, and you'll meet us on the way down!"

My first encounter with little people occurred in a dream I had back in the eighties. I was lying on a green, mossy mound in a beautiful forest. I had my ear to the ground, and my eyes were focused on the tiny world of the moss. Then a large finger appeared and gently stirred the moss. I heard giggles and laughter, as if children were being tickled.

When I looked closely, I saw a crowd of moss gnomes: plump, jolly little men dressed in red caps and blue and yellow jackets. They pressed into one another like bubbles, and it seemed that they liked nothing better than to be stirred by the giant finger.

Then, in 1997, I had a slightly more concrete encounter with gnomes. The pain in my body had made it impossible for me to travel to Calgary for Christmas, and I was disappointed. The family was pouring into the city from all over the continent to celebrate my father's seventieth birthday, and a big surprise party had been planned. One snowy afternoon, I went into an art store looking for Christmas presents to send to my young nieces and nephews, and I came across something called Model Magic, a sculpting clay made by Crayola.

I bought the clay and brought it home, intending to wrap it up as a gift, but I couldn't keep my fingers out of the foil package. I had to get the feel of it. The stuff is white, made from calcium, soft, pliant, and light as a marshmallow. No sooner did I have a lump in my hand than my fingers started flying all over it with an intelligence all their own. In fifteen minutes, a little man had formed in the palm of my hand. He had a gigantic nose and wore a beret, an elegant suit, and a little bow tie. He held a big orb that looked like a magical planet, and he winked at me as if to say, "There's many more folks where I come from, my friend!"

That Christmas I received a gift beyond anything I could have possibly imagined. A skill was given to me that I never knew I had. It came out of my own earth, fully formed, like one of those seeds in the meadow. The whole time I was making the gnome, I felt no pain. No painkiller had worked so well as the intense delight of seeing a little person take form in my hands. Needless to say, after the first gnome appeared, the store could not stock enough modeling clay.

"What are you doing with all this clay?" the cashier asked me.

"I'm making little people!" I announced.

His eyes lit up. "Well, that's great. I'd like to meet them one day."

Before long, I was taking my little people with me on visits so I could share their delight with others. While the gnomes were content to be invisible, nothing tickled them more than to be seen and recognized, let alone to be flattered and extolled. They were wonderful little narcissists—as full of themselves as I was when I stood in front of that mirror in my tutu at the age of four.

One day, my father came to Toronto on business, and when he dropped by for a visit, I took him upstairs to see the gnomes. At this point, I had made nearly fifty of them: elves, gnomes, dwarves, trolls, goblins, and leprechauns. I had purchased a little gilded oak tree that stood about four feet high, and I had placed it on a round, oak coffee table. The little people swung from the tree branches, played in the shade, and chatted with one another, every one absorbed in his own wee world. My dad, in spite of his commanding presence, was instantly enchanted. He bent down to look more closely, and I watched to see who would catch his attention. It was a very shy little gnome named O'Shucks who blushed easily and hid his face behind his hands.

Dad blinked. I don't know what he received, but something happened there. He straightened up and cleared his throat.

"They're a little disturbing," he said.

I laughed. The gnomes had their own way of speaking to people, and I think he had just been spoken to.

"What are you going to do with these? Is there a market for them?"

Being my father's daughter, I too had wondered what to do with the gnomes. What was their purpose? It would be great if they could make me a little money, as I had no other source of income.

A few months later, I carried half a dozen gnomes down the street to Lib 'n Ido's Rose Emporium and showed them to the store owner, a young woman named Katherine. She was charmed instantly, and was particularly attracted to a little troll who licked salt off a long baguette and called himself The Breadwinner.

"How much would you charge for them?" she asked.

I had no idea. I couldn't put a value on them—$1,000, $2,000? I had given certain gnomes up for adoption to dear friends who had formed a strong bond with this or that one, but to sell them ... hmm. I left the little troupe with her, and she put them up on her shelf above the cash register. People asked how much they were, and she gave them my card. When they called, I didn't know how to answer them. Finally, a little activist gnome came out of the clay to clear things up. He bore a sign and it read: "Save the Gnomes!" I went back to the store, gathered them all up, and took them home.

It wasn't until I myself arrived Nowhere that I understood the message of the gnomes. They had no purpose other than themselves. They did not come into this world to make money. They came here to give me whatever gifts I would be able to receive—humor, pain relief, insight, and, above all, delight. Delight is something that comes from being "surprised by joy", in the words of C. S. Lewis.

Over and over, they delighted me. I never knew who was going to come out next. Each little person took shape around one or several deformities—a large nose, big ears, fat lips, beady eyes, stubby legs, round bellies, or big hands and feet. Abnormalities were their defining features and the ones in which they took the most pride. Some were chatty, and they gave me their names and even their stories. Others were quiet and held their secrets close to their little chests. As I allowed them, they kept coming. Sometimes a face would form that would trouble me too much to bring it out entirely. They almost enjoyed pushing the limits of my acceptance.

One day, I coaxed out a troglodyte from way down in the earth. He lived in a hole at the base of a tree root and had never seen the light of day. With his long, haggard face and gray skin, he had a desperate need to be loved. He came out of the clay hunched over and down on his knees with his hand out, begging for every kindness he could possibly get. It would take a long time for that poor little troglodyte to warm up, but he, more than anyone, showed me the face of things buried deep in the earth.

Wild Geese

By mid-October, the skies were alive with gathering birds. The red-winged blackbirds filled the branches of barren maples and shrilled to one another from across the meadow. Wild geese landed in the field and fed on the corn left over from the harvest of the year before. The intelligence of the flock was everywhere—and the birds were caught up in the annual excitement of gathering and leaving.

Everything, it seemed, was converging and landing, and I had landed too. But what about the godmothers? Where were they? Had they landed? I missed them, though I hardly dared admit it. Every now and then I would receive some kind of message, or one would whisper in my ear so I knew they were not far away, but I couldn't make any contact with them. I had become confused about who they were and what they meant, if anything. What sort of purpose had they served?

Then one night I had an odd dream. The sky was washed in turquoise and splattered with golden stars. A flock of pink cranes descended from the heavens, floating down to earth on wide wings. In wave after wave, they streamed down and settled on the quiet, glistening waters of a Florida Key. The setting sun turned the sky into an ice-cream swirl of pinks, tangerines, and lavender blues. I had never seen anything so beautiful. The scene was more heavenly and real than anything I'd ever seen on earth.

But the process hadn't finished. The birds continued their descent even after they had lit on the waters. They sank through the marsh, which was just another cloud. They had a long way to go to reach solid ground. Their descent continued like a long song, the *ahh* of a deep, deep settling.

The cranes found their final landing place on the front lawn of a suburban bungalow. They were no longer heavenly beings. They were objects—pink flamingo lawn ornaments, to be exact, mass manufactured in varying shapes and sizes, all standing on one leg like your stereotypical crane.

Then a red pickup truck rounded the corner and stopped in front of the house. A little old crone hopped out. It was Tatatee! She stood no more than three and a half feet high. (How she saw over the dashboard was beyond me!) She wore a shiny pink raincoat with a plastic hat to match, and tromped over the lawn.

"There you are!" she said to the flock. "I've been looking everywhere for you. Come along, my pets." She began to gather them up and dump them into the back of her truck. Then she drove away. And I woke up.

I had no idea what the dream meant. But more than ever, I felt the pink flamingoes around me, landing and gathering me up in a spirit of buoyant euphoria and hope. Perhaps I would soon be in the pink!

But where had Tatatee gone with her truckload of birds? I had the recurring idea that maybe I could follow that truck. I waited for the inspiration. I couldn't conjure them up. The godmothers existed just outside of what I could invent, and I only knew one way to contact them. Make a wish and wait.

One night, when Ian had gone to the farm and I was alone in the city, I took myself out for dinner at Red Lobster. I sat by the window at a table that was bathed in a pool of fuchsia light emanating from the neon sign outside. I had a sudden inspiration to follow Tatatee's truck, so after placing my order, I pulled out my notebook and began to write my way back into the dream.

> I get into a car, and I follow Tatatee's truck as she heads out of the city. I follow her onto the freeway. She turns onto the off-ramp at Ferry Crossing. Then we drive north along a country highway. We drive till the sun goes down. We turn east onto a country road. Then we head north and then east again. The road narrows. She's leading me into the depths of a coal-black night. At last we pass a sign. It reads: "NOWHERE."
>
> Oh, wouldn't you *just know* it!
>
> I flash my lights and pull over to the side of the road. Tatatee slows and stops. She slides out of her truck, and we meet in the headlights of my car. She stands no higher than my pelvic

bone. She smiles at me and waddles to the side of the road, where we sit between my white headlights and her red taillights. She arranges her shiny pink raincoat around her. I am charmed by her, of course, but no less frustrated.

"Why do you keep doing this to me?" I demand.

She blinks in the strong light of my car. "Doing what, dear?"

"Leading me Nowhere! I try to follow you, but you just take me around in a circle! This is nothing but a wild goose chase." Tears sting my eyes. I've hit upon a hard truth.

"Yes. A wild goose chase," she says, nodding.

"That's just what it's like!"

"Well, that's exactly what it is."

"Right. Well, maybe I should just stop this. What's the point of going around in circles?"

"No point in a circle," she says, nodding her head.

Oh crap. I was never any good at riddles. I make a move to stand up, but I feel a tug to stay put. She searches my face with tiny, penetrating eyes that seem to shed more light on me than the headlights of my car.

"What I don't understand, dear, is why are you following *me*?"

"What?"

"You're the lead goose," she says. "We're just the *flock*."

The waitress arrived with my salad, and Tatatee dissolved into the pink neon light of the sign. At last, I understood. I was leading this expedition. So where was it headed?

For days, I walked around gathering my thoughts. I had begun my journey with the wish to know the princess—to bring her to life. Then the godmothers intervened. They snatched me up and carried me straight into the fairy world. At first, I thought my heart had been broken, and then I thought my mind had been shattered. For some time, I felt betrayed by my love for the fairy realm. But I had asked to understand something, and the godmothers had given me an under-

standing. It's a felt experience. P. L. Travers described it beautifully in her book, *What the Bee Knows*. To understand is to stand under a thing, she wrote:

[T]o understand, I come to something with my unknowing—my nakedness, if you like: I stand under it and let it teach me, rain down its truth upon me. That is, I think, what children do.

I had taken a stand with Lucy. I had resolved to look after myself and become grounded in a body that I often wanted to leave. But the journey hadn't ended. In fact, it had hardly begun. I still wanted to understand the princess. Who was she, how was she missing in the world, and why did I feel so strongly that she needed to be seen again and reinstated?

I knew one thing: the only way to know her was to meet her. On her own ground.

I look around me in this inner place I call Nowhere. It is a settlement in the middle of a desert, collecting all the fallen spirits who have finally settled into themselves. It stretches outward in every direction, greening the desert around it. Unlike the urban mountains of Somewhere that gobble up the wilderness, the people who live Nowhere are bringing the wilderness back. They are reclaiming their own lost ground, "following their bliss" to use Joseph Campbell's words. They are leading their own quests, greening the world from the inside out.

I walk through the streets of Nowhere until I come to the edge of the desert. I put my foot down on the sand, and the land greens under my feet. With every step, a garden springs into being, and before me, the gates to fairyland open.

I have a sense of fear and trepidation. It's akin to the feelings of Eve approaching the Tree of Knowledge. What I'm doing feels somehow forbidden, and yet the eager little shoots running ahead assure me that the way is good. Like the little gnomes, this world wants to be known and is bursting with delight at the footfall of a human being.

I walk over a little bridge that spans a wide stream. Thousands of fish of every color flash in and out, threading their way to the sea. Before me, the mist lifts, and I enter a forest of towering softwood trees—pine, redwood, and spruce. Their trunks are as wide as my arms outstretched and their branches brush the sky. I stand in their wind song and inhale the peace.

CHAPTER SIX

THE TOWER PRINCESS

The Tower Princess

I climb a little hill, and I see it, glimmering below: a circular spring reflecting the open sky. A waterfall pours into the well from its source in the mountains to the north. To the south, the sea breathes in and out, heaving her sighs upon the beach.

As I make my way down to the water, tripping over little stones that roll under my feet and leap down the hill ahead of me, I consider how I will travel in this world. Fairy tales have a magnetic power. They draw you in. The stories aren't meant to be skimmed and put aside. They're meant to provoke you, inspire you, prompt you to wonder. They invite you to dwell in the scenes, walk in the forests, and attune yourself to a different atmosphere.

There is a story drawing me to its heart. I'm not sure what it is, but I can feel the pull. I come to the well and stand on the wide, flat finger of rock that juts out over the water. It is smooth and rounded like a river stone. My feet, I notice, are bare, and the stone is warm and sunbaked. I lie down on my stomach and press my cheek against its smooth surface. The wind seems to have gone to sleep, leaving the water as still as glass. I look over the edge of the rock, expecting to see my own reflection, but instead the image of a maiden in a tower comes into view. I recognize her immediately as Rapunzel from the Grimms' fairy tale. She's singing from her prison tower.

That's surprising. I always assumed that Rapunzel was crying for help from her tower window. But no. As I run over the details of her story, I can plainly see that it's not a cry but a *song* that draws the prince to the tower—her exuberant, heartfelt, *happy* song.

Somehow, Rapunzel has found a way to be happy in her confinement. How? The image in the water gives me no more clues. All I have is a paradoxical picture of a joyful spirit singing from a prison tower.

I did not go any further into the story of Rapunzel at that point. Instead, I went wandering around in the country I had opened up, looking for other tower princesses. I soon found that Rapunzel is one of many maidens trapped in prisons and towers. In the region of the Grimms' collection alone, there are at least half a dozen tower princesses. Briar Rose met her fate when she came to a ruined tower in the castle, pricked her finger on a spindle, and fell into a deep sleep. Maleen was the daughter of a king who wanted her to marry the man he chose. She refused, and her father threw her into a prison tower with no windows or doors. He kept her there for seven years, hoping to break her will. Her faithful maid went with her. When seven years had passed and no one had come for them, Maleen and her maid chiseled their way out. They broke through the wall and found the kingdom in ruins—burned to cinders by the king's enemies.

The most confined of all the characters I found was the queen in a story called *The Pink*. She was accused of murdering her baby when she fell asleep in the garden. She woke to find blood on her chest and her baby gone, and she had no idea what had happened. In a rage, her husband sealed her inside a prison tower with no provisions and only the tiniest window grate high above. She lived in complete darkness. It was not only a physical darkness, but a spiritual one too. She didn't know what had happened to her baby. Did she deserve to be punished?

Doves arrived at the window grate and they brought her food. Years later, when the culprit who stole the baby was found, the king broke into the prison of his wife. He expected to find her decomposing body, but instead he found her alive. He held a feast in her honor, but she ate nothing. She had no further reason to stay in the physical world, and soon after, she died.

I spent a long time studying the stories of tower maidens, princesses, and queens. A whole year passed, from one fall to the next. Some princesses were very proud and lived in large, imposing towers. They would not lower themselves to marry mere mortals. But I was drawn to the ones for whom the tower had become a prison, a crucible. My encounter with chronic pain had put me in a tower, and I often described my body as a prison of bones. Like the queen in *The Pink*, I wondered what crime I had committed to receive such a punishment.

What goes on within a person whose body has become a prison? Medicine focuses on the outer symptoms of illness in the body, but there is much to be learned from the patient. How does the spirit respond to a state of mysterious, prolonged confinement and suffering? How does one spiritually survive such an ordeal?

The tower stories did not readily give up their secrets. Briar Rose does not tell us what she dreamed. We are left to imagine what Maleen and her maid talked about while they spent seven years in the dark. How did the queen in *The Pink* meet the demons of guilt and self-doubt that must have plagued her in her cell? And where in the world did Rapunzel get the passion to sing so joyfully from her tower window? I kept looking for clues, but I found none. I could not penetrate the stories' surfaces.

One fall morning, I was sitting upstairs in my office, lost in yet another tower story. It was called *The Sea Hare*, and it featured the proudest, mightiest tower princess I had ever encountered. She lived in a tower that rose so high it dominated the landscape. It had twelve magic windows that went all the way around, and through her windows she could see everything going on below. No creature—not even the tiniest mite—could conceal itself from her. Marriage, of course, was beneath her, but she did condescend to give her suitors a test. She promised to marry the one who could successfully conceal himself from her view. When the story opened, ninety-nine suitors had tried and failed. Their severed heads had been thrust on stakes, and they stood before her tower as a grisly warning to anyone fool enough to lose his head over the princess.

One day, a suitor came along who took up her challenge. He asked for three chances, not one, and she gave them to him because he was charming. With the help of his forest friends, he turned himself into several little creatures, which the princess easily detected from her magic windows in the tower. With only one chance left, a fox turned him into a tiny little creature called a sea hare. The fox put the sea hare in a glass jar and carried him to the marketplace.

The princess soon came walking along, and when she saw the wondrous creature, she had to buy him. She took the sea hare back to her tower. He crept out of the jar and climbed up into a place where she couldn't see him: the braid down her back. She went around her tower looking for her suitor through all her windows. Where was he? She couldn't detect him. Finally, in a rage, she slammed the windows shattering all the magic glass.

What a strange story, I thought, sitting with my book. What did it mean? It reminded me of a dream I once had about being in a tower. I had climbed to the very top. My head was squished into the tapering spire, and I was still trying to get higher. I looked out through a little window and saw a huge storm galloping in from across the plain. When it reached me, it would break the tower like a matchstick. Why, I wondered, had I chosen to make my home in a tower? Why had I not chosen to live close to the ground, in those rambling shanties I saw below?

Suddenly, Ian let out a cry from downstairs. "Michelle, come quick!"

I rushed down the stairs to find him standing in the living room in front of the TV, and we watched in horror as a plane plowed through the second tower of the World Trade Center. What I had seen in a fairy tale was happening before my eyes—the shattering glass, the tower's collapse, the unreeling saga of agony and terror....

For months on end, the event played and replayed on television. As the United States invaded Afghanistan and led a war against terrorism, everybody was talking about towers: the Twin Towers, the tower in the tarot, the tower as a symbol of the changing times.

I began to see towers everywhere. They were the dominant feature of our outer and inner landscapes. Every major city in North America had its tower. We worked in office towers and climbed the corporate ladder. We went to school in ivory towers. It seemed that in one way or another, we were all in towers. Our very bodies were towers, and no one brought that home more vividly than the Afghan women in their burqas. I was riveted by their images. They walked along the streets of Kandahar like ghosts, invisible to others. Who were they inside the confines of those garments? How did they come to terms with *their* predicament?

One day, I saw a picture in the newspaper that was taken by a journalist named Laura Rauch. It was a photograph of an Afghan woman who was waiting in line to receive wheat and oil from a UN bakery. She stood among a crowd of other widows who were described in the caption as "the most vulnerable group in the city." The women around her were hidden under their burqas, their eyes gazing out through netted windows. But this woman had raised her burqa to reveal her astonishingly beautiful face. Her eyes shimmered, and she smiled mischievously. She had put a finger to her lip as if to say to the reporter, "Shh, don't tell anyone."

That was *her*. The heart of the world.

I put her image beside my computer where I could see her all the time. Sometime later, I happened to catch an interview on television with a nun who had worked with the women of Afghanistan. The interviewer asked the nun why the women still wore burqas even though the Taliban were no longer in control. She said, "You would know the answer to that question if you ever wore a burqa. The minute you put one on, you feel safe."

Safety had become very important in our world. But safety wasn't the way of the princess. It wasn't the way of the heart. The way of the princess was written on the face of the woman in Laura Rauch's photograph: a free spirit in a desperate situation.

Now I knew the story I wanted to follow. It had been Rapunzel all along. She was the one who could show me how a change of heart occurs in a prison of bones. I was being drawn into her story like a bee to a flower. The nectar was there.

Flight to Rapunzel

I stand on the flat rock by the well and turn in each direction, hoping to sense the way into Rapunzel's world. I face the east and hear the sounds of the forest. I face south and smell the sea. I turn west to see the fresh expanse of the plains and north to feel the chill of the mountains. When I come round again to the east, I see a bee, hovering in midair between the east and the south. It flies in a big circle, and when it comes back around, it makes a beeline for the southeast.

As far as I know, there is nothing out there but sea. I walk down a narrow sandy path that winds through a stand of trees between the well and the beach. The sand on the shore is warm, and the setting sun, flickering through the trees, flecks the rocky coast in gold.

I notice white tail feathers sticking out from behind a large boulder at the shoreline, and when I approach, a huge bird pulls his head out from under a wing and gawks at me. He stands up and shakes himself, releasing a cloud of downy feathers. He is more than seven feet tall and pure white with a rust-orange beak and black eyes. My first thought is, *It's a snow goose.*

He preens his feathered chest, sending me the distinct message: "S'no goose, but a gander!" Then he drops his long neck as if to say, "At your service, madam."

What sort of service has he come to provide? I have the strong sense that he is supposed to deliver something. Deliver what? He cranes his neck toward me. *Me?* Deliver *me*! Where? Over the sea, apparently. I look out at the water, hoping to detect the outline of a distant shore. Nothing. There is a possibility that he will deliver me somewhere other than the place I want to go, which is into the story of Rapunzel. He could be some trick or diversion. At times like this, I have a hard time trusting my active imagination to carry me anywhere. What am I doing? Where am I going? This is really nuts!

With grace and an exceedingly gentle air, he lies down so I can climb up on his back. It's like climbing into a luxurious feather bed, perfectly safe and supportive. I put my arms around his neck and tuck my feet into the underside of his belly. I feel like Mother Goose. It has never occurred to me that the goose would ride the gander, but now that I've actually assumed her position, it makes perfect sense and fills me with inexpressible delight.

The gander extends his powerful wings and beats them against the air. We rise heavily and gradually climb into the sky. His flight is labored and his breathing loud. *Nnyhah, nnyhah*, he rasps on the in-breath, like someone suffocating. It takes enormous effort for him to get into the sky, and I feel guilty for being so heavy. I want to become lighter, but I can't. I don't know how.

One by one, the stars come out winking, and the sea turns a teal blue, velvety and smooth. The feathers of the gander are sweet-smelling and soft as rose petals. I soon find that I don't have to hold on so tight. I can let go, and I won't fall off. As I release my grip on the gander's neck, a wonderful thing happens. He accepts me as part of his own weight, and I start to feel lighter and lighter until I seem to weigh nothing at all. Our two beings become one. I have the odd sensation that we're leading a whole migration, that we're part of some very large movement known only to geese. I want to experience more of the goose and the migration, more of what the goose and the gander know—but the gander's descent has begun. Land appears in the distance, little lights glimmer under a heavy cloak of forest and cloud. I don't want to go down, but the gander continues his descent. As he does, I find myself clinging to his neck once again, feeling fearful and heavy, separate and oh so utterly human. When his feet touch ground, he gently shakes me out of that warm nest.

I land on a beach covered in rounded flat stones. A clump of sweet grass grows thick at the shore. I remember what my aboriginal counselor taught me about thanking the allies. I pull some grass for him and offer it by way of thanks. He gratefully accepts it. I stroke his wing feathers several times, but he shakes his head. For reasons known only to the gander, strokes are not what he wants.

I bid him adieu and start through the forest that leads into Rapunzel's world. It's getting dark, and I'm beginning to feel uncomfortable. The story is familiar to me, but not the details. I have never walked on the actual ground of a fairy tale. Acorns, hickory, and beechnuts roll under my feet, making my footing insecure, and as the sounds of the day give way to the hoots and caws of the night, I think perhaps I've had enough for one day. I'm not keen on the idea of meeting that old witch just yet. Maybe the gander is hers, in which case, my goose is cooked! Does she know I'm here? Will she snare me the moment I set foot on her turf?

I think I'll leave the search for today and return to the comforts of the here and now, where it's three o'clock in the afternoon. I wouldn't mind getting outside for a good old-fashioned walk. But then, I come to a tree with a wooden sign hanging on it and paths leading left and right. The sign is written in pink neon letters, and reads:

FAIRY GODMOTHERS LEFT

Just when I figured I had things under control! I stand there at the crossroads and consider the sign. I appreciate that they have given me a choice. Do I want them on my adventure or not? If I take them back, I will have to be very clear about my direction. I don't want to get caught up in their campaign. On the other hand, maybe they can help me. It wouldn't hurt to check them out.

CHAPTER SEVEN

HELP FROM THE FAIRIES

The Picnic

Fireflies flash in and out of the trees as I walk along the path in the twilight. I sense the presence of other beings. In fairy tales, everything is animate and has a story, including the rocks and the plants and the trees. I pass a large, moss-covered boulder and run my hand over its lumpy limestone surface. What imprisoned spirit might it hold?

I come into a meadow and find the godmothers seated on Gangee's sprawling cloak. They're having a picnic under the full orb of a rising moon. The flowers glow, dotting the meadow like a thousand little rainbow-colored spotlights. Fireflies blink in and out of the stars on Gangee's cloak, and she rocks happily back and forth, her crinkled brown face dwarfed by the spread of her magic robe. Her hands are busy with knitting needles. Tatatee is kneeling down and unloading a big picnic basket, while her luminous white elephant steals peanuts from her pocket. Willow floats above the group like their own personal cloud, and Greta Greatwaite has dropped her head onto a big book that lies open on her lap. I can't tell whether she is reading it very closely or has gone to sleep.

"Hello, dear!" creaks Tatatee without looking up. She carries on, pulling sandwiches out of the basket. "Come and join us. We've only just arrived."

I kneel on the blanket. Gangee puts down her knitting and greets me with an outstretched arm. My white, and her brown hands meet in the starlight between us, and our fingers intertwine.

"Hello, precious Hope," she croons.

"How did you get here?" I ask.

Gangee chuckles, causing the stars on her cloak to shiver. "Fairy tales are known territory for us. We have always inhabited them. They are a meeting place for many worlds."

"We're very excited about your present direction," says Tatatee. She stands up and brushes the crumbs off her jeans, which I notice are folded up at the cuffs because her legs are so short. "However, you may be comforted to know that we have established some ground rules. Indeed, we have reinstated a very old noninterference policy, or NIP. All the fairies who are present here have signed it." She pulls out a scroll from her picnic basket and unfurls it. The air becomes very still as each little point of light hovers in space.

"We, the undersigned members of the fairy world, who have traveled by train of thought from Somewhere to Nowhere, hereby vow not to interfere in human affairs. We shall not forget that we are, and ever shall be, servants of humanity, and we shall return to Nowhere the moment we are bid to do so."

She rolls up the scroll. "We have quite comfortable lodgings in Nowhere, and we will take no offense whatsoever if you wish to send any or all of us back. Simply direct us to the Wayside Inn."

"If you send us there," says Willow, settling on the blanket, "we won't be able to get out without your permission." She has an airy, melodious voice that is very pleasant to listen to, like listening to a child sing.

"Perhaps we can be useful to you," says Tatatee. "You have opened up a country that is home to us, but we have been away for a long time. Undoubtedly, much has changed. We understand that you are here for your own reasons, and we too have questions to investigate, which have to do with the matter of our displacement and its cause, which we have previously described to you as the ... ahem, I had better spell it out ... the S-E-R-I-O-U-S effect."

"The *serious* effect? So you didn't mean a real star?" I ask.

"Fairies are not meant to be taken literally," Greta barks, pulling her head up from out of her book. "That sort of top-down thinking is nothing but pure superstition."

She looks at me—or rather, through me—as if she doesn't see me at all. I'm so gobsmacked by what she just said that I have to suspend the action for a moment, and go look up the meaning of the word *superstition*. To my surprise, it means "to stand over," as opposed to the word *understanding*, which means "to stand under." If I *understand* Greta correctly, she's telling me that the fairies look at the world from the inside out (and the bottom up) and not from the outside in (and the top down). That sheds a whole new light on the star they're speaking about. From the outside, it's *Sirius*, but from the inside, it's *serious*. From both points of view, it's a star, and the fairies clearly believe it's the reason for their separation from human beings.

"Why have you come here?" Greta wants to know. Her tone is off-putting, but I decide to meet her head-on.

"I want to know more about the story of Rapunzel."

"You're going to tell the story?" Willow wraps her cloudy form around me like a cat. "Are you going to take us through it?"

"Where did you find the story?" Greta wants to know. She licks her thumb and flips through the pages of her great book, making it clear that if the story carries any weight whatsoever, it will be found in her book.

"Well, technically speaking, it's from the Grimms' collection."

"You're not going to *read* it, are you?" Willow sounds disappointed.

"No, that's not exactly what I had in mind. I was thinking, actually, of reading *between* the lines."

"Eh?" Greta leans toward me, cupping her ear.

"I said I want to read between the lines!" I shout boldly.

"I heard you," says Greta. "How do you expect to read what isn't written in the lines?"

"I won't ignore the lines, but I want to see what is going on with my own eyes. I want to walk around in the story. I mean, aren't we here already?"

"We are most certainly in the vicinity," says Tatatee.

"Well, it is important to pay attention to the lines," says Greta. "The patterns are very old." She closes her book and drums her large square fingers on the cover.

Oh dear. Greta seems heavily weighed down by that book. I want to free my imagination and go into a story to experience it for myself. I want to touch things and be touched. Otherwise, a fairy tale is just a museum piece. Respected, maybe, and preserved—but not alive.

"Don't mind her gruff tone," Willow whispers in my ear. "She's supposed to be the keeper of the lore, so she's having a hard time of it. She'll come around."

Just then, there is a big explosion overhead and a burst of fireworks. Lucy comes plummeting down on a red and white striped parachute, and lands—*kerplunk*—in the middle of the picnic, sending sandwiches flying into the air and scattering

Willow all over the place. The elephant screeches happily at the shower of pink and green stars that shoot into the sky, while I'm thinking, *Oh no. Lucy. Has she signed the NIP?*

"Ahem, pardon me ... oh dear ... Came in a bit too fast there—my apologies." Her rich, old, thunder voice crackles in the air. She gathers up her parachute and packs it into her carpet bag, which I notice has a new travel tag attached to the handle. It reads "NOWHERE" in red letters. She wears her signature pink tutu, patent leather shoes, a sparkling purple wig and green freckles. Her wings are there, but they seem too small to support her. Evidently, she prefers parachuting tonight.

"Not a lightweight at this very moment, I'm afraid," she mutters. "Hope I'm not interrupting anything." She notes the sandwiches that have gone flying into the field. "Oh dear, I've made a big mess. I'm too much!" She laughs heartily.

"I trust my appearance will not upset you, my dear, but I am pleased to be able to give you a gift which has been *much changed*." She bends down and draws a glowing wand out of her bag. "I expect it will help you on your quest for Rapunzel."

She steps forward, bows deeply, and presents me with the wand. It no longer sparkles with dazzling blue-silver light. It's golden, with the calming effect of candlelight, and it smells sweet, like honey.

"It is your very own wand," she says. "It's also collapsible." She pushes on the glowing tip, and it shrinks into an object the size of a pen. Then she taps it on the little golden bulb at its tip, and it shoots out again. "Pretty nifty, wouldn't you say?"

"Downright phallic, Lucy," I mutter.

"Well, there you go ... something from me," she says triumphantly.

It feels very warm and friendly in my hand, and I know it will be a comforting companion in the dark.

"You will note, it does not have the power of sorcery," says

Lucy. "It cannot change one thing into another on a whim. I'm afraid that the days of witches' sticks are over, at least as far as the Nowhere crowd is concerned. However, what it can do is show you a thing for what it really is.

"Well, I best be off before you're tempted to use it on *me*!" She claps me on the shoulder, and before I can thank her, she has disappeared in a puff of green smoke. I have to wonder what she would turn into if I did use the wand on her. No sooner do I think that thought than I see a green fairy, so tiny as to be invisible to the naked eye. It flashes away.

Gangee's Cloak

Several days and nights went by, during which time I lounged on Gangee's cloak in the meadow under moonlight. Every time I went into the inner worlds, there we were. Nothing much was going on.

Meanwhile, I felt increasingly uneasy. I woke up at three in the morning three nights in a row and couldn't get back to sleep. I stared at the ceiling and wondered why, if fairy tales were supposed to be so irrelevant and unimportant, was I experiencing so much fear and anxiety going into Rapunzel?

I felt a lot of pressure in my head. My thoughts tormented me. What the heck are you doing? Leave this alone! they cried. Don't go there! Didn't you read the signs? What signs? The signs over the gate to the fairy world! "No Trespassing." "Thou Shalt Not Enter." "Here Be Dragons." I didn't see any signs, although I was moving against an inner resistance for sure. From the moment I took my first step into Rapunzel's world, I knew that you can't tiptoe into this place unnoticed. I had sent out a signal, and right away, I felt its report. The witch knew that I had arrived, or at least that something was afoot. How would she react? I didn't have to be very well studied in fairy tales to know that certain characters—like witches, devils, griffins, and giants—have a nose for humans, and they don't welcome them. Who can forget the giant in Jack in the Beanstalk roaring, "Fee fie fo fum. I smell the blood of an Englishman!"

It was comforting to have the wand. I imagined planting it in the ground like a streetlight and resting under the lamp. The light was calming, sweet scented, and warmly knowing. On those unsettled nights I would fall asleep naming the qualities of the wand. Roused by my appreciation, the light grew stronger, and long after I had fallen asleep, it was still chasing the shadows away.

Three days passed—uneventful November days. A steel-gray sky put a weight on the city. Traffic lined up every morning across the street, as cars snaked their way to work. I had instituted a routine that would keep the pain down to a dull roar. Every morning, I did my physiotherapy exercises and then went out for a walk through the park. I climbed a long hill to get my heart rate up and then wandered past Casa Loma, a spectacular castle built in 1911 by Sir Henry Pellatt who made a fortune on the Toronto Electric Light Company. He had a monopoly on all the street lighting in the city, and he put $17 million into his dream house. Unfortunately, his dream was too big, and he couldn't finance his expansion plans. His funds dried up, and today his home is a public place, an anachronism to which tourists are drawn, attracted by the Disney magic of the castle on the hill. Alas, they find nothing more than a museum and empty rooms reserved for weddings and private affairs. No fairies there.

My walk took me past the high stone walls of Casa Loma and down a long series of steps to the street. Cars rushed by, and angled to get around one another. In spite of the pain and the anxiety of not having a life, I was grateful for the opportunity to step away from the nine-to-five routine. Without it, however, I felt that I was drifting like Willow, cloudy and diffused, sometimes almost dissolving. Strange to say, but the ground within had become firmer than ground under my feet. At least, in the fairy world, I had set a course. I was going somewhere!

On the fourth day, when I returned to Gangee's cloak, I was ready to move forward, and a change had begun.

The stars on her cloak have stopped moving. They glow like hundreds of tiny suns and hum. We all rise into the night air, leaving Greta on the ground below, sitting with her closed book on her lap and staring ahead. I strain to see through Gangee's cloak, not wanting to leave Greta behind, but she has become too heavy to carry.

The meadow underneath us melts away, and the next thing I know, we're landing on a cobblestone street in the village where Rapunzel's parents live. It is just before dawn.

"Nice neighborhood," Tatatee remarks, stepping off Gangee's cloak and onto the street. "Yoo-hoo, come along," she says to her elephant. "We have much to explore before sunrise."

Willow remains sleeping on the cloak, but Gangee is awake. She has been gazing at me for some time.

"You are not meant to hurt yourself, my child," she says quietly. "Remember that, above all. This is the mirror world. It may reflect the truth, but it is only a mirror. You can break the spell at any time."

Relief sweeps through me. "How do I do that?"

"Make the sound of two hands clapping."

I put my hands together. "Clap, you mean?"

"Yes, that's right. The sound of two hands clapping will shatter the mirror. Fairies like nothing better than a good round of applause. Everyone will remember that they are just actors in a play and that the scene is done."

"I have to wonder how many people are attending the show these days."

Gangee smiles, bemused. "People have been going to this show for a long time. For as long as humans have reflected, they have been coming into the mirror. Now there are many mirrors, and not all of them are true."

"Rapunzel feels very true to me, though I don't know why," I muse.

"Then all the more reason why you must say what you see." We are quiet for a moment. "What is the matter with Greta?"

"Dear Greta ..." Gangee squeezes her eyes shut for a moment. Then she says, "Well, you know what is the matter with Greta."

"All I know is that she carries many stories with her, but she can't get at them."

"Go on," says Gangee. "Say more of what you see. What do you imagine has happened to Greta?"

"She has lost them somehow. Maybe she lost sight of them when the stories went into print. A connection was broken there ..." I know how hard it is to be a storyteller in a literate culture. Once the stories have gone into print, it's not easy to lift them off the page and make them real again. If you're afraid of offending the ancestors or the folklore community by making the story your own, then it's impossible to let them climb into your heart.

"Yes, Greta has lost sight of her stories," says Gangee, absorbed in her thoughts. "She cannot see very well anymore. What else are you seeing?"

I consider her question. Images are forming. I grasp hold of the thread. In Gangee's presence, I feel that I can trust the strength of my insight. "Well, I am seeing a great stone standing on a wide plain. Once upon a time, people passed the stone on their journeys. That's where they camped and exchanged their stories. The stone absorbed all their experience, and Greta was that stone, remembering everything."

"What happened then?" Gangee asks.

"The people began to leave the land. They started going to live in towns and cities. They forgot the stone, and soon, even Greta left it and began to wander around, trying to follow where the people went. As she wandered, her stories began to fly away from her. She began to forget them. But then she was given a new gift."

"Ah, yes, there is always compensation," says Gangee, rocking back and forth. "What was her new gift?"

"She learned to write. So she wrote down every story she could remember in her big book. She traveled with her book, but it grew heavier and heavier with the weight of her recorded stories. Nobody was particularly interested in her book ... and as they became disinterested, she lost her eyesight—and with it, her *insight*. She forgot what the stories meant. But she continued to hold on to her book. It was her only remaining connection to the past."

"Well done. And now it seems that with the loss of her sight, Greta has acquired yet another gift." Gangee plunks her knitting on her lap with satisfaction. "She has situated herself in the meadow, and though there is only one story to tell, she now has the power to amplify it. She will project it outward in the form of images, so we can all watch the show."

"So she's like a *broadcaster*?"

"Just so!" Gangee exclaims. "That is precisely what she is." She giggles like a delighted child. "Just so, just so ..."

Gangee begins to blink rapidly. The sun rises like a ruby over the distant hills, and she fades in the light. I have the funny feeling that she doesn't go anywhere, but in the light of day, she and the other fairies can't be seen. I stand up and look down the hilly cobblestone street to see if I can spot the house belonging to Rapunzel's parents. There's a tug on my sweater, and I turn around to see a young woman standing beside me. She is maybe fourteen years old, with a mass of curly white-blond hair, green eyes, and a dusting of freckles on her nose.

"Do you know who I am?" she asks.

I recognize the voice. "Willow?"

"Yes, it's me! I haven't come to light for such a long time. How do I look?" She runs her hands over her face, torso, and hips. She wears a white blouse and an emerald bodice that is laced to reveal the gentle curves of her breasts and hips. She swishes her legs back and forth under a gauzy ivory skirt made up of several layers of organza. A drawstring tapestry bag swings from one arm.

"You're gorgeous! Wait, though. I can still see through you a bit." I touch her shoulder and feel a little resistance, but I could break through it if I pushed hard enough. She's still slightly ghostly.

"Well, this is quite enough material for me. It's confining, don't you think? But very grand! I feel so solid and strong. I wish I could see myself in a mirror, but I don't dare. I might not be there!" She laughs. "Oh, I almost forgot. Look what Gangee made for us." She pulls open her bag and draws out two lapis blue robes, studded with flecks of gold. "Cloaks of invisibility!"

We put them on, and with their hoods, they cover us from head to toe. We saunter down the street, arm in arm, enjoying our invisibility as we pass villagers who are pulling carts full of produce up the hill on their way to the market. I feel safe in my cloak, and can't help but think of the Middle Eastern women in their burqas.

Willow squeezes my arm. "If things get too scary," she whispers, "don't forget to clap!"

CHAPTER EIGHT

THE FISHWIFE

A Terrible Craving

It's not difficult to make out the house where Rapunzel's parents live. It stands at the base of a hill and looks very much like all the other houses that are pressed into one another, all in a row. They remind me of clothing on a line, painted in pretty, soft colors: lavender, blue, coral, yellow, and sage. They have pottery roofs and lead paned windows. Most of them have three floors, and are quite narrow with small flower gardens in the front and cheerful blooms growing in window pots.

The house belonging to Rapunzel's mother and father is yellow and leans into the shoulder of the magnificent house that stands squarely at the foot of the hill. Unlike the wooden houses, the mansion is made of gray stone and asserts itself against all the others. Its ample front garden is surrounded by a high iron fence, and on opposite sides of the gate, two marble lions snarl at passersby.

Next to the mansion, the yellow house looks pale and sickly. We walk down the path to the house, creep in through the front door, and tiptoe up a narrow staircase that leads to the second floor. In the room at the back of the house, overlooking the garden, we find Rapunzel's mother and father.

Her mother stands with her back to us, looking out the window. Her lush red hair has been swept up off her shoulders, plaited expertly and fastened with combs that are decorated with pearls and shells. She wears a teal dress made of shiny rustling silk. The sleeves puff at the shoulders and narrow to points on the back of her hands. Her small breasts are pushed up by a coral bodice embroidered with copper vines. Even through the reflected glass, her beauty is dazzling, and we can see that she is pregnant. Her belly, round as a pumpkin, swells under her dress.

Her husband stands behind her, resting his hands on her shoulders. He's a lanky man with a faded brown beard, and though he is handsome, he looks haggard—rough weather at sea and at home has prematurely aged his face.

"Come away from the window, Kate," he says gently.

She shrugs him off. "Leave me be, Jacob."

"It's no use pining after something you can't have."

"I said, leave me *be*. Why must you always be telling me what I can't have?"

"Come on, Kate, try to think of something else other than the rapunzel in that garden next door."

He tries to draw her away from the window, which is a mistake. She elbows him in the ribs. "If you loved me, you would get me those greens."

"She's a sorceress, Kate! You know as well as I do that if I steal her rapunzel, she'll make a meal of *me*!"

Kate hauls herself to her feet. "I *need* that rapunzel, Jacob, and if I don't get some to eat, I will *die*."

"Don't say that."

"I will die! And I will take the child with me!"

"You're acting like a fishwife! You go too far!" he shouts. He leaves the room and she lunges after him.

"How dare you call me that!" He ignores her, heading down the stairs. Steadying herself on the banister railing, she hollers, "If I'm a fishwife, then you're a maggot! Do you hear me? A *maggot*!"

Her words ricochet off the walls of the house and rattle down the street. She sinks into a hill of taffeta at the top of the stairs.

Willow and I slip around her, and follow Jacob as he stumbles along the road. He's holding his head and wailing, "She'll never be happy—never. Why didn't I see it before I married her? I can't do this. I can't."

He kicks the stones and sends them rolling before him on the road. As he trudges out of town, a strong wind from the sea flies up. It pushes against him, howls in his face and whips his thin, gray coat like a flag on a pole. He puts his head down and continues walking into the wind, away from the village. The wind grows ferocious as he pushes up a long hill. It blasts him with rain and hail until he can go no farther, and he falls to his knees. "Aaaaaaaayyyyyy!" he cries. Burying his face in his hands, he sobs.

After some time, Jacob tips his face to the sky, water streaming down his cheeks. "What difference does it make whether or not I go over the wall?" he says. "Either way, I am beaten."

He gets to his feet and drags himself home like a broken animal.

The Fishwife

Willow and I take refuge from the storm in a cave that overlooks the sea. We make a little fire in a stone circle, arranging the kindling around half-burned logs. Willow instructs me to point my wand at a small piece of wood under the heap of kindling, and it bursts into flames.

She shudders. "I had no idea that it would be so stormy in your story. The lady of the house is very troubled. Why does she demand that her husband do such a dangerous thing? What is so enticing about the rapunzel? Why can't she be happy with the little one who is growing inside her?"

I pick up a stick and poke at the little blaze that keeps being buffeted by the winds outside the cave.

Her questions are mine, too. It occurs to me that Rapunzel's mother is a pretty clear portrayal of the modern consumer. She's always looking outward at the grass that's greener on the other side of the fence.

Willow rubs her right ear and stretches her long, white hands over the fire. She doesn't look comfortable. We have taken off our cloaks, and they lie beside us, glimmering in the firelight. The day has darkened with the storm. The sea pounds on the rocky shore below. She rubs her ear again.

"Lucy's here. She's in my ear. She picked up on that word. *Consumer.* She says she hopes that you aren't using the word to mean humanity ... because *consumer* is not a good way to spell humanity."

I'm taken aback. "Can Lucy read my thoughts?"

Willow cocks her head to one side. "Some of them ... but her pickup isn't very good. I wish she'd settle down in there. If you don't quiet down, Lucy, I might squish you!"

We laugh. I ask Lucy if she wants to join us, but I get no reply. She seems content to stay in Willow's ear. Maybe, like the others, Lucy can't appear in the light of day. The sun hasn't gone down yet. Maybe it isn't dark enough for her to come to light.

"Lucy wants you to explain what it means to be a fishwife," Willow says.

"Well, what's coming to mind is the story of *The Fisherman's Wife.* She and her husband also lived by the sea. Heck, they might have lived in this very village. But I'm not sure you want to hear that story, Willow. There's another storm in it, and it's an even bigger one than this one!"

"But we need to know the story," Willow insists. "You can tell it. We'll be safe in the cave."

"All right, but clap if you want me to stop, okay?"

"I will, but I won't," says Willow, settling in.

"Okay. Well, here goes. Once upon a time, a fisherman and his wife lived in a house by the sea. It wasn't a beautiful house. It wasn't even a house. It was a pigsty. The fisherman's wife hated her life there.

"One day her husband went out fishing, and he caught a flounder on his line. This was no ordinary fish. The flounder could speak! And he said, 'Please don't kill me. I'm not a fish. I'm a prince under a spell!'

"The fisherman was amazed. 'Gee, you didn't need to tell me you were a prince,' he said. 'I would have thrown you back into the sea just *for speaking* to me!'

"He quickly released the fish from the hook and tossed him back into the sea. The flounder swam down into the deep, trailing a line of blood behind him.

"When the fisherman got home that night, he told his wife what had happened.

"'You let an enchanted fish go?' she cried. 'Why didn't you ask it to grant you a wish?'

"'What kind of a wish?' he asked.

"'Well look around you, man! Can't you see that we live in a pigsty? You go back and find that fish, and you tell that fish that we want a decent house to live in!'

"The next day, the fisherman went down to the shore and gazed out over the water. It had turned a sickly yellow-green."

"Like the sea here," says Willow, peering out of the mouth of the cave. "It's the same color."

Sure enough. The clouds are swirling over the waters, agitated.

"Yes, well the sea wasn't very happy that day. The fisherman called to the flounder. He had to shout over the noise of the crashing surf:

'Flounder, flounder in the sea,
Come, I pray thee, here to me;
For my wife, good Isabil,
Wills not as I'd have her will.'

"The flounder heard the fisherman's call, and he rose out of the waters. 'What does your wife want?' he asked. The fisherman explained that she wanted to live in a nice house.

"'Well, then go back home, and you will see that she has the house already,' said the flounder.

"When he got home, the fisherman found his wife standing outside the house and jumping for joy. She took him inside and showed him the porch, the parlor, the bedroom, and the kitchen with a pantry. The house was well furnished and fitted up with beautiful things, and they had a small yard with hens and ducks, and a garden with flowers and fruit."

"That's a pretty generous fish," Willow remarks.

"Yes, he was, and everything went well for a little while, but before long, the fisherman's wife grew restless again."

Willow scowls and stirs the popping fire. "Why? Why wasn't she content?"

"I don't know, Willow, but she wasn't. She found the house and garden too small. She figured she ought to be living in something better, like a castle. So she pushed her husband again, and he went back to the sea, and this time, the water had turned purple and dark blue.

"The fisherman called to the flounder and asked him to grant his wife's new wish. The flounder granted the wish, and the fisherman went home to find a castle with a great hall made out of marble and chandeliers hanging from the ceiling. A feast was laid out on a grand table, and he walked around and found a courtyard, stables with horses and carriages, and a magnificent garden—the whole nine yards!"

"Surely she is satisfied now!" exclaims Willow, wide-eyed.

"She was for a while, but then she grew restless again. She wanted to be king of the land."

"King?" Willow looks at me, aghast.

"That's what the story says. The fisherman stumbled back to the shore, muttering, 'It is not right, not right.'

"The sea had grown angry. But once again, the flounder granted the wife's wish and made her king. So now she had all this power, and she sat on a throne made of gold and diamonds. She had servants working for her and who knows what else—a whole army to order around. But it wasn't enough to wear a crown. She wanted to be emperor!

"The fisherman went back to the sea, and now it was black and boiling. The waters foamed at his feet." (At this point, I leave out the raging wind because the storm outside has intensified, and I don't want the fire to go out.)

"Again, the flounder granted the wish of the wife, and she became emperor. But then she demanded to be pope. The fisherman had grown very much afraid, and he went back to the sea."

Winds are gusting around the cave, and the flame doesn't have a chance. I hurry through the tale, shouting over the roar of the sea as it pounds the rocks below. "The wind had gathered hurricane force. The ships in the distance were being tossed around like bath toys, and the poor sailors were crying for help. But still he called to the flounder, on behalf of his wife:

'Flounder, flounder in the sea,
Come, I pray thee, here to me;
For my wife, good Isabil,
Wills not as I'd have her will!'

"She got to be pope, and she ruled the hearts and minds of the whole world. But she still wasn't happy! She wanted to order the sun and the moon to rise. She wanted to control all of nature!"

"Nature? Control *nature*?" Willow shouts.

"Her husband fell on his knees and begged her to stop, but she flew at him in a rage, tore open her bodice, and shrieked that she could not stand one more moment of this torment.

"'What? What would you have me ask for?' he cried.

"'Make me like *God*!' she yelled.

"The poor man pulled on his trousers, and he ran away like a madman. He could hardly get to the shore, the wind was blowing so hard. Houses and trees were toppling and falling into the sea. Even the mountains in the distance trembled, and the sea had gone pitch black. The sky boomed with thunder and lightning, and the waves rose as high as church towers. He called to the flounder, and he couldn't even hear his own voice over the roaring sea.

"'What does she want now?' shouted the flounder.

"'She wants to be God!'

"'Then go to her!' cried the flounder, and he swam away."

"I know where he found her," says Willow. "Right back in the pigsty."

"Yep."

The wind drops, and we fall into silence.

"Now I understand what it means to be a fishwife," says Willow. "I never saw anyone so unhappy."

Just then, Lucy materializes, fully amplified, in the darkest part of the cave. She looks worse for wear, as if she has been out in that big wind with the fisherman. Her tutu is tattered, and her wig has blown off, revealing a bald, speckled pate, bent antennae, and the natural green freckles that spatter her nose. "You might have warned me the story would have no good ending," she mutters.

"I'm sorry, Lucy. I didn't know you would be so affected by those sea winds."

"I'm affected by *everything*," she says dramatically. "Well now, go on, tell us ... Have human beings become fishwives?"

I'm not sure how to answer that. The Rolling Stones line, "I can't get no satisfaction," comes to mind. That's basically where we've been for the last half century. We never have enough. Something better is always hanging in front of us, just out of reach, tantalizing us like the salad greens in the witch's garden. Through the window of television and computer screens, we see a happier, more luxurious lifestyle than our own, which could be ours if only we worked harder and made more sacrifices. Advertising keeps us in a state of constant dissatisfaction and anxiety. Our clothes, homes, gardens, spouses, *selves* are never adequate. In the 1950s, the advertising industry consciously set about to create dissatisfaction so that we would feel a need to buy soft drinks, junk food, hairspray, and a raft of other unnecessary items.

A television commercial from last night plays back through my mind. It portrayed the face of a very unattractive woman (your garden-variety hag, actually!) with long pieces of hair coming out in unsightly places. The narrator said: "Are you *embarrassed by* those ugly black hairs that appear on your upper lip and chin? Are you *worried* about being seen with those unsightly hairs?" And on it went. I found my hand going up to my own chin and thinking, *Gee, is facial hair really that embarrassing*? How harshly will I be judged if a whisker sneaks past my notice?

Lucy stares at me, aghast. "What kind of mirror is that?"

"What are you seeing?" Willow asks Lucy.

"A picture of a hag with mole hairs ... a piece of the shattered mirror, I warrant ... Oh drat, now I've lost it ... all scrambled ..." She adjusts her antennae like we used to adjust old television sets.

"Why would you want a mirror that reflected you as a hag?" Willow asks.

"It's not a mirror. It's television."

"Tell-a-vision? What sort of vision does it tell?" Lucy gives up on her antennae and looks at me, blinking rapidly as if she is now trying to clear her eyes.

"Television is a technology that broadcasts images and stories. People use it to sell their products, and they do that by making their stuff look tantalizing. If you don't need the stuff, they instill the need in you by making you feel bad about yourself."

Lucy frowns. "Dastardly bit of sorcery, if you don't mind me saying. Let us hope that the telling or spelling or whatever it is—stops at hair removal."

"Well, actually ..."

Lucy blanches. "Don't tell me it doesn't."

I try to explain to them that in our world people are always trying to sell us stuff. That's what it means to be a consumer. We consume things. And yes, we are persuaded to buy things we don't need, because we think we'll look ugly or stink if we don't have them. But it's not all bad. Technology has enabled us to improve our lot in many ways. As I speak, Willow stares blankly at me, and Lucy madly swats flies or bees or whatever it is that buzzes around her head and creates interference. This isn't working. If I want to communicate the idea of technology to the fairy godmothers, I'm going to have to speak in terms they can understand.

Finally, I say: "Technology is like a wand that gives us the power to transform the elements into things we can use."

"So you do have wands," says Lucy.

"Well, sort of. We have machines."

"And what do you use them for?" Lucy has grown quite pale all of a sudden.

"Well, to build houses, harvest food, make clothing, cure diseases, travel, communicate—you know, improve ourselves."

"To what end?"

"To live more comfortably, I guess. To be happy."

"But where is the *end*?" Lucy asks, exasperated. "How much do you need to be happy? Is it enough to live like kings, or do you need to become emperors and popes?"

The question is disturbing. "I don't know if we have set any limits. We're faced with many ethical problems at this time. Many people feel that our power over matter has outstripped our spiritual development. Our minds keep racing forward in the name of progress and material comfort, but we haven't come to terms with our impact on nature … So I'm not sure about limits."

Lucy shifts around. She looks extremely uncomfortable, as if she were sitting on an anthill.

"So there's no end, then."

"Not really. No."

Lucy scowls and moves the dirt back and forth with her speckled hand. "There's no end to the story, either. How will the spell of the fisherman's wife be broken? There's nothing more to that story, is there?"

"That's all I know, Lucy."

She shakes her head and stares at the ground. "The fish prince is powerless to help her. He is caught in a net, and so is the husband. Everyone is floundering, so to say …"

She bats those invisible things around her head like she has pulled down a hornet's nest. No question about it. Lucy is *bugged*.

Bugged

Ian and I were driving back to the city from the farm. Winter had arrived. Outside the car window, the sky was slate gray and featureless. I slumped in the passenger seat, dispirited. We had had a difficult time during the three days we had been at the farm. Ian always had something to do there. He worked in the basement in his workshop, puttering over blocks of wood and joinery, teaching himself to work with wood—to make shelves, cabinets, and frames.

I, on the other hand, had way too little to do. I had been slowly increasing my range of movement by walking every day and swimming when I could. I had started a healing-through-movement class that took place once every week. The facilitators kept the lights down low so no one felt self-conscious, as we attempted to reconnect with bodies that had betrayed us in a variety of ways. For the most part, however, I was still very limited, still struggling to accept the profound confines of a body that was full of complaints. Constant pain in my back, neck, and hips. Noise, noise, noise. In the mornings, I could sit up a little to study, but by noon, my back would no longer support me. I would have to lie down until four o'clock when I rose again to make the evening meal.

As we were driving along the freeway headed back to the city, I dropped my forehead on the cool window and revisited the last few days at the farm. Things had come to a head. I could no longer bear rattling around the house. Reading books. Journaling. Trying to figure out what I was doing on the planet. I could no longer bear being exiled from the working world, stumbling aimlessly through hill and dale, comfortless. I wanted out of my body, but I couldn't get out. My spirit felt trapped like a bird in a cage. I couldn't get rid of the pain, and I couldn't live with it either. I had no way to channel the building frustration and rage.

Lately, I had been doing things that scared me. I would have a sudden impulse to jab a butcher knife into my chest or plow into a passing train. I couldn't tell Ian about those impulses. They were too terrifying, and besides, he had taken enough grief. I wanted to give him some better part of me. But this mad woman was all I had to offer. I hated myself for not being able to rise above the madness, for the fact that I always ended up unloading on him. Some time ago, he had realized that I couldn't stop dumping my burden when it became too great to bear. He couldn't fix the pain and depression. He could only take me into his arms and let me melt there. I loved him for receiving me as I was … for staying true and sharing the burden, for maintaining a happy spirit, and continuing to build our dream house even though it was making less and less sense to both of us.

The night before, the lucky guy had gotten another load dumped on him. We had come into the living room after dinner, and we were sitting across from one another on our new chenille sofas. He had placed a candle between us that lit up the fire in his warm brown eyes.

Rapunzel's father looked like that, I thought. They were both bearded men with laugh lines and gentle faces. But I couldn't keep my upset contained. "This isn't working!" I burst out saying. "I don't feel at home here. I'm disconnected and lonely, and I need friends. I need community. I don't have anything to do here. I can't live here." I had a dinner napkin in my hands, and I was twisting it into little knots. I went on about how I had never felt settled anywhere in the world. I needed to settle somewhere. Home was so important to me. But we'd gotten it wrong. We needed a home in the city where we could be with people, not in the country where I was alone.

He frowned. He knew the farmhouse was too far away from friends and that I felt dislocated with too little to do. But hadn't I asked to get away from the noisy toxic city? Hadn't I needed the quiet? He wondered what all his work had been for.

He said: "My fear is that we're going to find a house in the city and spend all our money buying it and renovating and furnishing it, and then you will be no more settled than you are now. You are like a bird without a nest, all flighty and restless. I'm afraid you will never be happy, no matter where you live."

I was horrified. What was he saying? I was nothing better than a *fishwife*! There I was in the beautiful home that he had built for us, and it wasn't enough. Build me another home. This one isn't good enough. Would I ever have enough? How much was enough? I was so disturbed, I took my coiled, twisted napkin and stomped upstairs. On the way up, I remembered something Joseph Campbell had written in his book, *The Hero with a Thousand Faces*: "Generally we refuse to admit within ourselves, or within our friends, the fullness of that pushing, self-protective, malodorous, carnivorous, lecherous fever which is the very nature of the organic cell."

I was definitely seeing the carnivorous part of me—and I couldn't bear it. I couldn't bear being a fishwife. Now, sitting in the car with my forehead on the cool glass, I wondered if anything would ever satisfy my hunger—quiet my unrest. Would I ever come to peace?

Sudden tears welled up, borne on an unexpected tide of love. It moved outward in waves, embracing everything.

"A penny for your thoughts," said Ian quietly.

CHAPTER NINE

GOTHEL'S GARDEN

The Capture

"Take a look at this rapunzel." Tatatee peers into the lush, broad leaves of the rampion (otherwise known as rapunzel) that grows in Dame Gothel's garden. She has her nose on the leaf like some very nearsighted person trying to read a book. The plant is easily four and a half feet high, taller than Tatatee herself.

The sun has gone down, and the moon has risen—a slender arc of shining copper in the eastern sky. Tatatee has no fear of being seen by the witch, and neither does Willow, who has dispersed herself into a fine mist that hangs over the thickly growing flowers and herbs. I am hidden safely under my cloak, although I can't say I'm at ease trespassing on the witch's property.

Last night, after the sun set, Jacob climbed over the wall. He grabbed a bunch of the rapunzel and got back to his wife undetected. She made a delicious salad, but then her appetite grew three times bigger. She would give him no peace until he went over the wall again. He did her bidding, but on the third morning she wanted more. He wouldn't do it and the shouting had gone on all afternoon.

"Use your wand," says Tatatee.

"Isn't that a bit of a risk?"

"Do it quickly!"

I shine the wand on a small clump of the lush rapunzel. Under its light, the plants wither and shrink to a brown-green mass.

"Just as I suspected," says Tatatee. "She's put a spell on it."

We hear a scrabbling sound on the other side of the wall, and Jacob's fingers appear at the top, groping for the other edge like the legs of a white spider. Then his head looms up, and we see his brown, disheveled hair and his shocked, white face. He heaves his body over the top of the wall and tumbles down on our side. For a moment he crouches in the shadows, and then scuttles toward us on all fours. Reaching into the rapunzel patch, he grabs the plants, twists the leaves from their stalks, and stuffs them into his shirt. When he turns to creep back to the shadowy side of the wall, he runs headlong into the witch.

Dame Gothel stands no more than four feet tall—a twisted knot of fury, dwarfed by the plants in her garden. She wears a black cloak, with a hood that makes her look like a small figure of death. Spikes of black hair spring from her head, and her hairline nearly meets her heavy eyebrows. She has a long nose and sharp, feral eyes. Her back is rounded and hunched, giving the effect of a scarab beetle standing on one end. A cold wind slices through me, and I back into the recesses of the wall, clinging to my cloak of invisibility.

"You thief! How dare you come into my garden and steal my rapunzel!" she rasps. "You shall suffer for it!"

Jacob, still on his hands and knees, immediately starts shaking out the greens he has crammed into his shirt. His whole body is trembling as if he's freezing to death. He tries to explain that his wife is pregnant and has developed a craving for rapunzel. She has to have it, or she might die and take the child with her.

The witch crosses her arms and thrums her long, gnarled fingers on her forearms. "I will tell you what I will do. You may come into my garden and take as much rapunzel as you wish, on the condition that when the child is born, you give it to me. I will raise it well, I assure you—better than its own mother."

"Please, not the child," he begs.

"Go now!"

Terrified, Jacob scrambles up the wall, legs and arms flailing, taking every hold available. He drops down on the other side with a thump and a crack. I can only hope the sound is a twig and not his leg!

The sorceress surveys the damage done to her garden. Her beady eyes search the darkness, and her long nose twitches as though she has caught some foreign scent. I look around for Tatatee, but she has disappeared. Willow isn't here, either. I am alone apparently, backing against the wall in my cloak of invisibility.

"Who goes there?" she demands, starting toward me. "You can't hide from me. Nothing hides from me!"

I am not about to let this happen again. It was one thing to be approached by Lucy, but I refuse to tangle with a witch. Icy winds slash the air, whipping around me as she closes in. They're asps and adders, poisonous energies roused by my fear. That's how she'll see me, I realize. She'll see me by my snakes.

I think of using the wand, but then I hear Lucy in my ear saying, *"Not* the wand! You'll reveal yourself!"

Then, what? I remember that Gangee told me to clap. But I'll be heard if I do! There's no way to make a tiny sound when you're clapping, so I go for it. I clap heartily. I shout, "Bravo!

Bravo!" At first, I feel dreadfully exposed, but then I hear another pair of hands and another, and then a whole crowd bursts into thunderous applause. The image of the witch, her garden, her house, the wall, the stars, and the moon above—shatters. The last thing I see is the startled expression on the witch's face, who, for a split second, has seen that she's nothing more than an actor on a stage. All made up!

A warm wind catches me, and in a great *whoosh* I'm carried somewhere, along with all the other bits and pieces of the scene that are being gathered together and recomposed. I find myself with the other godmothers, floating in the night sky on the magic carpet of Gangee's cloak. I look down through her cloak, and I can see treetops and pottery roofs. Willow has settled above us as the wisp of a cloud, and Tatatee rests her head against her dozing elephant and gazes up at the diamond sky.

"Well done!" says Gangee, her deft brown fingers clacking happy knitting needles.

"I'm not sure our sister has ever been so well received!" Lucy chirps from inside my ear.

"Is she related to you?" I ask the godmothers.

"She is a godmother, to be sure," says Tatatee, "but she has a different mission than ours."

I'm not sure I understand that fully, but my main concern is the danger that Gothel now poses to me. "Do you think she saw me? Did she hear the applause?"

"We don't know exactly what she heard or saw," says Tatatee. "But for one blessed moment she failed to believe in herself."

"Sorcerers rarely have moments of self-doubt!" Willow sings from above, where she's rocking like a kite on a flirty breeze.

"Why don't we just clap them out of existence?" I ask.

My question positively titillates the godmothers, and Gangee's cloak rocks with their laughter. "You can't clap anything out of existence, dear!" says Gangee.

"Use that appreciation sparingly," Tatatee advises in a rather sharp tone. "Nobody wants a witch with a big head."

The godmothers seem to find that uproariously funny. But they've lost me. As we float along, I become increasingly concerned, so concerned that the magic carpet of Gangee's cloak sinks, skirting the rooftops.

"What is weighing you down, child?" Gangee inquires.

"It worries me that the witch has seen me. At the very least, she knows that someone invisible has been poking around in her garden. I know this is all my own make-believe, but I have a feeling that there is something in nature that doesn't want to be seen. I'm worried that characters like Gothel will fight to stay hidden, and retaliate if exposed."

"Dame Gothel is in your nature," says Gangee gently.

"It's your story," says Tatatee. "And she's your witch."

That's not very comforting, but I think I understand what they're getting at. Gothel is expressing a dark part of me. Another person might imagine a different witch or see Gothel in a kinder light. But I'm investigating this particular expression of what Carl Jung called "the shadow," and my Gothel is grasping, furious, suspicious, and self-protective.

As we continue our descent, Tatatee removes a little brown bag from a satchel strapped to the side of her elephant. "Look here," she says. "While in the garden, I took some samples." She removes some leaves from the bag and spreads them out before her on Gangee's cloak. "Here is the rapunzel as it truly is, and here is the rapunzel that your Dame Gothel grows. You can see it has been artificially greened."

Gangee inserts her monocle and peers at the greens.

"What do you make of that?" Lucy inquires from inside my ear.

"I'm not sure. Maybe she's a genetic engineer. She's altered the nature of the seeds."

"Why?" asks Tatatee. "Why would she interfere with the nature of the seeds?"

That seems clear enough to me. "She wants to have the best garden on the block." But there's more to it than that. Something more malicious. Suddenly, I understand. "It's a lure!"

"Go on," says Lucy. "Tell us more."

"She wants her neighbors to crave what she has, what they can't have. She's like a drug dealer, making drugs, creating addictions. That's how she sets her trap. People will give her anything to get the fix—even their own children."

"What we have here is living evidence of the serious effect," says Tatatee, studying her leaf samples. She squints at me. "Tell me, *does star power* mean anything to you in your world?"

Seeing Stars

Super stars. Movie stars. Rock stars. Media stars. Stars on ice. Stars in your eyes.

Starstruck.

Yep. We've got all kinds of star power in our world.

I had a full-on experience of star power just the other night when I watched the Oscars on television. The movie stars (especially the women, of course) were doll-like in their perfection. The beauty industry is geared toward hiding the smallest defect, and drawing attention to silicone breasts, plumped lips, surgically altered noses, and flawless skin. Sitting in the shadow of all that starlight, I thought, *Gawd, I'm a mess.*

We settle on the ground in the meadow, and Greta comes up again, quite literally, right up through Gangee's cloak. There are stars everywhere—fairies that look like stars, stars in Gangee's cloak, stars in the sky, stars in my eyes.

"Look, snow is falling!" Willow exclaims, looking up.

"Not snowflakes," says Greta brusquely. "Starflakes. Don't get any in your eyes."

Willow circles around and folds herself before Greta. "Greta, are you remembering something?"

Greta stares straight ahead through sightless eyes. "I am getting a rather long flash," she says. "It concerns a wicked hobgoblin. He created a powerful mirror that made everything that was beautiful appear ugly. If you looked into the goblin's mirror, you would hate what you saw."

"Sounds just like tell-a-vision," says Lucy from inside my ear.

"One day there was a big explosion, and the mirror shattered into millions of pieces. Pieces of that star flew everywhere, and before long, the whole world was surrounded by pieces of the broken mirror. Tiny splinters flew into people's eyes and hearts, making them see things differently. They became critical of one another and themselves. They would focus on a nose that was too large, or teeth that were too yellow, or an unpleasing body shape, or a pimple on their forehead. They developed an increasing intolerance of all disfigurements."

"That's *The Snow Queen* by Hans Christian Andersen," I exclaim.

Greta ignores me. "Due to the splinters in their eyes, people became obsessed with their appearance. They tried to improve themselves by any means they could. One of the people affected was a little boy named Kay. He was playing in the garden with his sister Gerda when all of a sudden, a piece of the mirror stung his eye. Then another stabbed his heart. Gerda said, 'What's wrong?' Kay looked at his sister's face all twisted up with concern, and he said: 'Don't screw up your face like that. It makes you look ugly.'

"His remark cut deeply into Gerda's sensitive heart. Then Kay looked at the roses and flowers of the garden, in which the children had previously taken so much delight. This flower was slug-eaten. That one was stunted. Everywhere he looked, he saw problems and defects. Nature disgusted him. His heart grew cold. He began to spend more and more time in his own company, drawn to the perfection of the hoar frost on the window and the snow that fell from the sky. Without even knowing what was happening to him, Kay was drawn out of the natural world and into the perfect world of the Snow Queen who lived far away in the north.

"Kay stayed a long time in her beautiful, frozen world. The longer he remained, the colder his heart became. He lost all affection for the hearty, courageous efforts of the flowers and the plants. He would rather create an artificial rose than submit himself to the imperfections of the natural one."

Greta stops. "That is all I see," she says. "I can only conclude that Kay does not return to the natural world. He stays in the critical, frozen land of the Snow Queen."

"Hang on, Greta," I say. "That's not how the story ends! Gerda goes on a long journey to find her brother, and she discovers him in the realm of the Snow Queen. She melts his frozen heart with the warmth of her love, and her tears wash the splinter out of his eye."

"I cannot see that. And because I can only see things as they *are*, I must conclude that the ending of the story was not, or is no longer, true," says Greta.

"Have we completely lost our endings?" asks an exasperated Lucy, batting around in my ear.

Willow encircles me. "Is it true? Are there no happy endings anymore?"

How can I answer? When I look into her ghostly face, I see the face of future generations, children who are not yet born, wanting to know if there's any hope for humanity, any reason to come into the world.

"Yes, there are happy endings," I say firmly. "But we must believe in them. Gerda will make it to the realm of the Snow Queen. She will warm Kay's heart and wash the splinter out of his eye. And though it may not be apparent how it will happen, Kay *will* be rescued from the clutches of the Snow Queen. You have to believe that, Greta. We are all making the journey—right now. But we've only just begun. We must keep on going."

A single tear escapes from one of Greta's sightless eyes. It rolls down her hard, square face and splashes on the cover of her book. "It is perhaps too painful to believe in happy endings," she rasps.

The days following my experience with the godmothers were powerful. I had gone beyond them in some way. I was definitely the lead goose, flying into the dark passages of the story on the wings of a strengthening conviction that we could recover the princess, along with our belief in happy endings. They seemed to go hand in hand. Lose contact with the princess and the meaning of happy endings, and you might as well shred the tales and put them in the recycling bin.

Of course, it's not reasonable to believe in happy endings. It is much more reasonable to believe that the world is falling apart. Certainly the images we receive in the mainstream media support that conclusion. Faced with war, terrorism, and environmental disaster, not to mention the abuses perpetrated on women and children worldwide, who can believe that we are progressing? But someone has to believe in the nobility of humanity and the possibility of getting out of this mess. Otherwise, what hope do we have?

A few days later, our friend Arash came over for dinner. Arash was a very spiritual man who worked as a research scientist for a technology company. He was an amiable, portly fellow who was Danish on one side of his family and loved the stories of Hans Christian Andersen. We enjoyed a lively meal together, and then we settled in the living room to continue chatting after dinner.

Out of the blue, Arash said, "People at the office say that I'm always critical. I stand back and judge things all the time. Do you know of a word for that?"

"Cynic," said Ian.

"What does *cynic* actually mean?" Arash asked.

"Well, let's look it up." I pulled a copy of *Funk and Wagnalls* off the bookshelf over the sofa and flipped through the pages. When I came to the definition, I read it aloud:

"A sneering, fault-finding person; especially one who believes that all men are motivated by selfishness. adj. 1. Cynical. 2. Pertaining to Sirius, the Dog Star."

I could not believe what I was reading. While the men debated whether or not Arash was actually a cynic, I sat there in a state of speechless wonder. Generally, I went around thinking that the inner world of the godmothers was separate from the outer one and that their choice of words, like the *serious effect*, was fanciful. But here, once again, they had alerted me to their real intelligence!

Several days later, one of my few godmother-savvy friends drew my attention to the fact that Jesus had been a Cynic. The Cynics were a philosophical school originating in Greece, whose proponents upheld the highest virtues of humanity. They wanted to direct humanity's attention away from materialism to the essential nobility of nature—to the kingdom within. But around the fifteenth century, the word *cynic* changed. It became associated with a disgust in humanity—which, oddly enough, coincided with the witch burnings and the total extermination of pagan beliefs by the church. The spirits of nature were driven out of the world, and we all underwent a disenchantment. We entered the Enlightenment. We began to look at nature with a cold, critical eye. Under the dissecting gaze of reason, we dismissed the idea that nature was an expression of the divine mind. We saw no intelligence in nature. We saw a dog-eat-dog world where nature blindly selected the strongest and the fittest. We looked up into the heavens, and we saw the stars and planets orbiting like clockwork, without the need for divine intervention. We had no stories to warm us to the spirit of the rose, the gentleness of the deer, the wisdom of the fish—no stories to show us the beauty of our own nature. Everywhere we looked, we saw ourselves reflected in the goblin's distorted mirror. We sought refuge in perfection, and that's where Greta saw us, locked in that cold, hard place.

For all her power, she could not see us free.

CHAPTER TEN

RAISING RAPUNZEL

Rapunzel's Birth

Kate's labor comes on suddenly in the middle of the night. She wakes with a start from a deep sleep, screaming loud enough to wake the dead and certainly loud enough to wake the witch next door. By dawn, her contractions are strong and regular, and Jacob runs down the street to fetch the midwife.

Willow and I hide in the corner of the bedroom and watch as the midwife strides in through the door. She's a matron with silver hair, a heavy bosom, and large, capable hands. She doesn't seem to be in the least disturbed by Kate, who has backed her naked body into the headboard and looks like a frightened cat who won't come down off the roof.

"Give me something! Make it stop!" Kate shrieks.

The midwife, unperturbed, speaks to her softly. She hands Jacob a small bundle of herbs and instructs him to make the tea. With soothing words, tea, and the confidence of ages, she leads the fretful mother through her excruciating labor. By early afternoon, a baby girl is born. But Kate is spent. All she wants is to cover her eyes with a cold compress.

"Don't you want to see the child?" Jacob asks.

"Later," she mumbles from underneath the cloth.

The midwife washes the baby in a warm bath, wraps her in a soft, blue blanket, and places her in her father's arms. He sits on the bed and rocks her, cooing to her sweetly, telling her how beautiful she is.

Has he forgotten his deal with Gothel? Maybe he's hoping that she didn't mean it or that she forgot or, better still, that she forgave him. One thing is for sure—he hasn't told Kate. Lying there with the white towel over her eyes, she shows no signs of worry that her baby is in jeopardy.

Suddenly, the bedroom door bursts open, and the sorceress blasts into the room like a cold wind. The shutters bang and the curtains snap against the wall. She aims her wand at the parents, and they momentarily freeze. Then she grabs the baby out of her father's arms.

"Ha! Now you are mine. All mine! Rapunzel. That's what I'll call you—a reminder of your mother's greed."

Jacob comes to, sees his baby in the witch's arms, and bolts for the door, barring the exit. Gothel spits at him like a cat, and he staggers backward, rubbing his eyes as if she's struck them with poison. She kicks the door open with mighty force and speeds out.

We follow her down the long flight of stairs and out the front door to the street. She flies toward her house like a crow, her black cloak flapping around her, and she passes through the open iron gates to her garden. We dash in through the gates behind her, and then the whole house—along with the fence and gardens—whirls up into the air, spins us around, and carries us away.

Willow grabs me by the cloak. We tumble through the air, churning in a dark funnel cloud. Faster and faster we spin, at a dizzying, then nauseating speed. At last, the churn slows, and patches of mustard and green cropland come into view. A forest appears below with a small lake and several houses dotting the woods. The flying house lands, followed by the garden, the wall, the iron fence, and the gate, and everything is restored to order. The wind puts us down in the backyard. The landing is surprisingly soft, and it occurs to me that though the wind might be enslaved by the witch's will, it is nonetheless kind.

The Education of the Princess

We are in witches' country. Here, the natural world is unnaturally bright. The sky is too blue; the sun is too yellow. The flowers in the witch's garden grow to heights of four and five feet—crimson poppies, pumpkin-orange tiger lilies, and a blinding palette of tulips. The broad, green leaves of the plants, the petals of the flowers, and the skin of the berries on the vines that creep along the red brick wall have a waxen texture, and look as if they have been computer-generated in hyperreal colors.

Strangely, for all their splendor, the flowers have no fragrance. The garden is eerily quiet. There is no insect buzz, no birdsong, and no scent of water in the soil. I can't resist bending down to touch the ground. The earth is chocolate brown and looks rich, but when I rub it between my fingers, I can't feel it. I have no sensation. How odd. It's like we're on a production set. Everything here is simulated—nothing is real.

"Do you want to stay here?" Willow asks anxiously. "We have a lot of time to move through. If we settle, we'll solidify." She claps her hand to her mouth, blushing. "Sorry. I think I just broke the noninterference policy."

"That's all right," I tell her. "I won't be sending you Nowhere anytime soon."

"You did want to see Rapunzel grow up, didn't you?"

"Of course." I yank myself away from the weird ground. "Okay, let's go find her …"

"At what age?"

"Well, four maybe …"

I feel the sensation of melting and becoming like water. We flow through the house, and though I'm not able to get a fix on any of the rooms, I feel a thickening of the current as we pass through the walls. We arrive on the other side of the house and reconstitute ourselves in the front garden.

It too boasts an array of weirdly colorful flowers, even more exotic than those in the backyard—tropical flowers, orchids, and hibiscus; flowers with large cups and downright obscene stamens; blooms that are so extreme in their beauty they have crossed over into the hideous. They strike me as something insect-like and predatory. I do not like the front garden—not at all.

But then a child comes out the front door. She wears a cerulean dress with white leather boots that have little covered buttons running up the sides. Her wavy copper hair is thick, and many strands of gold stream through it—but it is absolutely unruly! It curls around her head and tumbles down past her shoulders, shrinking her little face, which is exquisitely fair and tender. She has bright red cheeks, shining blue eyes, and an expression of wide-open wonder. Her sense of mischief and uncontrollable aliveness makes me want to clap my hands with delight, run up to her, and sweep her into my arms.

"Come outside too, mother," she insists, holding out her little hand to the shadowy figure behind the door.

"Oh no," says the hidden one. "You go out and play by yourself. The sun is too strong for my delicate skin."

"It's nice here." She stomps around for a moment, trying to get the feel of her feet on the wooden porch. Does she too have no sensation? Then she stares up at the sun that has climbed to the summit of the sky. "Why does the sun not like you, Mother?"

"Many things do not like me," says the witch from behind the door. "I am not beautiful. But you are, so go now and play."

The little girl is silent for a moment. Then she goes to the door, and she says, "I am sorry the sun doesn't like you, Mother. It is very mean of the sun to make you stay in the dark."

She turns and clumps down the steps, frowning at the sun for his unkindness. As she wanders down the path, she greets the flowers that bob above her. I notice Gothel watching her from the doorway.

A sparrow lights on the top of the iron fence by the gate. He chirps, and the child's face breaks into a happy smile. "Hello, friendly friend!" she cries. "I have missed you!"

She stretches out her hand and runs toward the sparrow who hops excitedly on the railing, as if there is nothing he would rather do than light on her hand if only she would come closer. But she never gets to the gate. The wall keeps retreating as she runs toward it. She stumbles, gets herself up, and runs again, flushed by the heat of the sun. After falling several times, she cries out: "I shall never reach you, friend!"

The sparrow seems to understand and flies away.

"I don't know what is wrong with me," she mutters, wiping her tears with the back of her hand. Then she gets up and returns to the house.

What a mean spell. I'd like to say a thing or two to that witch. I reach for Willow's hand. "We better keep moving before *I* start interfering."

"What age this time?" Willow asks.

"Let's say ten."

We become like water again and flow into the house.

"Aren't there any girls around here who are my own age?"

THE TOWER PRINCESS

Rapunzel sits on a pile of huge books, legs dangling. She wears a white slip, and her hair has been plaited into four long braids that fall over the books and swing below her knees. She has not yet grown into a woman, but she will soon. Her limbs are long and gangly, her breasts undeveloped.

The parlor is cold and bare, its gray stone walls comfortless. There are three volumes stacked underneath Rapunzel, bound in red leather and each a foot thick. *How many pages in a foot?!* I wonder.

Gothel sits in the corner behind Rapunzel, crouched on a large, carved dining room chair that resembles a throne. A long, dusty table has been pushed up under the front window, and the center of the room is occupied by a square wooden platform. The hearth, covered by an iron grate, has never seen warmth—not from fire or even the light of day.

"No, there are no girls your own age, and if there were, they would not be a proper influence," says Gothel, sliding off her chair and hobbling to the window. She pokes her fingers through the gray, spider-webby curtains.

"Where is Cantata?" she demands. "The woman is late."

Rapunzel sighs heavily. "Do we have to make another dress, Mother? They are so tight and warm. I can hardly breathe in them."

I notice that the great books have a title running along their spines: *The Education of a Princess: Volumes I, II, and III.* I am shocked to think Rapunzel is going to have to learn *all that.* But then, I guess, if you were to record what any girl has to learn in unwritten social codes, maybe it would amount to all that.

"Every article of clothing is necessary, my dear, no matter how binding it may be. You must have a queen's carriage if you plan on *riding* in one." She crosses her arms, vexed by the tardiness of her visitor. "I wish I could make it easier for both of us, but unfortunately, you will have to learn the hard way."

Gothel turns away from the window and limps over to her daughter. She has a bad right leg, twisted at the hip, so she rocks sideways when she walks. "With you, everything has to be spelled out. I can tell you, my girl, it is a damn nuisance." Her eyes dart in the direction of a polished wooden wand that stands in the shadows of the closet near the foyer. "We must develop each of your attributes: your posture, your hair, your clothing, and your wit (such as it is). We are raising you above the rest, so you will attract a prince. I have it all planned. But you must not fail me, or we will have no future at all."

Cantata, the seamstress, arrives at the gate and pulls the rope that jiggles the bell above the door of the house. Gothel hobbles down the garden path to open the gate, and to my surprise, I notice that the flowers along the path have wilted. They have dropped their heads as if they're ashamed of themselves.

Cantata is very tall and thin—I am tempted to say anorexic. She is long past her youth, but she's trying to hold it all together. Her plum-red hair is pulled back into a tight bun, and her white skin has been stretched over her face like a mask. She wears a long burgundy skirt covered by a vest made out of gold netting, and cinched at the waist with a wide, red girdle that is laced cruelly up the front. Her long breasts sag over the clashing girdle, and her hands and forearms are encased in fingerless gloves. They are made of silver netting, not unlike the webby curtains on Gothel's windows.

"You're late," Gothel grunts, opening the gate.

Cantata ignores her and marches into the garden. "Well now, this is a sorry sight," she says.

"Leave it be," Gothel mutters as she locks the gate behind her.

"Haven't been able to put out her light, eh? It's only going to get brighter. And that won't serve you well." Cantata carries on up the path and goes in through the front door, without even acknowledging the barefoot Rapunzel who stands on the porch in her slip.

"Go inside. You have no clothes on," Gothel hisses, shooing the girl into the house.

Rapunzel follows Cantata into the parlor. While the two sorceresses chat by the window, she steps onto the platform that stands in the middle of the barren room. "I am ready for the fitting," she says, stretching out her arms. "Do with me as you will."

The fitting goes on for hours; it is a torture that Rapunzel has grown to endure. Cantata, with her mouth full of pins, loses patience many times and on occasion draws blood. "I don't know why you don't just use your wand," she grumbles to Gothel when she has finished pinning the hem.

"You know why," says Gothel. She is crouched on her throne in the corner of the room, her legs tucked underneath her like a little bat. She chews on her nails constantly, anxiously. You can practically hear the whirring of her thoughts: planning, testing, and changing plans, wondering and worrying, never at rest. Interruptions are never welcome.

"Is this all there is to being a princess?" Rapunzel asks when Cantata is finished and packing up her things. "To look pretty, wear fine clothes, and speak with perfect elocution?"

Dame Gothel gives her a fierce look. Then she smiles, in a strained attempt to cover up her instinctive contempt for the child's guilelessness.

"There is much more to it than that," she says. "You must look your best, sing your best, dance your best, and always say clever things. You must perform, day and night." She and Cantata exchange a knowing glance, and Cantata arches her dark eyebrows, which are painted on, I notice, and not the color of her hair.

"Then what?" Rapunzel asks, longing to relax her arms.

"Then you will be a queen."

"And what will I do when I am a queen?"

"You will not need to do anything, my dear. We will all be rich."

Rapunzel frowns, confused. Now set free of the dress, she pulls a loose periwinkle coat over her slip, ties it at the waist with a braided golden cord, and runs outside to the back porch. Quickly, she gets down on her belly, reaches underneath the porch, and draws out a wooden box that contains dry bread. She grabs a handful, and slides the box back in its hiding place. The sun hangs low in the sky, orange against the deepening blue. She runs out into the middle of the garden and throws the bread out to the birds. She may not be able to touch them, but she's determined to feed them. The swallows swoop in first, announcing their arrival, and after, sparrows and finches appear. They don't eat the red berries on the vines or the seeds in the garden, but they do accept what Rapunzel offers them. When they finish feeding, they linger on the high walls, and Rapunzel speaks to them, unselfconsciously chirping and twittering in their own language.

The sun sinks below the wall. The birds depart, and Rapunzel walks back up the path to the house. On her way, she pauses to speak to a clump of lilies that are sadly slumping. "What is the matter with you, lilies?" she asks. "Why are you so sad?" She touches the trumpet of a single flower that has been standing up bravely, with what seems to be an Olympian amount of effort. Feeling the touch of her hand, the lily sinks to the ground and withers.

The child does not understand her effect on the flowers. Tears well up in her eyes and run down her pretty cheeks.

The witch, standing at the back door, is not happy about what she sees going on in her garden. Not happy at all.

THE TOWER PRINCESS

After Rapunzel has gone inside, Willow and I stand on the garden path, lost in reverie. I have a lot of questions. Who is Cantata, and how is she wrapped up in the business of raising Rapunzel? Why isn't Gothel using her wand to raise the child?

"I've never seen any witch like Cantata!" Willow exclaims. "Is she a new character in the story?"

"I think so. She isn't in the original story. She just strode in between the lines."

"Oh." Willow's green eyes widen.

"I'm pretty sure she has an investment in Gothel's plan to make Rapunzel top princess. I bet she'll get top dollar."

Willow frowns, uncomprehending. "Do you mean she is to be sold?" The idea shocks her so much that her solid form wobbles, and I think for a second she might vanish.

"I want to know how the two witches got together in the first place. What do they have in mind for Rapunzel?"

We move into the past, to the early days soon after Rapunzel was taken. We find ourselves in the kitchen on the ground floor of Gothel's house. It is a long, rectangular space with wide wooden planked floors and a window (which is covered by black shutters) to the back garden. It's the middle of the night. The house is dark, and the only light source comes from two lanterns on the mantle in the living room. Little silver sparklers crackle inside a pair of glass jars—not exactly electricity, but close. Willow goes to the kitchen door and gazes at them, fascinated. Meanwhile, my attention is drawn to little Rapunzel who sits naked on a roughly hewn harvest table under the kitchen window. She can't be more than two. Her pink flax nightie lies beside her, and the two sorceresses hover over her like bats. The table stands adjacent to a wall of shelves cluttered with bottles that contain potions of one kind or another. On the other side of the table, some foul steam emanates from a cauldron on a brick hearth.

Rapunzel rubs her eyes while Cantata finishes examining her skin.

"What are you looking for?" Gothel snaps. "The baby is cold."

"Birthmarks," says Cantata. "I don't imagine you checked for birthmarks before you took her?"

"Leave her be," says Gothel, approaching the child. Cantata strides into the front parlor wearing an ugly, green dress while Gothel puts the nightie back on the girl. "We'll be right back. Don't move," she commands.

She limps into the parlor where Cantata stands in front of the window. A full moon is rising.

"Why did you choose a mere mortal? That's what I'd like to know. Why didn't you go and steal some child from the court? They've already been altered for beauty and longevity. She's not going to live longer than seventy years, and she'll only have thirty good ones, at best."

"Thirty is all we need," says Gothel. "And besides, I don't mind her mortality. It's different."

Cantata stands there thinking, her bony fingers fluttering on the slash of her painted lips. "What are you going to use on her?"

"Enhancements, potions. *No* alterations."

"So you're not going use any wands?"

"No. I want her to grow up naturally. She'll have a much more powerful allure."

"You're planning to enhance her *natural* light? Why? It will counteract your spells. It's already happening. Your spells are weakening. Any fool can see it. Your garden is a mess."

"Are you with me or not?" Gothel snaps.

"Well, of course, Cousin."

"Then focus on your duties. Make her magnificent clothes, conjure up fabrics from the Far East, and dress her up to entice.

That's your art. And use your wand to spruce up my garden from time to time. But don't use it in her presence. Do I make myself clear?"

"All I'm saying is, it's not going to be easy—"

"Are you with me or not?"

"Yes, of course ..."

"Good. Now get out." Gothel herds her out.

"All I'm saying is ... Her light is only going to get stronger... Wands will become necessary one day ... Don't say I didn't tell you ..."

Gothel pushes her cousin to the foyer and out the front door. She shoos her down the path to the gate, like she's getting rid of a pest.

Back in the kitchen, Rapunzel is lying on the rough table. Curled up like a kitten. Fast asleep.

Memory Lane

A whole crowd of godmothers (the Nowhere crowd, I presume) has gathered in the meadow to listen to Greta tell them what is going on in the story. In the course of broadcasting it, she has become so large and heavy that one might mistake her for a stone and climb up on top of her. Yet, she is able to produce a kind of hologram of the story that plays out in the middle of the field, while the godmothers and other fairies gather around it in a large ring.

In her deep, authoritative voice, Greta can deliver every nuance of the tale. I can't tell if she's enjoying her new gift—her attitude seems rather pragmatic. She sits cross-legged, with her eagle staff planted behind her and her great bird watching over the crowd. Lucy has plunked herself to my right and stretched her legs out before her, her big, black patent leather shoes flashing in the moonlight. Gangee hovers overheard, rocking back and forth, her cloak making a blanket that spreads out around her. She busies herself with her needles and yarn that is coming to her from the images in the story. For all I know, she's turning the tale into sweaters and socks. Fairies dart through the air, and gnomes clamber up the edges of Gangee's sprawling cloak, vying for a comfortable spot.

Willow has assumed her night form—a featureless ribbon of cloudy light—and she settles on my left, folding in on herself like the Christmas candies that my mother used to put in our stockings. Willow is starting to feel very familiar. When I'm with her, I have the sense that I'm with my younger self, a ghost from the past who existed before my identity solidified, before habits were formed, before I was schooled and spelled into a working, workable person. She reminds me of what it was like to be an unbounded spirit—happy, unknown to herself, and looking to the world to help her solidify. In a word, she is my innocence.

Greta stops speaking, and the hologram of the story vanishes. A round moon sails over the treetops through smoky veils of cloud, and everyone is caught up in a state of wonder—washed in that sweet maple fragrance that I have come to associate with the godmothers' love.

"That's all we know so far," Greta says plainly. "You are free to explore the place where we find ourselves in the story, providing, of course, you do not interfere." The fairies, bristling with excitement, shoot off in various directions.

"Well, maybe *now* is the time," says Lucy, clapping her gloved hands on her lap.

"Time for what?" I ask.

"A walk down Memory Lane. You did want to walk down Memory Lane, did you not?"

I haven't thought about Memory Lane since I first met Lucy

in those ballet clothes. She had reminded me of the time when I was four years old, and I was taken out of dance class for staring in the mirror at my tutu. She had made reference to Memory Lane at the time, but I didn't think it was an actual *place*.

"Of course it's a place," Lucy barks in her old, cracked voice. "Well, time's a-wasting. Shall we go?" She gets to her feet in her usual ungainly way and gives me a hand up. Then we head to the edge of the forest. "All you have to do is use your wand. Say *Memory Lane*, and then we'll see what we see."

I remove the wand from my pocket and tap it on the end. It springs to life and begins to glow like a robust little sun in the dark. "Memory Lane," I announce.

The trees around us petrify into white columns, and the avenue opens. Under our feet, paving stones shine milky white, like huge pearls. I can't see the end of the lane or anything in the darkness beyond the luminous pillars and the twinkling golden lights that border the path. As we make our way down the lane, I have the urge to stop and look between the pillars. Maybe I will see something. But Lucy seems quite intent on taking me somewhere.

She still wears her tutu, although it has become rather tattered and stained, and she's lost her wig. Maybe it just fell off, and she forgot to put it back on again. She's been scratching her head constantly since the fisherman's wife episode.

"I haven't walked down Memory Lane in a crone's age. Now, mind you, I won't be able to see much. The looking is up to you, but I might be able to pick something up ... get a little look-see ..." With her free arm, she swats the air around her head to ward off those invisible bees or bugs that seem to torment her.

"What are those things around your head, anyway?"

"Bees in my bonnet, so to say." She stops for a moment and cocks her head to one side. "Too many thoughts distracting me—more now than ever before. Not all mine, but they come to me like bees to a flower." She threads her gloved fingers together, presses them into her chin, and flutters her eyelashes. "I simply am *too* sweet."

Ha! Lucy, sweet? She's more of a shit disturber. I'm beginning to suspect that the closer fairies get to humans, the more troublesome they become. They can influence your thoughts or get you going on some wild goose chase, and they don't seem to be able to help themselves. I can't fault Lucy for her enthusiasm. Her intentions are admirable. But she's got a powerful personal will and no sense of mortal limitation. Humans have to know their limits to deal with fairies like Lucy. If they don't, or they want the power of the fairies, they can be taken over. That much I've learned from Lucy.

She smirks, reading my thoughts. "Well, then perhaps *sweet* isn't the word," she remarks.

We resume our walk, and I decide to venture a question. "Tell me, Lucy. Are the bees in your bonnet anything like the bugs in Gothel's garden?"

"Very good question! I daresay we are experiencing what happens when one comes into the mortal atmosphere."

"What do you mean?"

"Well, one cannot think clearly here … It is difficult to get close to your thoughts because there are simply too many thoughts to think! But that is another subject. Here we are. We've arrived."

She turns me sharply to the left, and we stand before a full-length mirror that hangs in space between two pillars. What a pair! Me, wobbling in the moonlight, thin and willowy in plain jeans, with brown hair curling about my shoulders. And Lucy, my height exactly, with a fuller bosom and a crazy, pink tutu sitting askew on her hips, not to mention a green, speckled head and bobbing antennae.

"Here is where it all began," she says with satisfaction.

"Where what began?"

"The Separation. I'll step aside so you can get a better view."

She takes a big, leggy step to the right, leaving me the only one in the mirror. Then my image changes, and I see myself as a four-year-old girl, the way I looked in most of the pictures from childhood. I have short brown hair. I wear brown corduroy pants, a red plaid jacket, and a yellow T-shirt. I look exactly like my four brothers—indistinguishable as a girl.

"That's me at four," I say.

"It's when the Separation usually occurs," says Lucy. "Sometime around four. Step through the mirror, now. Go on. Have a look at yourself from the other side." She gives me a little push in the back, and I step through the surface of the mirror. It yields as if it is made of mercury, and reforms into another looking glass on the other side.

There I am again at four, only this time I'm wearing my tutu, a little theater pink leotard, tights, and black patent leather tap shoes. I can feel exactly what I felt as a child. I am completely, unapologetically smitten with myself! The fairy princess is a lot more like me than the person I see every day in the mirror. I don't want her to go away, and I'm afraid that if I move, she will disappear.

That's why I couldn't dance. I didn't want the fairy princess to disappear!

Lucy reaches through the mirror, takes my hand, and pulls me through to the other side. "There you are, you see. You might remove the girl from the princess, but you cannot remove the princess from the girl! Now that you've found her again, I daresay you are getting more than you bargained for!"

I think about the princess who collapsed in the clearing under her burden of grief. If she has been with me all my life, what brought her down? What is her story? I want to follow that line of questioning, but Lucy is off on her own track.

"After the Separation, you were lost to us. You never stood again before the mirror—not that one. Oh, you would catch a reflection from time to time, but we never saw you well. I had terrible pickup."

"What kind of mirror are you talking about?"

"The mirror that reflects who you *are*. And when you see yourself as you are, we see you. It's as simple as that." She wipes her hands together, as though she's completed her business. "But then, you disappeared."

"Are you saying I'm some sort of princess?"

Lucy looks confused.

"Oh dear, I haven't gotten through." She cranes her head to the side like she's trying to pick up a new signal. "My dear, I'm speaking about what you see when you *reflect* ... What I mean to say is that you can only be seen through your reflections. I'm speaking of the inside mirror, of course, which is not same as the outside mirror. The outside mirror is a physical thing, you see. You might dress to impress, but which of the expressions are you? Who can tell? Since the inside mirror has been shattered, it is very difficult for you to see who you truly are. And until you see who you are, how can we possibly see you? Do you see? Oh, sometimes I get too exasperated trying to speak to you! I'd give anything to have my old powers back ..."

"Let me see if I can understand what you're getting at, Lucy. Are you saying that we must restore the mirror that shows us who we are?"

She scratches her head. "Yes, that's it."

"And when we are looking into the outside mirror, we are looking at reflections that don't express who we actually are."

"Precisely!"

"So am I able to see in the inside mirror?"

"Another very good question!" She raises a gloved finger to

answer it, but then she snaps her mouth shut as if she's just caught a bug. She looks at me sheepishly. "But say what you see."

"Well, something just came to mind. I imagined the frog king looking into the mirror of the pond. He's forgotten that he is a king."

"Oh, yes! Terribly deep spell," she says, shaking her head vigorously.

"But then, when he remembers that he is a king, he starts to feel really uncomfortable in his frog skin. He wants to shed it because it doesn't nearly express who he is."

"That's it! Must be miserable," says Lucy, wide-eyed. "All that wriggling and wiggling … and those bugs that were sweet to the frog must taste *awful* to the king." She starts smacking her lips and gagging dramatically.

"Yes, Lucy, and in the midst of it all, there's nothing but confusion. Who am I? How did I get to be a frog, and what does it mean to be a king?"

"There you go! That is the question—what does it mean to be a king? To answer that, one must keep looking into the inside mirror, you see, because one has begun to put it all back together again." She flashes that overly sweet smile. "All the king's horses and all the king's men couldn't put Humpty together again, but there's nothing to say a princess can't do it!" Laughing heartily, she takes my arm. "We'd better return now, or I'll be charged with interference!"

"Lucy, *did* you just interfere?" I ask as we speed along the lane.

"I don't know, but I am *pleased* that we're clear about the mirror!"

CHAPTER ELEVEN

THE TOWER

Rapunzel's Light

As Rapunzel nears the end of her childhood, Gothel's plan becomes clearer. She wants to heighten all of Rapunzel's allures to ensure she catches the attention of the king's eldest son, a comely young prince who lives in a castle up the river, on top of a hill. Gothel has images of him in her big books—maddening images that portray him at a distance in silhouette, riding on horseback and leading armies. In Gothel's view, Rapunzel must snare him if she is to have any worth at all, and to do so, she needs to make herself more attractive than any other girl in the kingdom. To Rapunzel, it seems like an impossible task.

How can one improve on the princesses sauntering through the pages of the books, who, in their lavish castles and gardens, are utterly flawless?

Because Rapunzel is a lonely child, she seizes hold of Gothel's dream. She wants to be loved, to meet the approval of the court, and to be selected by that distant knight. She is determined to do everything required to leave her mother's walled world with its iron gates and high, retreating walls. Even though her lessons require her to invent a false story about herself and where she comes from, she embraces her destiny. A princess she will be. She focuses on learning how to eat properly, walk properly, dance properly, and speak properly. She endures Cantata's endless fittings, putting up with her critical eye that is forever sizing her up and finding her wanting.

However, the one gift she has that needs no improvement whatsoever is her singing voice. It is powerful, natural, and spellbinding all by itself. Even Gothel has to admit that, alongside her magnificent and unruly mane of copper-gold hair, Rapunzel's voice is her main attraction. Gothel herself, however, cannot stand it. It chagrins her to hear the girl pouring her heart out in songs that she improvises while in the presence of flowers and birds. All that ridiculous sentiment! Worse still, the light that radiates from her when she sings has the effect of reversing all her spells. Her cohorts, like Cantata, sneer at her stunted, bug-eaten flowers and the decrepit state of her house. Dame Gothel does not relish the physical labor required to exist in the material world. She would much prefer to make potions, and use wands to reorganize matter according to her will, but she has chosen to cultivate the natural attractions of the girl, and those include her voice, her hair, and her innocence.

At this stage, it's the birds that are most attracted to Rapunzel. They're lining up on the garden walls to listen to her sing, which has prompted the sorcerers in the area to wonder what's going on behind Gothel's high walls. The local wizards have sent out spies and, lately, Gothel has noticed a shrewd-eyed crow lighting on the wall and staring keenly at the eleven-year-old girl.

Gothel's paranoia is mounting. She doesn't want people prying into her business. Rapunzel is her project, and she will brook no intruders coming round to glean her secrets or steal her property. To make things worse, Rapunzel has been asking questions and digging into matters that are off-limits—memories that must lie dead and never be exhumed.

One afternoon, Rapunzel is lying stretched out on the hardwood floor, reading a section from *The Education of a Princess, Volume II*. She's been reading for hours about the bloodlines of various noble families, but she's not following the words anymore. Her thoughts have wandered elsewhere. She turns to her mother who is sitting on her high back chair, pouring over her accounts.

"How exactly did I come into the world, Mother? Where did I come from? And who is my father?"

"I've told you before. It's not important," Gothel snaps.

"But it is to me." Tears pool in Rapunzel's eyes, and she wipes them away quickly so her mother won't see them. Her mother hates tears—all forms of upset are forbidden to a princess. She says tears will contort a perfect face and make it look hideous.

"Stop whimpering," Gothel commands. "I didn't give birth to you. I found you. Your mother put you in a basket and placed you outside my gate. I took pity on you because you were ugly. If you think you have beauty now, mark my words, my girl, it's all because of me. I brought you back to life, and I made you pretty with my potions."

Rapunzel becomes thoughtful. She has heard this before. "But who was *your* mother? Don't we have any relations? Besides Cantata, I mean."

"Oh, don't bother me anymore." Gothel examines a chewed finger, now blistered and raw.

But Rapunzel can't stop herself. She sits up, and wraps herself around the arm of her mother's chair. "Tell me something about yourself. Please, Mother."

Gothel frowns and sniffs. She draws a cloth from her pocket and blows the horn of her nose, which chronically drips. Her little dried-up heart is beating rapidly, and those old corpses don't want to be woken. Still, she might be able to tell the girl something if it would serve to demonstrate her good fortune.

"My mother was a great lady, but she didn't want me, if you must know. I wasn't pretty enough, so she gave me to the servants. They sent me out to beg for them, but when I didn't bring home enough money, they took me out to the woods and left me there. I had to fend for myself from an early age, and I can tell you, my girl, nobody loved *me*." Her mouth stretches into an awful grimace; her long, yellow teeth chatter, and her nose twitches uncontrollably.

Rapunzel, shocked by her mother's monstrous grief, runs to the kitchen to fetch a shawl. She wraps it round her shoulders and apologizes for the upset that her question has caused her.

"See what you've gone and done now. You've made me think about it," Gothel whimpers as she composes herself.

Rapunzel doesn't ask any more questions about her mother's roots, but it seems that even a little insight has made it possible for her to tolerate her mother's mood swings and neglect. Gothel is always busy with her recipes and potions. Apparently, she makes a living for herself by making and selling beauty potions. Over the years, orders for her products have increased, so she's had to work harder—not that she gets any richer because the merchants who buy her potions are constantly harping about the price being too high and that other, younger witches are making better stuff. Her busyness makes her miserable, and she constantly grumbles.

The merchants aren't selling her products to ordinary mortals, of course. Her customers are the women and men of high society who are desperate to maintain their youthful appearance and longevity because, without them, they will lose their social position. They rely on powerful concoctions and the occasional, more dramatic intervention of the wand. But the older they get, the more difficult it becomes to maintain the illusion of youth. Magic may give them a temporary gleam, but they soon look more aged than before. Gothel herself is well over two hundred—sometimes she mutters a figure closer to three hundred, so none of her wands or potions are of any use to her. She has exhausted all solutions.

One day, after making a delivery, Gothel comes home to find Rapunzel out in the backyard. The crow has shown her a way up the wall, and Rapunzel is sitting beside him, chatting away while stroking his tail feathers. Gothel goes berserk. She crashes into the garden, swinging her walking stick around her head like a propeller and whacks the bird, who takes off shrieking. As a cloud of feathers settle upon Gothel, it becomes clear to her that the time has come to put Rapunzel away.

Fatal Attraction

When I was Rapunzel's age, I lived in a middle-class neighborhood in Calgary, Alberta. I had two good friends who lived on the street. Dora was a very frilly girl. She had a trunk full of Barbie dolls and dance clothes (tutus, leotards, and theatrical paraphernalia), a canopy bed, and a doll house. My other friend, Lee, was a tomboy. She would rather practice her violin than pick up a doll, and on rainy days, we hung out in her room and played board games like Mousetrap and Operation. During the summer, we ran around the park climbing trees, playing baseball, and exploring the nearby ravine.

I experienced a fair amount of tension growing up between those two girls. Who to be, Dora or Lee? When I was twelve, my dad moved the family to the States, to an upper middle-class neighborhood in a suburb of Denver, Colorado. There I met a perky thirteen-year-old girl who lived across the street. Sarah taught me several things that were valuable—most memorably, to do the hula dance. She loaned me a grass skirt, and showed me how to stuff a brassiere with tissue paper. I relished being an exotic hula girl and trying womanhood on for size.

During the summer, we spent our days by the pool at the country club down the street. There, among the semi-clad sunbathers, I couldn't hide the fact that I was far off womanhood. I didn't care that much, until a beautiful girl in a white bikini sailed into view. She was fifteen, fully developed, vivacious, and blonde, and everyone fell in love with her—girls and boys.

I wanted to get a bikini like hers, and I did—or rather, my mother bought me a two-piece bathing suit with brown and green stripes. When I put it on in front of the mirror and squinted, I could at least imagine that I looked like the shapely girl at the pool. The first time I went swimming in my new bathing suit, I jumped off the low diving board and surfaced with the top bobbing before my eyes. Mortified, I grabbed it, put it on under water, and waded furiously to the shallow end. I figured that next time, I would dive headfirst into the pool, so I went back round to the diving board and took the plunge. On re-entry, my bottoms slid off like skin from a snake. Profound mortification. I don't remember anyone witnessing that little drama in the pool—or maybe I just slammed the spectators out of my memory.

In any case, I did a lot of fantasizing about being as feminine as Pool Girl. If that's what it meant to be a woman, I couldn't wait to become one. Who wouldn't want that breathtaking, disarming beauty? She gave me something to look forward to—something that offered the promise of being loved and cherished. Increasingly, I separated from my brothers. I didn't belong with the boys who spent their days firing off Estes rockets and taking potshots at frogs with BB guns. I imagined that, after boys grew into men, I might find a truly gentle man. The first poem I ever wrote was about that Gentle Man. He was an Indian brave, a warrior who defended the vulnerable members of the tribe.

Then one day, my friend Sarah rang the front doorbell. Her pretty, gypsy face was streaked with tears. Something horrible had happened. The girl at the pool had been found dead under a bridge nearby. She had gone missing after school the day before, and her body had been found in the morning. She had been raped and beaten to death. My friend spewed out the news and reeled away, sobbing.

I ran to my bedroom for cover—covered my ears, to protect them from the horror that had crashed in; covered my mouth to mute the screams. The news stormed my little Barbie-doll world, washed it down a swollen river, and crushed it like an aluminum can. I couldn't get the dark imagery out of my mind. I kept replaying the scene, slowing it down, trying to imagine how it could happen. Step by step, I went over it—his attraction, her trust, his hand in hers, their walk under the bridge, his betrayal, her horror, her resistance, his beating, her terror, his rape, her tortured death. It went round and round in my head—a record with deepening grooves. Later that day, I heard the news report on the radio in the kitchen. The family was going to play "Bridge over Troubled Water" at her funeral. That had been her favorite song. It was mine too.

I don't remember talking to anyone about this incident. I didn't know what to do with such dark and overpowering feelings. My mother was busy with the younger children in the family, and I just figured that I would be able to take care of myself. Also, because rape is a sexual crime, it was not a topic for polite conversation. You couldn't exactly talk about it at the dinner table. It belonged in that drawer of unmentionables that was starting to get overcrowded. They weren't pretty lacey things. They were a twisted knot of old stockings, gray panties, discarded bikinis, and fantasy bras that would never fit. I would never let anyone look in there. I put all those dark things about womanhood under lock and key.

I learned a huge life lesson from the death of the girl at the pool. I took it in deeply and stored it in my body. It was dangerous to be attractive—lethal to have the light of Pool Girl. The fascinating, curvaceous, dancing body that I had admired so much could get a female killed. I stopped wearing my bikini to the pool. I turned against my femininity, Barbie dolls, and the whole girlie fantasy. I distrusted the opposite sex, and recoiled from their sexual hunger. I recoiled from my own as well. I didn't want to attract attention or be pursued or caught, but it seemed that I couldn't avoid it. Increasingly, the eyes of men were on me.

When I was fourteen, I went traveling with my grandmother to Britain. In Scotland, my grandmother bought me an emerald and teal tartan kilt of the Douglas clan. I wanted it to be fashionable, which meant that it had to be shorter than anything my mother would allow me to wear. My grandmother had no qualms about letting me show my long legs. She bought me a white blouse, a tie, and knee socks to go with the outfit, and I found some high-heeled platform shoes to wear with the skirt. Then one day we went for lunch at a very fancy hotel. The waiters kept coming to the table, pouring the water, asking questions, and making excuses to hover around like flies. Finally, I said to my grandmother, "What is up with these waiters? Why won't they leave us alone?"

My grandmother looked at me and smiled sweetly. "It's because you're *attractive*, Michelle. Didn't you know?"

No, I didn't. My stomach ached. I twisted the napkin, making the first twist in what would be a lifetime of twisted napkins. I knew then that I would never be free again. Those waiters were taking something from me that I couldn't get back. I didn't invite them to hover around the table. I hadn't given them permission to make assessments, and to judge me according to how good I looked, or how well I measured up to their bedtime fantasy. I had no wish to be their appetizer, and I didn't consider it a compliment to be appetizing! From then on, I would struggle against the claim of men on women's bodies.

Like Rapunzel, I had loved to sing. I could stand up and belt out any song to any audience, wholeheartedly and without restraint. But now I was seized by self-consciousness and debilitating stage fright. How were people seeing me? Did I measure up? No, I didn't. My voice wasn't cool. It wasn't the voice of a rock singer, hard and crusted. It was a silly sentimental, operatic voice. I lost the power I once felt inside me, and my voice shrank into a tiny place. Bit by bit, I sealed myself off from the world. I put myself out of reach.

While having these memories, I was riding the subway. A young woman came in and threw herself down on the seat across from me. She was dressed in black leather, with fishnet stockings and black army boots. She had spikes on her jacket and studs in her nose and eyebrows. She wore pale face makeup and purple lipstick, and her fierce eyes were pooled in dark lines and shadows. "Stay away from me," she signaled. She was what people called a goth. Daughter of Gothel. Progeny of the lost feminine. Dispirited. Thorned. All that was left of the princess was her defiant, impenetrable hedge.

The Tower

Gothel has become busy—very busy. Her plan is to put Rapunzel in a tower deep in the forest, and right away she begins investigating the spells required to make an edifice from a rubble of stones. She locks herself in her dark, musty room on the second floor where she sleeps (or rather, lies down, because Gothel never sleeps), and she pours over a large book of spells and incantations. She works to unlock the word *tower*—extract its power, make it cower.

For days, she hobbles around in the forest, chanting bits of verse and striking her wand on stones, boulders and trees. She gets the trees to petrify, and that's a step in the right direction. She hasn't used her wand for years, she's out of practice, but the farther she gets from Rapunzel, the better it works. In fact, it's eager to do her bidding after idling so long in the closet.

Once she is deep in the wood, she finds the perfect spot. It's not easy to reach—one has to go through a dense and buggy bog, and then cross over a river. Gothel spells herself a bridge and scrambles over it, and as she climbs the hill on the other side, she whips her wand back and forth like a scythe to scatter the thorns, and part the tangled underbrush. She keeps sniffing the air because she senses that she is not alone (which, of course, she isn't.) Her fierce little eyes dart everywhere, looking for proof to warrant her fears.

The site is a flat area on top of a low, rising hill. Magnificent hardwoods—oak, ash, cherry, and maple—are rooted to the crown of the hill, and reign there like kings. But they have no power against Gothel who whips her wand back and forth through the air. The trees, struck by the cruel, cutting light, pull themselves up by their roots and skedaddle out of there. Then she positions herself in the middle of the clearing, points her wand at the ground, and summons the stones:

Stones who cower
under my power
build me a tower
Here!

She cracks the wand on the earth, and a rubble of stones heave up from below. She keeps repeating the chant until she's made a hill of rocks, but it's nothing like a tower. Gothel doesn't enjoy exerting herself, and this is too much like work. She grows enraged with the stones that are shuddering and tumbling inward at every command. They're clearly trying to follow orders, but aren't able to arrange themselves into the tower that Gothel has in mind. In her frustration, she growls,

You stones belong to me
Make the tower I want you to be
Do it, you must
Or I'll turn you to dust
And blow you away with a sneeze!

The stones blast off the ground, and hover mid air in a wide circle. Then they fit themselves into place by squeezing into the holes that open up before them, as the tower surges into shape. The air is choked with their dust and the high-pitched sound they emit as they conform. In only a few minutes, the tower is complete. It rises eighty feet high, and its sullen, gray stones are all perfectly uniform, and neatly stacked. The walls cannot be scaled. The tower has a black, pointed roof with slate shingles, and it stands upright before Gothel, like a soldier waiting for the next command.

Now all Gothel has to do is attend to details, and that is easy work for her wand. She opens up a door, and creates a spiraling stone staircase that leads to a circular room at the very top. She provides the apartment with all the amenities she can dream up. A pretty arched window looks out over forest and hills to the northeast, with just a glimpse of the sea to the south. She produces a soft, goose down bed with many brightly woven comforters, and installs a wardrobe containing beautiful gowns.

Gothel scratches her hairy brow and glares at the window. She would be happier to see no natural light coming in, no access whatsoever to the outside world, but then she herself would have no way to come and go. The opening is necessary. What a bother. No spell is ever airtight. There is always that infernal hole in the matter—that window of awareness when a spelled thing can remember its original state.

She sighs and turns to other duties. She puts in a lavatory, plumbing, a hearth, and a magic cupboard with preserved food that will restock itself after being eaten. She mumbles some inaudible words, and an ornate, full-length mirror appears by the bed. It looks fit for a queen, with its gilded frame and cut crystal edge. Gothel smirks with satisfaction (though she doesn't dare look at herself in that glass). She covers the floor with a thick bear rug, and adds a square wooden table plus a couple of chairs for Rapunzel's lessons.

Gothel has only one more problem to solve: to figure a way to get herself in and out of the tower, once she has sealed the girl inside. On her way back home, she considers the escape. No good. What else? Why, Rapunzel's hair, of course. She could use her braids to make a rope. It isn't nearly long enough, though. She will need at least seventy-five feet. Oh, bother. Well, Cantata can do it. She hasn't been in Rapunzel's company long enough for her wands to be influenced by the child's natural light.

When she gets home, Gothel tells Rapunzel that the time has come to go to a place where her learning will be intensified. It will be a slightly confined situation, she adds, providing a great deal more focus on her studies, but it will all pay off in a few years. Soon, Rapunzel will be introduced to the court, and everyone will be enchanted by her, especially the king's eldest son who will be looking for his bride right around the time she arrives. He will make her his queen, and they will live happily ever after.

Rapunzel has endured many tortures during her upbringing, but none is so cruel as the spell that Cantata puts on her hair. It comes to pass one sunny afternoon, when Rapunzel is sitting in the parlor with an embroidery hoop, and using the light that comes through the dirty window to see her tiny stitches in an intricate pattern of gold and green ivy.

Cantata rings the bell, and Gothel goes out to let her in through the gate. Cantata knows what she is there to do; she marches up the path and into the house without saying a word. She will permit no distractions; not one ray of Rapunzel's light will interfere with her duties. She sets a polished mahogany box on the table under the window and removes her wand. She waves it to and fro as if she's testing it. Then she hisses at the tip, and the instrument bursts into chaotic, hard, and crackling light. The wand is even more powerful than the one Gothel used to make the tower. Its noisy light scrambles the mind, and incites absolute terror and compliance.

Rapunzel shrinks into her chair. "What is going on, Mother?" she whimpers. She has never trusted Cantata. She has experienced her deliberate pin jabs, and she knows how cruel the woman can be. Until now, however, she has trusted that her mother will protect her.

Before Gothel can speak, Cantata utters the words that fix the spell: "River of hair, *go*! Fast now, dash now, *grow*!"

An image of herself with bountiful hair flashes into Rapunzel's mind with the force of a strobe light, and her hair begins to grow. It springs from the roots of her head, and there is no end to the flow. The weight of her hair drags her head to the ground, and she lies on the floor, captive. "Stop! Stop it!" she screams, but the hair keeps on growing.

Once Gothel herself is practically covered in hair, she grabs a bolt and wraps it around her arm to test its strength. "That will do," she says tartly.

Cantata stops the spell by reversing the words: "Grow now, dash now, fast now. *Stop*."

Gothel carries a candle into the room, holding it away from her as if handling some vile thing, and Cantata thrusts the noisy wand into the flame. Both lights go out, leaving a stink in the air. Then she returns the rod to its polished case, shuts the lid, snaps the lock, and leaves the house without saying a word.

"Mother, what have I done?" Rapunzel sobs. All that can be seen in that mass of hair is her pale, shocked face, and she holds her poor head, which is sore all over, inside and out.

"I am sorry, my dear, but your hair is the only way I will be able to reach you in the months to come. You will thank me, to be sure."

The next morning, Cantata returns with a couple of horses, and the group sets off to the tower. They're an odd sight. Gothel stumbles along on foot, leading the shaggy gray horse that bears Rapunzel. The girl's hair has been tightly braided into two ropes, and Cantata rides behind her, carrying the ropes like reins. She is mounted on a blue-black stallion that is her pride and joy because she broke him herself (which is unfortunate because the horse is skittish and limps).

When they arrive at the site of the tower, Gothel leads Rapunzel up the stairs to her room. She finds it beautifully appointed, and all her things are there. Gothel ties her hair to an iron hook above the window, releasing her from her burden and giving her enough slack to move freely about the room. What a relief!

After Gothel has gone down the stairs, Rapunzel sits at the window. She drinks in the beauty of the scene below—the sea that glimmers to the south and the high, golden peaks of the snow-capped mountains to the north. From within Gothel's high-walled garden, she never saw the glory of nature—never felt the wind on her cheeks or smelled the sea air. Now that she has been raised up, she can hear the wind and the sea, and gaze on all the strange creatures in the forest. It is the most wonderful place in the world, and she calls down to her mother. "I do thank you, Mother!" she cries. "It is lovely here!"

The old sorceress hobbles to the edge of the clearing where she cannot be seen, takes out her wand, and utters her final incantation. "Having risen, be a prison!"

The stairway disappears first and then the door, trapping Rapunzel inside. As Cantata readies the horses for departure, Gothel admires her finished work. She has achieved the perfect capture. Her prisoner has no idea that she is not free.

CHAPTER TWELVE

THE WINDOW

The Gathering

"I believe the audience would like you to take their questions," Greta announces, interrupting the story that she has been broadcasting to a crowd of fairies. They shoot up like a spray of fireworks and land in the trees, dangling their leafy legs. Gnomes crowd around the perimeter of the tower hologram, and everyone is speaking at once.

I find myself once again riding along on Gangee's cloak, accompanied by the usual suspects. We're hovering at the edge of the clearing, joined by elves in the tree canopy. The fairies seem to be trying to figure out the story that I've been telling. The gnomes are fascinated by Dame Gothel. She's got gnomish peculiarities, but she's not happy about them, which is perplexing because the gnomes are proud of their odd features. Their powers are stored in their oversized mouths, feet, hands, and noses.

The fairies have been fluttering around Dame Gothel's garden, trying to speak to her mute plants. They're wondering what's the matter with them, and what sort of power has been harnessed by Cantata's wand.

The light-footed elves, who love the trees and high places, are interested in Rapunzel herself and can't wait to hear her sing from the tower window. They've been vying for front-row seats in the trees around the tower. Even the dwarves are making an appearance, coming up from under the earth and blinking in the starlight. They're concerned about the stones of the tower. *How long will the stones hold together under that kind of force?* they wonder, scratching their heads. Unlike the other little people who are, more or less, directing their questions to me, the dwarves gather in little groups like somber rabbis dressed in dun colors, and try to work it out among themselves.

I recognize many of the gnomes because they first came to me through the modeling clay. Boomer and Yarn are there. Boomer is a round, jolly little fellow, and Yarn is a thin and boyish jokester. Whenever Yarn tells a really good story or cracks an especially funny joke, Boomer bursts into laughter, slaps his friend on the shoulder, and shouts, "That's a *real boomer, Yarn!*"

In the midst of that raucous crowd, overwhelmed by their questions and the pure delight of being in the thick of it, I look around for the troglodyte. Perhaps my wonder summons him, because right away he comes up out of a hole, panting and throwing the weight of his little self onto the ground at the edge of Gangee's cloak. He has travelled a long way with his question. Deep down in the earth, he has experienced the hollows left by the departed stones and the collapse of inner earth. I only need to look into his ashen face and drawn-down yellow eyes to know that he has felt the depletion.

"Why take the generous earth by force?" he asks. "Why give nothing back?"

There are too many questions to answer—not that I could, if I tried. Then I realize that the fairies don't expect me to answer. The story will provide the ground for them to find their own answers. All I need to do is tell the tale—and, for the moment, let their questions wash over me. *Take* their questions!

When all their voices have been heard, the fairies sigh in relief, covering us all in a light rain of gold dust. We breathe together, floating on Gangee's rippling cloak with its edges rolling in and out like waves on the shore. We merge into one being—strange and beautiful, teeming with personality, deformities and wonders, limits and expanses, mischief and love.

"Indeed," says Gangee, putting her knitting down on her lap. "Let us consider the questions." She flows to the ground, sending fairies tumbling down the sides of her cloak. They scatter to rearrange themselves once she has settled at the base of the tower image. We can all see Rapunzel at the window, and then Gangee says, "Let us see how Dame Gothel reaches her daughter."

Dame Gothel appears in the picture, climbing Rapunzel's hair like some sort of malignant growth.

"Ah, now where do we find the human heart?" Gangee asks in her gentle, thin voice. "Rapunzel has been shut into a tower. She is sealed in from the outside, and out from the inside. Her only access to the world is through her stepmother, who is controlling everything that comes in and out."

"That is correct," says Tatatee coming forward, hobbling on her cane and leading her little elephant. "Rapunzel is being used by our sister to get back into power after being shut out for so long."

Greta, Gangee, and Tatatee, who have gathered round the circle, nod thoughtfully. Then Willow, in her wispy form, flies into the middle of the circle and wraps herself around the tower. "She has made Rapunzel very comfortable and safe. She is keeping her very busy. Her mind is always on, never off. She is always trying to please. She is never good enough." Willow begins to blink rapidly. "She is always on," she repeats. "She has too much daylight, not enough rest. It has a terribly scattering effect."

"Do not get too close to that light, Willow," says Gangee rather sternly. "It is too hard on you. Let us find out how Lucy sees the picture. Where has she gotten to?"

"I'm here," says a wee voice. Lucy, in her fairy form, lights on top of the tower like a tiny ballerina.

"We can't hear you from up there," says Greta. Planting her staff before her, she launches herself to her feet and moves heavily through the crowd to the base of the tower image. "Amplify yourself, Cousin."

Lucy plunges downward, transforming into a human-sized fairy. She lands on her belly with a thump, and for a moment she can't be seen, lost in the white feathers flying. "I'll never get used to landings," she mutters, standing up and smoothing out her tutu. "Well now, you asked me a question. What was that again?"

"We asked you where you had gotten to," says Willow.

"Well, I'm here," says Lucy. "Somewhere in Nowhere, I expect, at the Heart of Rapunzel."

"And before that, we asked for your perspective on Willow's suggestion that Rapunzel has too much daylight," says Gangee. "You are our resident genius, Lucy. You understand matters related to light."

"Yes, well." Lucy primps her wigless head. Her antennae bob around as if they're gathering thoughts from the air. "Gothel is far too brilliant."

"Go on, Lucy," Willow prompts.

"Yes, go on!" cry the fairies, tittering with excitement, above and below.

"Well now," says Lucy, looking surprised and flattered by all the attention. "You want me to say something about that?"

"Yes!"

"Very well, then. Most of you will understand what I mean, when I say that it is not easy to give up one's witching stick." She clears her throat. "I myself thought it would be easier than it actually was. In the beginning, I did say that we were not going to use sorcery here, and that we wanted to come up with a creative and loving solution." She waves away some bugs around her head. "But the problem was, I took charge of the plan."

"What about Dame Gothel?" Willow whines.

"I'm coming to that. I am not so different from Dame Gothel, though it doesn't please me to admit it. The fact is, we're both brilliant." She smirks. "However, what she will not accept is what I know I must accept … which is … that we are the servants of humanity, just as humanity is, properly speaking, the servant of the Earth … That is to say, we are not in charge, which is most humbling, as those of us who are brilliant must work within the limitations of a rather unevolved nature. It is not easy to follow the path of love, and go meandering down memory lanes, blind alleyways, and such—"

"Lucy, dear, you are getting off track," says Tatatee, who stands before Lucy, dwarfed by her stature. "Stop waving wands in the wind. Tell us about Dame Gothel and her light."

"Yes, indeed, there is much to say about our sister, but Cantata is my main concern. I've never seen anything like her wand. It is capable of granting wishes and intervening in the natural growth of just about everything. I see no end to it, and that concerns me greatly." She bends her head and points her antennae directly at Dame Gothel. "Our sister has not gone Nowhere. Not at all. She is most definitely on her way Somewhere. She wants Rapunzel to become something better than anything, just like one of her plants. I daresay, she does raise some beauties, but what I mean to say is that she does not want her daughter to know her own nature. She wants power over nature. Those engaged in sorcery see no advantage in knowing the heart, and are quite prepared to bypass the whole bloody business."

"I fear there is more sorcery in the world than ever," says Tatatee, nodding her head soberly.

"I don't deny it is dangerous, with all those wishes being granted, higgledy-piggledy (not wishes, but wants, not givings, but gets), and meanwhile, we have made very little headway with love...."

"Nurture your patience, my dears," says Gangee. "We have more to learn from the story of Rapunzel."

"Yes, but when is Rapunzel going to learn anything about her own nature?" Willow asks. She sounds exasperated. She has wrapped herself around the trunk of the tower and is gazing into the window. "Look how comfortable she is. Why would she wish to know her heart, when her destiny has been so clearly laid out and her future appears so secure?"

Greta raises a finger. "Ah, but Gothel couldn't seal her in completely. Like it or not, she had to make a window. Let us see what comes through."

With that, she takes her staff and shuffles her way back, tortoise-like, to her seat at the head of the gathering.

The Window

Every morning Gothel arrives at the base of the tower and utters the command: "Rapunzel! Let your hair down to me!"

Rapunzel releases her ropes of hair that are hooked above the window and throws the pile down. Two long braids are twined around one another and tied at intervals to make a ladder. Gothel scrambles up, and Rapunzel's instruction continues. She's thirteen now, and her course of study has intensified. She must become a convincing princess. Her speech has to be perfect and her performance impeccable. Gothel never fails to remind her that if she wants the world to receive her as a princess, she must not only act like one, but believe in her role with absolute conviction. Gothel feeds her a false history, a false family, and false titles, and as she matures, it becomes difficult for Rapunzel herself to separate what is made up from what is real. She is that princess with those noble roots, that faraway family history, and this mother-governess.

Besides, the role gives her the hope of freedom one day and acceptance in the world beyond. It also pleases her mother to see her excel, and she does love to please her mother. It would break her heart to upset or offend the ugly little woman who has led such a miserable life, and is doing her utmost to give her adopted daughter a better one.

During the day, Rapunzel does what she is told and complies with the lesson plan, but she lives for the hour at the end of the day when the sun sinks behind the mountains and the snowcapped peaks turn purest gold. At twilight, the birds stand tippy-toed on their branches and sing their prettiest songs. Rapunzel, safe in her tower, has no fear after dusk and loves it more than daytime because there are no rules at night, only the wild hoots and howls of the creatures in the forest, the dance of the moon's face moving through veils of mist, and the deep mystery of the stars that hum to her on the quietest nights. Wonder spreads itself before her in the evening, and she sits for hours by the window, often fighting sleep to be present in the dark. Sometimes the night draws in so close that she blows out her candle and lets herself dissolve into it. Her spirit expands beyond the tower, and she becomes queen of the forest. The wings of the owl beat in her breast, mice skitter under her tree roots, and the stars glitter in her hair.

As I gaze at the candle flickering in the tower window, I marvel at what is coming to me from the inner worlds. The story has a life of its own and is stirring up poignant memories. Rapunzel is thirteen. She has become a prisoner, and, at the same time, a window has opened to the mysteries of the night.

I remembered being thirteen. Thirteen was the piercing year—the year when the blood began to flow and the moon took me under her wing. We were vacationing in France when the flow started, or rather, didn't start because the follicle wouldn't burst to release the egg. Almost every month, I bled internally. Sometimes I couldn't breathe because of the ripping pain. Doctors wrote it off as *mittelschmerz*—a German word for painful ovulation, literally translated as "middle pain." Meaning what? Nothing to them, apparently.

The moon claimed me as it does all women, and I became more private and enclosed. A window opened in my soul that had not been there before. I spent a lot of time alone, longing for the love of someone whose heart I could trust because we were already, mysteriously, known to one another. I looked for that companion in every young man I met, and mistook others for him again and again.

Meanwhile, I began to write poetry. The poet had an entirely different voice than the learned voice that never wrote a sentence without thinking how it might be read. This quiet, free voice spoke in pictures, unfurling images from a timeless interior place. I often didn't understand what I was writing, having no familiarity with the language of myth. It was easy to dismiss the images as adolescent fantasies, and not just anyone's fantasies—*a girl's* fantasies, which made them even less valid.

At the time, my father had moved the family to a wealthy district in Colorado. Now we found ourselves wandering around in a stone mansion with two turrets, many rooms, servants' quarters, and a creepy attic that contained boxes of old photographs, paintings, dolls, and other remnants from times gone by. The house was so big that we six children were spread far apart and divided from each other.

I spent many hours alone in my bedroom, writing poetry and looking through the window that had opened up in me. I began to think of the blank, white page as a kind of messenger: a Page. The Page delivered that loving and gentle voice within me. The Page would show me things. The Page would say, "This is who you truly are," and "This is where you truly live." I hardly understood what the Page had to say because the Page spoke in poetry.

As I continued to go to school—and especially when I entered university—I learned that poetry would not further my advancement in the world. One English professor told me that if I wanted to excel in English literature, I would have to start listening to what the professors said, and give them what they wanted to hear. He said, "Take that creativity of yours and put it in a pack on your back where nobody can see it." I was alarmed and left the field of English literature. I looked for a more reliable ladder to academic achievement, and I found it in history.

I became interested in the history of science, magic, and religion and, in particular, the problem of how spirituality and science became divided. How did we come to live in a materialistic culture? What had happened to our spirits? I stumbled into a study of the witch burnings in Europe during the sixteenth and seventeenth centuries. The horror stories of the so-called witches yanked me into a tumultuous history, a tide of powerful emotions that threatened to drag me out to sea. To succeed in school, I needed to bury my emotions and so I veered into the history of science. My professors were rationalists and would not tolerate my use of metaphor and imagery. They demanded concise, logical, clear arguments. My essays were not to meander into reflective places. They were to be engineered to go directly from one point to another, on a track, like a train.

One day in the third year of university, I was standing in the hallway and waiting for my professor to return to her office so I could get my essay back. I had written a paper on the seventeenth-century philosophers and the implications of their view of the universe as a clock. My bespectacled young professor was all business as she strode down the hall towards her office. I rallied my forces as she approached. Must have wits. No frills. On the first day of her class, she had challenged us by saying that she hardly ever gave out As. After that, her class size shrank from thirty to six. I stayed, determined to win her respect.

She turned the corner into her office, remarking as she passed, "You want your paper, I suppose."

I followed in behind her, crab-like, wary. "Yes, if you don't mind … if you've marked it."

"Oh, I've marked it all right. I remember it well." She stood at her desk, licked a finger, and flipped through a stack of essays.

"Here it is. Yes, I liked this paper *very* much. There's some really good stuff in here." She began to read. "'The underpinning of the well-stitched fabric of seventeenth century thought leads one to believe …' That was one of my favorites. But there's more."

She flipped some pages. "Oh yes, now you're really inspired: 'In the blooming of thought that occurred during the spring of rationalism …'" She looked at me over the top of her glasses. "I went looking for the rain; thought for sure you would mention the rain …" More flapping of pages.

I was confused at first. I couldn't absorb what she was doing. What was she trying to say? Did she like my paper? She certainly seemed to be enjoying herself … but then I saw to my horror that she was not reading what I had written. She was not the least bit interested in what I had been trying to say. No, she was laughing at my metaphors, and not only laughing at them, but *devouring* them. Greedily shoving them into her mouth. Every last one. Until they were all gone.

"You get my drift," she said, thrusting the paper at me.

I clutched the essay and fled her office, flushed, chagrined. I wanted to crawl back in there and sweep away all last remains of those stupid, embarrassing, ridiculous, infantile, silly, and, worst of all, *revealing* metaphors. By the time I had reached the elevators and pressed the arrow *down*, I was resolved to go through all my writing and cleanse it of all unsightly metaphors. What use were they to me? They would only ever mess me up.

From then on, I began to look upon my poetry with disdain, the way a proud princess would view her unsuitable suitors. I felt ashamed after writing poetry, as if I had had illicit sex, and viewed the affair as a colossal waste of time. In turn, my poems became increasingly dense and incomprehensible. The desperate Page filled my head with images of lovers who had been cast out of Eden, flung to distant parts of the world, and mad women who wandered the beaches of fishing villages, wailing for their lovers long after they had been lost at sea.

Siren of the North Sea
She rebuilds the castles lost to the tides
And the fishermen pass her by in the dark
And mutter that builders must build where they must;
And they head for the markets along cobblestone streets
Where they sit in the rain and drink poteen
To keep from reviving
Lost delights in a rhythm of pain.

Not many build castles on the coast anymore
And the streetlights blink on the western shore
And the children slumber deeply now
For they do not know the tales of ghosts
Nor of the ships long lost at sea
Loaded with treasure from the deep

Her lover was a sailor who could not stay
locked in her land-bound ways
So she let him go
And he sailed to a place she could not know
But for the pain that makes her rise
To rebuild the castles lost to the tides ...

I did not know what my poems meant. My heart had become a stranger to me.

CHAPTER THIRTEEN
GOTHEL'S PROBLEM

The Prince

He stands at the edge of the clearing, eyes fixed on the maiden who sings from the tower window. He has been following her song all afternoon, and now, as the shadows lengthen across the forest, he has come to its source. He wraps one arm around the oak and leans against it, as if it were an old friend. His long, walnut hair curls around his shoulders; his loose, white linen tunic blows like a sail in the buffeting wind. He has almond-shaped eyes; a dark, sunbaked complexion; and a generous, sensual mouth. His breeches are made of deerskin, a bow and a quiver hang on his back, and a dagger is strapped to his hip.

Her songs are improvised, and she sings with unselfconscious abandon, inspired by light, wind, and birdsong. She has enchanted the whole forest. Even the brook has slowed to listen. But what is she doing up there in a tower?

After the sun dips below the hills, he creeps around the perimeter, investigating the edifice, looking for a door. A thorn bush has grown around the base, but he can find no entry anywhere. How strange. After circling the tower several times, he stops and puts the palm of one hand on the sullen, gray stones.

"What secrets are you keeping?" he whispers. "Tell me, who is your prisoner? Who is keeping her under lock and key?"

The tower provides no answers. He returns to the sheltering oak, hoists himself up onto a low, wide branch, and settles in for the night. The stars wink in, one by one, and the maiden stops singing. But she doesn't leave the window. He can practically hear her breathing.

"Where does he come from?" I wonder.

We're caught in a rush of air, and we land in a cemetery some distance away from a castle. A boy with almond-shaped eyes is standing over an open grave on a barren, windswept plain. An iron gray cloud hangs low and heavy over an expanse of dry brush, and a scattering of women in black are milling around the grave. The only man there is the king, an ash-bearded bear of a man in a purple cape. The boy clutches his coat to close it against the wind. The old king goes to his nephew and tussles the boy's curly brown hair.

"We will miss your mother," he says. "But from here on out, you're going to come and live with me, eh? Have no worry, my boy. I will treat you as well as my other two sons." The great, barrel-chested king looks awkward. He doesn't know what else to say to the stricken child. He turns and leaves the gravesite, followed by the other mourners.

The boy stands alone. "Mother, why did you have to die?" he cries, kicking the turf.

She has taken all the color and joy from his world. Who was his mother to him?

Again, we're pitched into space and sent back into the young boy's past. We land in a beautiful room where the prince, a child of three, is sitting on his mother's lap. They are look-

ing out through a stone arched window onto a garden that is enclosed by a low wall. It is right after sundown, and the pine forest beyond the wall has turned a deep shade of mauve. The stones underneath our feet glow with a warm, golden light, and the prince's mother looks like a fairy queen. She wears a turquoise gown, banded in gold at the neck and wrists, and her raven hair streams over her arms. She is singing to her son in a language I can't understand. He plays with his mother's hair, twining it round his little fingers as he sings the refrains. They are completely absorbed in one another, gathering the last flames of the day.

"Where are we?" I ask Willow.

"We're at the heart of his world," she whispers, as if she can't believe her eyes.

Then abruptly, the scene dissolves like a desert mirage, and we find ourselves back at the site of the tower.

Rapunzel, framed in the window, is listening to the sounds of the night. Up in the tree, the prince stretches his long, lean body along one of its broad limbs. He watches her intently.

He *knows* her.

Gothel's Problem

The next day, in the late afternoon, Dame Gothel bursts out of her house, kicking the door open in her usual manner. She has her wand in hand, and it is sparking dangerously. Muttering to herself, she hurries down the front path and thrusts the fiery end of the stick into the keyhole of the big iron gate. The gate springs open, and she passes through, making her way across the path and into a forested area. She hobbles down a trail, hopping over tree roots, her head crowded with thoughts.

Cantata comes up the hill from the other side of the woods,

and practically runs headlong into her friend. "Well hello there, Gothel," she chirps. "Where are you off to?" Cantata clutches a maroon woolen shawl to her chest. I don't know where she's headed—maybe to Gothel's house, which she frequently visits.

"I'm going to get supper," Gothel says. She makes a sharp left turn and heads down a steep ridge path that leads to a quiet lake.

"You're in a nasty mood. What's bitten you?" Cantata asks, trotting behind.

"It's the light, don't you see? The girl has too much light. She's always at the window. I can't get her to concentrate. All that infernal levity. She thinks her education is some kind of a joke."

"You're not strict enough," says Cantata, picking her way down the hill. "I've always said that's a problem."

They come to the shore of a small lake. A mother swan and her downy gray cygnets glide past. The mother puts her head under water, and Gothel, still absorbed in her conversation with Cantata, thrusts her wand at the bird. A ball of silver light barrels from the rod and hits the swan just as she pulls her head up. It kills her instantly.

"It's no use being strict with words," Gothel says as she wades into the water to fetch the swan. "Words have no power over her." She grabs her victim by the neck and ploughs back through the water to the shore. "I don't know where she gets all that light. It's the damnedest thing."

Neither Gothel nor Cantata pass a glance at the orphaned birds who have begun to swim round in circles and cry for their mother.

"I'm not saying that I told you so," says Cantata.

Gothel ignores her, arms full of dripping swan. "I need her to become absolutely certain about who she is."

"And she's not."

"No."

"That's because she knows the story is a lie," says Cantata, crossing her arms over her chest in a condescending manner. "You should have started much earlier."

"That's water under the bridge," Gothel snaps. "No use to me now." The old witch starts up the ridge, dragging the swan behind her.

"I tell you, you're too soft. You're no more a mother than a farmer is the friend of the cow he's taking to market."

Gothel grunts.

"You've got to find a way to turn her against herself. It's the only way. Turn her against her light and show her, once and for all, that it's *dangerous*."

Gothel gets to the top of the hill and turns to Cantata. "Go on, keep talking."

"Those plants in your garden. She withers them, right?"

"Reverses all my spells—you know that."

"Well, why not use that light against her? Show her that her light is bad, and not just bad, but deadly and must be put out! Then she'll get serious."

Gothel resumes her trek home. "That's not a bad idea. But how?"

All the way back, Cantata runs behind her, helping her devise the plan that will turn Rapunzel against herself, so she will put out her own light.

When they reach the gate, Gothel holds up the swan. "Staying for supper?"

"Don't mind if I do," says Cantata, plucking a plume from a wing. "And I'll take a feather for my hat."

What the Prince Sees in the Morning

The next morning, the prince, who has been hiding in the oak tree, sees the sorceress come along with her sack over her back. He knows what sort of creature is hiding under that hood—a dark one.

People at court will hardly admit that the sorcerers exist, let alone that they pay them for their charms and potions. Dark ones are masters of the art of deception. They can make ordinary people look like gods and goddesses. They grow the fattest produce and spin the finest cloth ... They can practically (but not quite) spin straw into gold. By their spells, they spread glamour everywhere, making it impossible to trust appearances. No one knows how powerful the sorcerers have become, because no one speaks about them or attempts to reveal them. They either fear their retribution, or they rely on their spells for their own deceptions.

She has a hobbling, uneven gait, and she grumbles constantly about the weight she carries, the long hike, the aches in her joints, the hot sun, her difficult chores, and the tree roots in her path. "Get out of my way! Out, I say! I'm too old for this ... Feathers in her hat, curses! I don't see her humping the sack and doing all the work. It's always up to me ... She does nothing. Give me way!"

She gets to the base of the tower and calls up: "Rapunzel! Let your hair down to me!"

It is a command that cannot be refused. The girl throws a pile of shining golden rope out the window.

"Hello, Mother!" she cries, leaning into view.

He sees her bright face, flushed cheeks, and a circlet glittering in the sun. Her hair seems to be caught on one side. Surely that is not her *hair* that the old woman is using for rope!

It is worse than he thought. But now he knows the way up.

All he has to do is to wait for the witch to leave. Then he will go and call, "Rapunzel! Let your hair down to me!" and she will drop the rope. He will climb up and take her away from that miserable place.

Snuffed Out

Before Gothel comes in through the window, Rapunzel has been standing in front of her full-length mirror, anxiously checking her appearance. It's midsummer, and the room is airless and stifling, yet she wears the elaborate costume of a medieval princess. A gold circlet rings her head, and her hair has been tightly pulled back, braided into a long rope and then attached to the hook above the window. Her dress has been fashioned in heavy silk, striped in bands of gold and silver with wide, winged sleeves. A green velvet bodice, loosely laced at the back, accentuates the volume of her layered, hooped and pleated skirts. To make it worse, a green velvet overskirt has been attached to the dress and it is lavishly embroidered, and horrendously decorated, with gemstones. On her feet she wears ivory silk slippers with little rose patterns sewn into them. *They will always remain white*, I think to myself. They will never touch the earth. Her rope of hair is long enough to provide her movement in the room, but she is no better off than a horse tied to the side of a barn.

Rapunzel goes to the window to greet her mother, who is climbing up her hair, grumping about being "too old for this." When her black, hooded form looms into view, all we can see from where we're sitting (on the unmade bed) are her shrill little eyes, round and peevish and possibly vicious.

"Take the bag," she grunts, hauling the sack up beside her. She crouches on the window ledge for a few moments to catch her breath, and then hops down onto the floor and sniffs.

"Smells funny in here," she says. She stares at the bed, blinking self-consciously, vaguely aware of her audience. For a fleeting second, I feel she is caught in that strange snare she experienced when she sensed us in her garden.

"Put the bag on the table," she orders. "Let's have a look at you now." She examines Rapunzel's dress, making sure that it fits properly. "Well, you do cut the image of a princess, if not the substance."

Rapunzel sighs. "I am working on it, Mother. It is very tiresome."

Gothel limps over to the table and starts pulling potted plants out of her bag. She puts a scarlet tulip on the table, followed by a yellow lily, a sturdy sunflower, two purple irises, and a poppy. Supporting herself with a knobby fist on the seat of a chair, she addresses Rapunzel.

"We have a problem," she says. "It has nothing to do with your appearance. What is not acceptable is your power."

"My power?"

"Yes, your power."

Rapunzel looks at the flowers and at her mother, and suddenly, she understands. She has forgotten about the power she had over the plants in the garden.

Gothel shoves the tulip in her direction. "Put your hand over this tulip," she commands.

"No, Mother, please. I know what you're speaking about …"

"Do as I tell you, my girl."

She reaches her hand out to the flower, her fingers trembling as if to say, "Please, please, please don't shy away." It's no use. When her hand approaches, the tulip faints, just like a person. It sinks to the ground and falls apart.

"That is your power," Gothel says. "It must be suppressed."

Rapunzel looks horrified. "What do you mean?"

"If you have this power over plants, what do you think you will do to people—not to mention the king's son? When you touch him, the same thing will happen. He will wither." She sniffs, vaguely amused. "He will die."

"I cannot possibly have that kind of power, Mother. I would never kill anyone. It's not possible! The birds come to the window, and I have never killed a bird. Never!"

"Well, that is going to have to stop. Eventually, the birds will die. Your light is getting stronger."

"I would rather die myself than harm anyone, even a tiny bird."

"Well *you* don't have to die. We have to get your light to die."

"How?"

"You must completely forget yourself—that is to say, you must step fully into this role that I have given you. You must forget your childhood. Replace all your natural memories with the stories you've been told. I don't want to see one flash of doubt in your eyes, do you hear me? Because if, for one moment, you imagine that you are anything other than your role, your power will slip like light through a crack in the door, and you might very well kill the person you are with."

"That can't be true!"

"I'm afraid it is, my girl," says Gothel, feigning sympathy. "It's very unfortunate, but I've known others with your light, and everyone around them became sick and died. I've tried to protect you from the truth, but I can't do it any longer."

"Do you have this power too, Mother?"

"Yes, but I have put it out completely." She passes her hand over the row of flowers, and they all remain erect. In fact, they straighten up like little soldiers passing inspection. "It takes years of practice to put out your light. But as I say, the key is to reject your nature completely. Control it. Crush it like a snake under foot. Aspire to be someone much better." She hobbles over to the mirror. "Look into the mirror. It will help you."

As Rapunzel turns to face the mirror, the witch begins to chant:

Disappear in the mirror,
Be only what appears ...
Disappear!

Rapunzel surveys her image in the mirror. "But who am I, really, Mother? I feel so many things I wish to express ..."

"Nobody cares how you *feel*," the witch hisses, yanking Rapunzel to her knees so that she can address her face-to-face. Her reeking breath has filled the room. No air moves through that stale swamp. "Feelings are your worst enemy. Put them out! The only one who has any hope of advancing in the king's world is one who performs without a flaw. You must not show defects of any kind. Never reveal your true nature."

"Why not?"

"Because it is *vile*!"

"How so?"

"Look at me!" Gothel shrieks, shaking her like a tree. "See how nature has deformed me?! Am I not vile? We both began ugly, but I did not have your advantage. Nobody raised me up! Nobody cared for me! I have made you beautiful. Use it to succeed! You can become the most powerful woman in the world. But you must never reveal me. And never reveal yourself. The mirror will help you. I will send it with you when you have been selected, and it will work its magic long after you are queen."

Disappear in the mirror,
be only what appears ...

As Gothel chants, Rapunzel goes into a kind of trance. She seems to pass into the mirror and acquire its hard surface, its reflective power to say whatever might please the person who is looking.

What the Prince Sees in the Evening

The day wears on, and the prince waits in the tree. First, he is impatient, but the long day gives him time to think. Why is the girl so joyful about being imprisoned, he wonders? Why does she not call for release? Has the old woman put some kind of spell on her? It doesn't seem possible. She is too exuberant to be under a spell, too open and trusting. Too real. She is the beauty that is missing from the world. And yet, what irony, that he should find her captured by a witch—and not just any old witch, but one of the most malignant. He can't wait to get to her out of that dreadful place.

At last, Dame Gothel clambers down Rapunzel's hair and leaves the clearing. The sun sinks beneath the ragged tree line, and the moon rises, full and frank. Not a sound comes from the tower. He can go up now. The way is clear. But he stays, held back in the arms of the tree. He has not solved the puzzle yet. Why is she so happy? Does she not know that her mother is a witch? Sorcerers often steal their children. From what nest has she been stolen, and at what tender age?

Suddenly, he understands. She knows nothing about herself. She doesn't know that her mother is a witch or that she is a captive. Who will tell her the truth? And what will it do to her? Will she ever sing again? No, she will become as disenchanted as everyone else in the dark world. The truth will break her heart.

He jumps down from the tree. "I cannot deliver you, my robin," he cries. "I would destroy you!"

He heads into the forest, away from the tower.

CHAPTER FOURTEEN

DELIVERANCE

Delivering Beauty

Early in spring, before the snowdrops or the crocuses had made an appearance, I walked along the slushy streets of downtown Toronto—running errands to the grocery store and the post office. I was thinking about the way the story was revealing itself to me, like a flower opening its whorl of petals.

    I had been able to read the thoughts of certain characters better than others. I could read Gothel, partly because she was always muttering to herself, and it was not difficult to catch her foul drift. Rapunzel was harder to find under all that *material* ... I had more connection with her when she was a little girl. The prince felt practically transparent to me. I could easily follow him back in time and understand his thoughts and motivations, maybe because he embodied my own yearning for beauty and innocence. The poet Robinson Jeffers once called our human sense of beauty "divinely superfluous." That never sat right. To call beauty superfluous seemed to express Rapunzel's painful removal from the world. Why had he not said, "divinely *intrinsic*"?

    Where is beauty present in our world? I could no more feel her in the concrete sidewalk than the child Rapunzel could feel her feet on the porch. Beauty wasn't present in the cars zooming by or in the utilitarian architecture of the buildings or the department store windows. Was that Beauty on the billboards, advertising clothing, cars, and chewing gum? If so, she had been put to work to sell products—to lure people into stores and restaurants. Maybe she hasn't been lost, I thought. She's just been employed.

What about the arts? I paused at a streetlight and stepped back from the gutter spray. Surely Beauty continues to thrive in the ballet, the opera, and the art gallery. Ballet. Ha. *Swan Lake*. How many dancers have been broken on the way to *Swan Lake*? Do you have to become prima ballerina to be considered a real dancer? Is Beauty only to be found at the epitome of an art form? Is every other artistic undertaking just a ridiculous, somewhat shameful derivative?

A classic test of the prince in fairy tales is that he's confronted by two princesses (or more) who look exactly alike. He has to distinguish the true princess from the other replicas. It's a fairly modern test when you think about it. If you knew a person and that person was replicated in every detail as a high-functioning robot, how would you tell them apart? The true prince, like the true princess, sees beneath appearances and recognizes the animate soul. Human beings have the unique ability to see into the depths and converse with Nature, but do we even know we have the gift?

As I walked toward the post office, a strange fusion took place. The streets became pathways through the forest, and the buildings morphed into trees. The story was being lived right here, right now. Like the prince, I earnestly wanted to know what feminine beauty had gone into exile in our fixation with flawless perfection and fitness.

But the prince was headed in another direction.

The Prince Turns Around

He takes long strides away from the tower, telling himself that Rapunzel is happy. Leave her with her innocent joy. What can you give her but terror and a broken heart?

At sunset, he climbs an old beech tree and sleeps in its arms until dawn. He wakes restless, upset, and tormented by his thoughts. He has no place to go. He can go neither back nor forward. His destiny is already tied to hers, just as she is roped to the tower.

He spends the day in the tree. Late in the afternoon, having no better idea, he climbs to its uppermost branches. Maybe when he gets to the crown of the tree, he will see something. He's an agile climber. He forces himself to ascend beyond his comfort zone to a place where he can think only about not falling. He dares himself, testing his courage as he moves out along a high limb.

When he has gone as far as he can, he becomes aware of a conspicuous absence. Something is wrong. It has been wrong all day. The air is silent, the forest sullen. Only the winding brook can be heard going about its business. Dispirited.

He listens. No song uplifts the mood of the day; no resonant voice stirs the songbirds and gilds the atmosphere. She isn't there at all. Where has she gone? His heart pumps hard in his chest, as he considers the possibility that the witch has taken her away.

He makes his way back to the main trunk, gingerly, reminding himself to go steadily along the high, narrow limb. He climbs down, focusing on each careful move. When he jumps to the ground, he runs swiftly through the forest and reaches the tower at nightfall.

There is no one at the window. No sound. Not even a flicker of light.

The Prince Comes In

Rapunzel sits by the tower window, staring at an edge of her wardrobe, a single vertical line caught between shadows and moonlight. She does not feel the cool air on her cheek. She derives no joy from the wind that teases threads of gold from her braided hair. Nothing can move her. The weight of the world presses in from every side.

It will be a long, uphill battle to become someone she isn't. She wonders if she will have the strength to carry on the pretense. Yet, she has no choice; it is either that, or face the horror of herself. How can her true nature be so awful? What cruel creator made her attractive only as a lure to destroy living things? It is inconceivable. Yet true.

Imitating the voice of the witch, he calls up from below. "Rapunzel! Let your hair down to me!"

She doesn't hear him at first.

He tries again. "Rapunzel! Let your hair down!"

What is Mother doing here at nightfall? she wonders. She never comes after dark. Perhaps the lessons have intensified.

Mechanically, she heaves the coil of braids over the window ledge and lights the lantern on the table. She's careful not to go near the flowers that her mother left behind. She needs no more evidence of her deadly powers tonight.

Tugging the heavy gown that took most of the morning to assemble, she moves back to the window. She is finding it hard to breathe in the corset. At fifteen, she has plump, round breasts, but her body has its own mind. Her waist wants to thicken, her hips to fatten. This must be her focus now. She must command her body to take the right shape. She must please the mirror.

She expects to greet her mother, but instead, a strange form looms up into the window. Shocked, she jumps back, tripping over her gown. The person is not her mother, not a woman, but a man. He has thick, dark hair and broad shoulders. There are glints of copper in the stubble on his face. He waits on the ledge, bracing himself, flooding the room with his presence. *Is he the raven who lit at the window just the other day? Or has the very Night come in?*

"Please do not be frightened," he says. His voice is warm, and his skin is casting a new fragrance in the room ... cloves and candle wax. "I only wanted to make sure that you were still here."

"Who are you?" Now she is sure that he must be the Night because his eyes are black and they shimmer like stars.

"I'm just someone who has been inspired by your beautiful singing. You've drawn me in."

"Then I am wrong to do so," she says, backing into the table and gripping it from behind. "You must go."

"Why?"

"I am dangerous."

He laughs. "Yes, I do believe you are!"

She frowns and drops her head.

"I won't stay. Not if you wish me to go. I was just concerned, when you stopped singing. I thought you had been taken away or that somehow you had managed to free yourself."

"Free myself? I don't understand." How could he possibly have such intimate knowledge of what she had been thinking?

"Your hair is tied to a hook. Do you not know that you are captured?" He tugs on the rope of hair that is attached to the hook above him. "Bound. You are not free."

"No. I am simply learning ... I am to be presented at court ... I am a princess."

He smiles. "I am certain that you are. The whole forest has been touched by your song—the birds, and even the wind and the brook have been inspired by your voice. But then you stopped singing, and the light went out of the world. Why did you stop singing?"

"I won't ever sing again."

He shifts uncomfortably in the window. "May I sit here?

Only for a moment...."

She backs into the dark room. "Yes, but you must not approach me. And you must not stay long."

He seats himself in the window, dangling his long legs, sweeping the stone floor with his calfskin boots. A thrill runs through her; a wish to wriggle out of her stiff clothes. He is a warm, living flame—rugged, fearless, and natural.

"Are you the Night, come to visit me? Perhaps you have come to take me away," she stammers. "Maybe it is best that you do."

"I am a Knight. Am I *the* Knight?" He laughs. "I hope so." Are you Rapunzel? Is that your name?"

"Yes," she says and then claps her hand over her mouth. She isn't supposed to utter her real name. Her made-up name is Ursula. She must tell him the story of Ursula. Her mother hasn't given her permission, but she has to tell him something.

She crosses her arms, and tries to focus on the story she is supposed to tell. "I come from a kingdom far away to the north. In my homeland, a princess is taken from her home and raised in a tower until she can be properly introduced to the court. Unfortunately, I have no court to return to because my father's kingdom was destroyed. My mother and I escaped, and ..." She blinks rapidly, trying to remember the details and articulate them in proper order. "She had a tower built for me here, so I could continue my education and become a princess fit to marry her intended."

"And who is that?"

"The eldest son of the king, sir Night."

"Hmm. That's a fine story." The prince pulls up his knees, rests his back on the side of the window, and rubs his bristled chin. "Quite convincing. Except for the part about the princess. You seem to be confused about whether or not you *are* a princess."

Blood rushes to her cheeks.

"There is truth in your story, but I do not think it is entirely true. It is learned." He frowns, and swings his legs up to the ledge. Leaning back into the wall, his eyes are lit by a secret pain.

She sees it. She must have let some of her true nature out. Already, she has hurt him.

"You must go," she says, turning away. She goes to the wardrobe for refuge and stands on the other side of it. She's feeling unwell, light-headed.

"What is true, and what is a lie? You are beautiful and pure, but do you think that your life here, in this tower, is natural?"

He's blocking the air from the window.

"You must go," she repeats. "I can't breathe."

"It's your laces," he says. "They're tied too tightly. Come. Let me help you. Please."

He swivels around, still sitting in the window. She moves to him, drawn in on another kind of rope. He loosens the laces on the back of her bodice. "No wonder you didn't sing today. You can hardly breathe," he says, resting his hand on her waist.

His touch sets her spine on fire. He has the power to undo her in every way. But no, she will undo him! She whirls around and backs away into the shadows of the room. "You must go now. Forget me, and never speak to anyone about the tower or what you have seen." How can she convince him to forget? How can she, when she would rather beg him to stay?

"I will. I swear it. But having let me in just a little, do you not wish to know something of the truth that has been kept from you?"

"Truth?" She tries to keep him in her focus, but her vision is blurred. He's going in and out of the moonlight coming in through the window. Is she dreaming? What does the Night know? "What truth do you have to tell me? Perhaps you know better than I do who I am."

"I cannot tell you who you are, though believe me, I would wish to know ... Sadly, however, I can tell you who you are *not*."

"Then say it. Tell me who I am not." She yanks off the uncomfortable bodice and flings it to the bed.

"You are not free," he says, sliding himself off the ledge.

She won't look at him. She blocks him with her hand. "Continue. But come no further."

"The one you call your mother is a sorceress."

"What does that mean, sorcer-cer-ess? Tell me."

"A sorceress is a person who can bend things into the shape of her will. She captures things, and makes them do what she wants. She doesn't care what her captive wants or feels."

Rapunzel winces. That does describe her mother. "Why? Why does she do that?"

"Perhaps she is trying to better her social position. She may have gone to the dark arts for that purpose and she is using you for her own gain—"

"That's enough. I don't want to hear any more. Please, move away from the window. I must have air." Rapunzel lunges past him to get to the window.

A warm mist has crept into the clearing, enveloping the tower and blocking the moon and the stars. She squirms in her dress. Her clothing is cloying. Is she really being used? It's unthinkable. But more unthinkable to challenge her mother. She fears her. She has always feared her. Yet, she loves her. She pities her.

She can feel his breath on her neck.

"Does my mother not love me at all?"

"I don't know," he says softly. "But she is not allowing you to become who you are."

"Who am I then?" She turns to him. "When I was little, I

had so many questions. Where do I come from? Who is my true mother? Why do I have to be so alone? My mother told me that we were both abandoned. She said we were ugly and unwanted. She raised me so that I would be acceptable, and not have to experience her fate."

He is standing so close to her that she can hear the drum of his heart. She has never been so near another human being, and it's like water to a dry, thirsty plant. He runs a finger along her forehead, across her temple, and down the side of her neck, lightly, as if she is exquisitely delicate. She is melting, wilting … She stiffens. Steps back.

"You have the power. You are deadly!"

"Deadly?" He grins.

"Yes! It's in your hands. I have it, too. Look."

She goes to the table where the flowers stand all in a row and passes her hand over one of the irises. The flower drops its head, and the petals come apart. "Now you do it."

"That's strange," he says. He goes to the table and crouches beside it to be at eye level with the plants. He studies the flowers, all standing straight, too focused on holding themselves together to emit any perfume. He rises, and slides the palm of his hand over the remaining iris. It comes down gracefully, folding into itself. "That is not death," he says, laughing. "It's relief!"

"What?"

"These flowers have been put under a spell. They're trying to match themselves to an image they can hardly attain. It requires great effort. When they feel the gentle light that flows through your hands and mine, they let go. They return to the earth. Let's hope that when they come up again, their growth will not be so forced."

Rapunzel begins to tremble. Even in her heavy clothes, she is cold—cold in the wet mist. She feels the weight upon her, the dragging, horrible weight of velvet and gems and cloth; so much cloth, cut to fit, with narrow seams forcing her to keep her shape, down the bone, leaving no more room for movement than she has in this room. She is shivering. Is it hot or cold? Is he real or imagined? Good or evil? She doesn't know. He's confusing her, and at the same time, she understands him completely.

"Are the flowers not real then? What is real? Am I real? And if I am not real, who am I?" She claws at her clothes. "You are the Night, truly! You've come through the window and you've thrown me into the deepest dark!"

This is exactly what he had feared. Now he can never take back the torment and confusion he has exposed her to.

"I am sorry, Rapunzel. I have no answer to all those questions. But I can tell you this: You are the flower of the earth. For reasons mysterious to us both, you have been removed from the world and from yourself. You must return, somehow, because if you don't, no one—not me, not the creatures of the forest, nor the stars in the sky—will be free. We'll all end up like those flowers, living under force. Don't you see? We are bereft without you."

She can't restrain herself for one more second. She throws her arms around his neck. "I know only one thing. You are real. You are real!" She kisses him, frantically, tearfully, running her hands all over him, touching him as she has longed to be touched, as the flowers have longed to be touched. They surrender to the power of love, which, though it may be deadly, they cannot resist. One by one, their garments drop like petals to the floor, and they melt into the shadows of the room.

Lady Shame

I had to go for a walk. I stood up, stretched, and went downstairs. Stared at the island counter in the kitchen. Tried to figure out what to make for dinner. Opened the fridge. No salad fixings. Must get to the store. It was getting to the end of a warm spring day. Put on your flip-flops and go.

I walked down the street to the noisy corner at Davenport and Dupont. Went into the Food Depot. Picked up a basket. Headed for the fruit and vegetable section. Paid for the groceries, and carried them home. Started the salad and threw a piece of salmon into a couple of ounces of water to steam.

I had been in the tower for a long time before I realized I wasn't free. When I finished graduate school, I married a history professor. It was time. I was twenty-four. My mother had married at twenty-four, and my grandmothers on both sides had done the same. When my father asked me bluntly, "Why are you marrying this man?" I told him that it was a rational decision.

We married, and set up house in the suburbs of Ottawa. I got a job in an advertising agency. I expected that in a few years we would have children and live a fairly conventional life. I gave little validity to my poems, though I continued to write them. If they couldn't be published or in any way purchased, I thought, what was their value?

My husband and I enjoyed camping trips, dinner with friends, the dog, and the day. But we rarely talked about our feelings. I grew increasingly lonely and cut off. I couldn't sleep. I would scream into my pillow at night, unable to bear the loneliness. One night, after trying to get to sleep, I couldn't take it anymore.

"Why don't we talk?" I asked him. "There are so many things I would like to share with you. Why don't you show any interest in what I feel?"

He rolled over and looked at me, his hair all tussled, his face unshaven. He said, "Look, you've been really hurt before in your relationships. Your heart is like a garden. Other people have gone in there and they've trampled on everything beautiful. I will never do that."

"Why? Why will you never do that?"

"Because I will never go into your garden." He laid back on the pillow and I knew why I had married that man. It wasn't for love. We had married as a *refuge* from love. Our real marriage was a contract to protect one another from feeling anything—until death do us part.

Could I survive a loveless marriage in order to seal myself away from hurt? Could I get through life walling myself in from the outside and out from the inside? By the third year of our marriage, I started to come apart. The line, "I am not what I appear," went round and round in my head. I felt like a porcelain doll, going through the motions, saying the scripted thing, and doing what was expected of me as a wife, daughter, sister, friend, and employee. But who was I? Who would I be if I were to become me? If I burst through the porcelain shell, what hideously eccentric form would I take? Would I frighten people? Would I be driven out of town like a witch, or shut into a lunatic asylum or laughed out of existence?

The only one capable of speaking to me about what was going on inside came through that old messenger of mine, the Page. The poems tumbled out, and I stared at them uncomprehending, thinking, *There is nothing in here worth anything.* Then one day, a poem wrote itself onto the page and practically knocked me over with the force of its truth.

The Poet and Lady Shame
In a hovel on the other side
Of the river that parts
The limbs of the city
From its heart;
The outcasts carry out their lives
I pay them a visit from time to time—
The poet and Lady Shame.

MICHELLE TOCHER

The poet is lonely, cut off like the limb of a starfish
To write these lines into the wide void
While the waters run out of the world
And the earth cracks, top-heavy, old and
bewildered.

And when it is done, and the thing conceived
I fly out, only to run
Headlong into Lady Shame
Who leafs through and leaves me;
Jangling away with her jumble of keys.
She has the final word, I cannot get
Around her into the world, she keeps her
Dobermans at the gate.

Are you good or evil, Lady Shame;
You with your jumble of keys
I thought that you would make good protection
    good direction when I took you on
    to be my good gatekeeper

And now, Lady Shame
The torrent in me
Will make you shameless
I have held too much
Water back in these unconscious cells
I need release

Gimmee those keys, Lady,
They're just an illusion I created
To keep me locked here
Fuming over miscarried dreams
And words that slide off the page
Like skaters off the ice

THE TOWER PRINCESS

I will throw you out with the metaphor: Shame,
You're an old tramp; I'm better off
Believing in my lunacy
Than to keep you here to tell me
I'm not enough, not right already
Not ever maybe
Damn you, Lady Shame!!

water in me
slams against the concrete world
I was not born to make more concrete
see my naked mind, Shame?

take it in, uncoil the beast
(she will not touch me, she walks away
she considers my thoughts obscene)

I throw it into your hollow face
Let the water flow
Down through your hollow body
Down to your hollow toes

I'LL DESTROY YOU, LADY SHAME!

(but keep the hood to hang
in the closet

Call you again maybe
on a too rainy day).

 By then, my removal from the world had been accomplished, and the old dame had acquired a hefty set of keys. I had locked myself into solitary confinement. I was desperately lonely, living a false life in a false marriage, and on some level—only dimly viewable through the glass of poetry—I was dying.

 I have heard it said that revolutionaries are born when people get a taste for freedom. As long as one is living in the tower and the tower is your whole domain, you don't notice that you are kept. But once I saw Lady Shame, I became aware of my confinement and my shocking passivity. What on earth had prompted me to live this life that was not my own? I could hardly recognize myself in the mirror. I lined my eyes with a thick, black pencil and extended the lines outward and upward like Nefertiti. I announced myself to the world in bold colors—mustard, purple, and red—but I had no idea who was making the announcement.

I was quite possibly the most banal person on the planet for all my exotic markings. Could I keep up the charade for the rest of my life? I began to notice the effort it took to keep the smile pasted on my face, when I pretended to listen to people prattle on about superficial things. I felt more and more brittle, terrified that at any moment the porcelain would crack, and the truth would burst through.

Then I started dreaming. Huge dreams came thick and fast. I dreamed of being in a tower. I stood at the window, only able to see through a tiny slit at eye level. I could see a storm barreling in from across the plain. When it hit the tower, it would snap it like a matchstick, and I knew that all my intellectual constructions would be flattened. Nothing would ever be the same again.

My dreams pushed against the walls I had constructed, pushed like water against a dam. One night I dreamed that I had died. My mother and I had gone to the Kmart store, and I got shot by a redheaded woman. My body was dragged out of the store, my skirt hiked up over my head. I flew into the parking lot and saw my corpse being dumped into a coffin and slid into a hearse. My mother came out of the store and got into her blue Thunderbird. I hammered at the window of the driver's seat, shouting, "Mom, Mom!" She turned and looked out the window, but she didn't see me. Her face was made of porcelain—no recognition at all. I woke up sweating. Who would I be if I allowed myself to be my true self? Would I become dead to everyone alive? Invisible? Or worse, exposed and then attacked?

I tried to hold myself together—to cover up the cracks, so they wouldn't show. But I couldn't. My eyelids twitched. The corner of my lip twitched. I couldn't stop the twitching.

I wanted to deny that I had seen Lady Shame—to pretend that she had not been exposed. But she stayed there, frozen on the page, photographed.

CHAPTER FIFTEEN

IN HIDING

Lost Ground

Willow and I amble through the forest that surrounds the tower. We have taken off our cloaks of invisibility, and put them away in her bag. We're just wandering, like the brook, through an open cathedral of woods. Here, the hardwoods stand tall and sturdy, with powerful trunks that shoot up from the forest floor to join the crowded canopy above. Their arms tangle, and their leafy fingers gather the light, leaving the forest floor open but dark. The sun shines through the canopy, splashing gold here and there and exposing unsuspecting butterflies, spiders, and mice.

"I suppose by now you have figured out who I am to you," says Willow, tucking a mass of white-gold hair behind one of her elfin ears.

I'm not sure I have. Willow is deeply familiar to me, though I can't say why. I'm tempted to say that she isn't another godmother. She's more like a ghost of myself from the past—a spirit that was split off in adolescence, and has been floating around ever since. She nestles up to me and we walk, arm in arm.

"Like the other godmothers, I can only be seen here," she says. "You have given us grounds, you see, grounds for existence. You've made it possible for us to be together again."

We pause under a grand old willow tree that bends over the stream. It's shedding its catkins, and the air is full of tree snow. We sit down on the pebbled embankment, and Willow raises her face to feel the catkins brush her cheeks. I can't imagine a spirit like Willow surviving in the dense atmosphere of the early 21st century. She is way too sensitive—and yet that extreme impressionability enables her to move around, shapeshift, and sympathize with every living being.

She trails her long, white fingers in the stream, and the water responds playfully, swirling around them. I can see her trying to summon her thoughts, straining to narrow her dreamy eyes into a single beam. I don't think it's easy for Willow to concentrate; she prefers to drift.

"I am trying to understand how we became divided," she says, shaking the water from her fingertips. "It's coming up through the story. I can almost see it, but not quite. Maybe you can help me. When Rapunzel learns that her light is deadly, she turns against herself. She distrusts her nature, which allows Dame Gothel to mould her into anything she wants."

She speaks haltingly, as if she's lining the words in a row, like beads, carefully arranging them in her own pattern. "Do you think Dame Gothel will be successful? Can Rapunzel live without knowing who she is? Is it possible for human beings to thrive when they become so divided?"

"Oh, Willow, what amazing questions." I know how our culture would answer them. We are quite able to live in a divided state. Many of us don't see the need to know ourselves. It's not like it's necessary for survival, or at least that's the general narrative. We need to learn how things work, so that we can get a job and become useful cogs in the machine.

"How does one perceive the world from the point of view of one who is divided?" Willow muses. "I can't understand how one would see it."

"Well, let's take the brook, for instance. You see it primarily as a living being, a spirit expressing itself as a meandering body of water. That's one way of looking at the brook. Another way is to see it as an element made up of many tinier particles. Each molecule has a function, and together, all the molecules are organized to make water. Then you name it according to its elements—two parts hydrogen, one part oxygen. H_2O. You don't talk about its spirit."

"H_2O. Do you forget the water after you spell it? Do you never speak to it?"

"No," I say with a snort.

She becomes downcast and dips her fingers into the water again, letting it glide through. "It must be terribly lonely for you. How will you ever know who the stream is to you? How will the stream ever know who it is to itself?"

I find myself getting a little defensive. "I don't know, Willow, but in my world people would laugh at you if you seriously suggested that the brook was a conscious entity, who cared about how it was being spoken to."

She frowns. "Why would people laugh?"

"Because the inner life of a stream—or a person, for that matter—is considered to be more or less immaterial."

"Of course it is immaterial—it's not physical."

"No, I mean it is *immaterial*. It's not relevant."

"Oh!" Willow lurches backward and looks at me with wide eyes, as if she has just seen me clearly. "Is that what you think?"

"Well, yes."

"Then that explains it."

"Explains what?"

"How we became divided!" Now the words just tumble out

of her mouth. "Once we lived together, matter and spirit. We met here. *Here.* This was our common ground. However, at that time, and this is no disrespect to you, there were many more beings here. Maybe too many beings—I don't know if you can have too many beings. But the fairies were here in swarms, and the forest was thick and carpeted in layers of moss and flowers, and all the colors and fragrances and sounds were the symphony that artists heard and painted ... Spirits were not cut off from one another, and through our converse, we learned about one another. We fed one another, don't you see? We belonged here, all together, on this ground, inside and out."

"But then, a clearing took place. That's what we called it, because we had no other name for it. We didn't know what was happening in the physical world to cause such an effect. But we lost our ground, the way the mist disperses in the early morning sun, and when we recovered our bearings, we found ourselves floating around in space, looking down on the Earth, which was surrounded by a ring of shattered mirrors. Several great explosions had taken place, and the debris was thick and dense, like the thorns around the castle of the sleeping princess. We couldn't get back in. We'd been locked out.

"So you see why I am so surprised by your word: *immaterial!* We never were material, so how could we become immaterial? But now I see. If you think that what is not material doesn't *matter*, then it would be absurd to speak of anything that doesn't matter. Yet your own spirit is trying to live here in this place that doesn't matter." She looks at me searchingly. "Do you really not know who I am to you?"

"I'm not sure I do."

Willow shudders. "You have made me a figment ... Perhaps I don't exist at all ..." She holds herself in her arms, shivering.

"Are you cold? We'd better go," I say, getting to my feet.

"Better go," she echoes as she begins to fade.

> "No, don't go, Willow!"
> "No, don't go...."
> Before I know it, she has washed away like a sidewalk painting in the rain.
> "That is not what I meant!" I cry.
> It's too late. She is gone. Just like that. Gone.

I stared at the words on the screen. What had I done? What did I say? It was my fault—I drove her right out of the story with my sneering attitude and my rational mind. I thought I was being so smart! Whoever Willow was, I didn't have what it took to keep her with me. I didn't have the sensitivity to carry on a relationship with such a tender spirit.

No wonder the fairies have departed the earth, I thought. It isn't just our great wars, our pollution, or even our materialism. It's our superior, defended, cynical attitude!

Over the days that followed, I felt that I had lost a part of myself, and that she was gone forever. A whole raft of stories swarmed up from out of the depths. The swan maidens, selkies, and mermaids haunted me—stories about feminine spirits who had tried and failed to make contact with humans. Stories like the one that Laurens van der Post told about the star maiden. He'd heard it from his old black African nurse when he was a small boy.

> There is a man who works hard farming his fields, but he starts to get the feeling that something is being stolen from him. One night, he goes out into his field and sees the most amazing thing. A group of maidens are lowering themselves down from the stars on a cord, and each carries a tightly woven basket. He catches one, and insists that she come to live with him. She agrees on the condition that he make a promise. He must never look into her basket without her permission.
>
> He agrees, but he's curious, and his curiosity grows. One day, when she's out of the hut, he thinks, *Oh, what the hell*, and he goes to have a look. Then he roars with laughter.

When she returns, she knows right away what he has done. "You have looked into my basket!" she cries.

"Yes, you silly woman, and why did you make such a fuss about it when there was nothing in it? The basket is empty!"

"You saw *nothing*?" she says, giving him a tragic look. She turns her back on him, walks into the sunset, and is never seen again.

"And do you know why she went away, my little master?" the old black nurse asked the boy Laurens. "Not because he had broken his promise, but because he could not perceive in the basket all the wonders she had brought him from the stars."

How would I get Willow back? I had to keep telling the story—to keep believing in the reality of the invisible worlds. I had to use the power of my own imagination, without relying on Willow's amazing ability to go wherever she willed. I could entertain no doubt, and absolutely no shame. I assumed a devotion for fairy tales I had never known before.

Caught Between Worlds

At the first ray of dawn, Rapunzel wakes to the cooing of mourning doves who perch on the window ledge and preen themselves in the light that breaks from the eastern sky.

The prince opens his eyes, disoriented.

"You have to go," she says. "My mother cannot find you here."

He twines his limbs around her in the soft nest of the bed. "Come with me."

"It is impossible. I am the Day and you are the Night, and Night must go. *Out*." She pushes him away.

"Yes, but first you must promise me that Day and Night will never part. Promise." They tussle and he pins her underneath him. "What would Night be without the hope of Day?"

She laughs. "Yes, and what would Day be without the relief of Night?"

"All true ..."

"Also true that my mother will soon be here."

She rolls away from him, and now he must find his clothes. He reaches for his shirt on the floor, and she throws herself over his bare back.

"Any more of that, and you will keep me here, whatever the cost!"

"I am longing for Night already." Sighing, she releases him. "I can't imagine what my mother would do if she found us out."

That hastens him. One last kiss, and he climbs down the rope of her hair. From the window, she watches him vanish into the forest. She stands there for so long that she almost forgets to pull up the rope before Gothel arrives.

The days pass, marked by a new routine. The prince arrives every night after the old woman departs, and he leaves just before dawn. Rapunzel finds herself in an awkward position, living in two opposing worlds. By day, she plays a role she has begun to loathe, dictated to by a mother she can no longer love. By night, she relaxes, sheds the costume, and climbs into her own skin. He adores her unadorned. There is nothing about her nature, inside or out, that he is not willing to know. He brings her to life, for better and worse, releasing within her a potent stew of new sensations, forbidden pleasures, and deeply buried pain.

Meanwhile, in the mirror, by daylight all the flaws and faults of Rapunzel's body are magnified. Dame Gothel's scrutiny intensifies. She focuses on Rapunzel's form—not her gowns, hair, or etiquette—but on her body parts. The nose is too long, the breasts too large, the lips too thin, the thighs too fat. In response, Rapunzel becomes obsessed with hiding—not only her defects, as Gothel requires, but any detail that might expose her; blood on the sheets, a hair on the table, soil on the rope, a smell in the air. She becomes adept at concealing, making up stories, and covering every possible track.

Hardest to hide are Rapunzel's emotions, which have now become truly dangerous. Who is this old witch? Who is my true mother? Did she really abandon me? Or did the witch steal me from the cradle? The more the prince tells her about how people live beyond the tower, the more clearly she understands the horror of her predicament. With every passing day, her life in the tower becomes more and more unbearable. Yet, she continues to pretend.

Only at night, in bed with her lover, can she allow her emotions free rein. Her body rolls in the flames of their passion, and the fire is never quenched. It only rests and then surges again, breaking sometimes into tears and often into rage. How can Gothel keep her like this? How can she be so heartless? What did she do to deserve such a fate? She might be beautiful on the outside, but she can't dispel the doubt that she was born ugly and wicked. There are times when she's thrown into awful turmoil, when it seems that Dame Gothel is right about love. It is taking her apart. She aches for him, and can think of nothing else. To be bound by her hair to the tower is nothing compared to her attachment to him!

At times, she feels powerless against them both, and what can she do but lash out at him? "You are both destroying me!" she cries. Her fury never lasts. Inevitably, it is drowned in grief and bewilderment. Over and over, she cycles through fury and grief, fire and water, rages and washings. He suffers it all with her, enduring a torment of guilt and helplessness. He knows that somehow, by some means, she will find her way through the painful labor of awakening, and that eventually she will know what to do. He won't press her. He forces himself to be patient and wait for the time of departure to ripen like the berry on the vine, but it agonizes him to leave her there every day with that shrew, when her freedom is so close at hand.

One morning, when the leaving has become too difficult and staying has gone on too long, he can no longer show restraint. Untangling himself from her desperate embrace, he says, "Leave with me *now*. I can cut you loose right away."

They're standing at the window. She's wearing nothing but her slip. "You would cut my *hair*?"

"One cut, and you are free," he says, reaching for the knife at his hip.

Until this moment, she hadn't fully grasped how easy it would be to leave the tower. Seeing the glint of the knife, she startles to the reality that he is no phantom, no dream. She has called him the Night. She knows he isn't, but she has never even asked him his name. She doesn't want to know. She doesn't want think about where he lives by day. She never asks to know details. He tells her about the forest, not the court. He has given her wings to fly but not the feet to land. How would she survive out there, exposed in that bright, critical place?

"I'm not ready," she says, shivering. "What would we do?"

"We'll go to my uncle's castle for a time. We'll marry properly, and the king will give me the land he has promised me. We'll be happy, my love. We'll be safe and free!"

He doesn't use her name either. He hates the name Rapunzel. It feels obscene.

"Dame Gothel is preparing me to marry a prince. Perhaps I could marry you."

"It won't be me. I am the adopted son of the king. I won't wear the crown. My father's land was overtaken by my uncle's family a long time ago. I tell you, none of this will matter after you're introduced at court …"

Now she's reeling. "I'm not prepared to be introduced anywhere! I have no story. What will I say? Who will I say I am?"

"Truth is not a criminal offense," he says gently.

"I don't know what a criminal is! I don't know anything! I will be a laughing stock."

"Perhaps we can—"

"I won't leave!"

He sheathes his dagger, cursing himself. She is so terribly caught. A mermaid who belongs in the sea. How can he possibly carry her to a home on the land? All he has done is destroy any certainty she might have had. He has stripped her of every defense. Just as he feared, she sings no more. The silent forest is bewildered by the absence of its joy.

She slides down the wall, wanting to disappear. All she can think of is the humiliation she will face when she fails to speak properly at court. Dame Gothel has told her what people in high places do to those who shame or deceive them. They are imprisoned, tortured, even executed. One must have beauty to survive out there, which she has to some degree, and title, which she has to no degree at all. That is why her mother has given her the role—to protect her and put her in good standing. What has he given her? Nothing! And that is what they will see. They'll see that she's weak and simple and ugly, and they will subject her to the worst kind of punishment.

Even if she does leave, Dame Gothel will come after her. Her mother has terrifying, inconceivable powers. She'll track her down like an animal, find her, catch her, and lock her away in the pit of the earth.

"I can't," she sobs. "I can't leave here ...."

They've lingered too long. He has to go. He kneels beside her, strokes her hair, and takes his words back. He's been presumptuous; he has rushed the time. "You need time," he says.

He runs his fingers over the coils of rope on the floor. The hair looks a little too worn, too used. Gothel will find out soon enough. How soon?

After he's gone, Rapunzel prepares for her mother's arrival, hurriedly dressing and putting the room in order. She knows her time is running out. She has to face her departure. It's going to happen one way or the other. She will have to face the cold, cutting atmosphere of the court. Removing the sheet that he had slung over the mirror, she remembers what her mother once said: "Think of the mirror as the court. What the mirror thinks of you, the court will think of you. What does the mirror think of you?" She does not even dare glance at it. She knows what the mirror thinks. If she is to survive the scrutiny of the court, she will have to assume a new dedication and focus. She must learn quickly—without rousing the witch's suspicions.

At the same time, she has got to strenuously hide her grief. Lately, it's been springing up unbidden. She's been remembering scenes from her childhood, times when she was baffled by what was going on, like the retreating gate in the front garden. Instead of explaining the world to her, the witch had told her bald-faced lies. She had said, "Oh, you're just imagining that the gate is moving, my girl. You imagine far too much that isn't so." She had almost stopped trusting herself, and, of course, it all came to a head in the matter of the light.

Over the days that pass, she wins praise from Gothel for her new attention and self-discipline. She sides with Gothel and scorns her body for its tendency to fatten. She accepts the new dietary regime, even though she is practically starving. She develops an almost too convincing and even somewhat hideous inclination to collaborate with the witch, which sometimes makes her fear that she really is going over to the dark side.

"I hate these plump thighs of mine," she says one afternoon, standing naked before the mirror. A strange pleasure seizes her. For a split second she feels that she has caught the hungry eye of a king—and she wants that eye on her. She wants him to eat her alive.

In her effort to prepare herself, to hide herself, to hide any trace of him (all the while hating herself for hiding), Rapunzel becomes utterly exhausted. One morning after he has left, when she's trying to pick up the pieces again and get dressed, she starts weeping, and she is unable to stop. She can't do anything anymore. It's all too much; she's cornered on all sides.

When her tears run dry, her mind clears. She sees herself in a different kind of mirror. Not the mirror of her mother, not even that of her lover, but in her own mirror. She sees how she is caught between night and day, pulled both ways and about to come apart. She has to make a decision. It is hers and hers alone. Which way will she take? There is safety in the witch's way. Yet, it leads to an artificial life, to learning many more of the wiles of witches, to a life made up of ropes and more ropes, and endless pretending. She will always be captured, but she will be safe. Or she can go the other way, toward freedom and love and mystery. There is no security there, none whatsoever. She will not be able to hold on to anything. She will not be able to hide herself. The truth will come out, and if people in high society find her unfitting, she will pay the price.

Yet, she knows what her heart wants to do. It wants to be untwisted and combed, freed of entangling lies and deceptions. Her heart doesn't care about consequences. It only wants to be true. So that settles the matter. She will leave the tower that very night. Relief gusts through her. She leans out of the tower window and waves her arms in the breeze. Feeling featherlight, she readies herself for flight.

CHAPTER SIXTEEN

LIGHTNING STRIKES

Cantata Lays the Trap

Standing in the woods on the roadside, Cantata sees the king's carriage coming around the bend and springs into action. Running pell-mell toward the carriage, she bangs on the side of the coach and begs the driver to stop. She's wearing a dirty, ragged kerchief and a plain, brown dress with an apron. The driver pulls in the horses. Panting, she tells him, "I was lost in the woods, when I saw the most amazing thing! I think it came from another world!"

The driver is a handsome, stern looking man with a gray beard and high cheekbones. He's on the king's business and looks perturbed by the disorderly peasant woman. The man in the carriage puts his head out the window. "Is there a problem?"

Cantata nearly forgets her lines, she is so bowled over. Here she is, face-to-face with the golden-haired prince himself! She can hardly hide the glitter in her eye and the spring in her step, as she approaches the carriage window.

"Your Highness," she says with a curtsey. "I don't mean to stop you on your important business, but I must tell you I have seen the most marvelous thing in the woods. Never in my life have I seen such a wonder."

"She's mad," says the driver. He starts the horses trotting, but the prince commands him to wait. The driver pulls the horses back, and they snort in their bridles while Cantata runs to catch up.

"I will hear what you have to say. It's been a rather dull day. Amuse me."

"Your Highness, I hardly know how to tell you this," she says, putting her hand coyly to her throat.

"Get on with it."

"I lost myself in the forest to the south of here. There must have been some sort of enchantment at work because I know that part of the woods, but all of a sudden, everything seemed so unfamiliar and I couldn't find my way home. I had to spend the night there, and in the morning, I heard the sweetest singing. I have never heard such a voice. I thought it must be the voice of an angel! I went looking for it and came to a hill where a tower had been built. Leaning out of the tower window was a princess, wondrous to behold, Your Highness, royally dressed, with hair so long that it spilled down from the tower window and fell all the way to the ground! She didn't look like a princess from this region, or anywhere on earth, for that matter."

"Did you speak to her?"

"No, but I did try to go up to see her. I couldn't find a door in the tower."

"No door?"

"No way up, sir."

"Where is this tower, did you say?"

"In the woods to the southeast, where the forest becomes very thick. There are no roads beyond the hills, only animal paths. There is a brook nearby. I'm all confused, I'm afraid, because I've been in the woods for two nights, and have only just found my way back to the road."

"Well, that's a strange story," he says.

"I assure you, it's more than a story," she says, rearranging her kerchief.

He gives her a coin. "No, I don't suppose it is. Good day, old woman."

The four restless brown stallions lurch forward, and the carriage rattles on its way.

"Old," Cantata sniffs, yanking off her kerchief. "I think not."

Meanwhile, Dame Gothel is in a real funk. She sits in her parlor on her massive walnut chair, holding her knobby knees to her chest. The tiny woman is dwarfed by the chair with its broad legs and claw feet. She bites her nails and mutters to herself, her eyes searching the room, searching everywhere, her nose twitching and sniffing. Twitching and sniffing.

The gate is unlocked, and Cantata lets herself in without ringing the bell. She carries a gleaming wooden case under her arm, and she hasn't changed her peasant clothes. She can't wait to tell Gothel what transpired on the road a few hours ago, but Gothel hardly notices her. She is too caught up in her paranoid twitching and sniffing.

"What's got up your nose?" says Cantata, putting her case on the table under the window. She doesn't want Gothel's problems to interfere with her exciting news.

"Something's not right," Gothel says. "I can smell it."

"Nonsense. Everything is going according to plan. Your bird has come over to our side at last. What could possibly be wrong?"

Gothel's eyes dart from side to side, and her nose twitches like a fearful rat.

"Something rotten's got in," she says, twisting in her chair. "Other than you."

"Oh bosh. Let me cheer you up." Cantata rubs her skeletal palms together to heat herself up in the chilly room. "Guess who I've just spoken to? One of the king's sons! And not just any son, but the eldest! His own heir! I had no idea it would be so easy to get to him, but I did, and I put the bug in his ear. Your fortune is about to change, Cousin, have no fear of that. All our hard work will pay off."

"I don't want things to go too fast," Gothel grumps. "She's not ready. I thought you were going to start a rumor among the servants and let it fly around for a while."

"I went straight to the top," says Cantata, arching her brow. "You should be congratulating me."

Gothel gets to her feet and stands on her chair, still not quite at eye level with Cantata. "I tell you, it's too early. She needs more polish. She's too fat, and she's not convincing enough." Gothel scratches her elbows and forearms.

"You are looking for defects that will never be noticed," says Cantata. "Everyone at court will be charmed by her."

"There's something else too," Gothel mutters.

"What's that?" Cantata asks, fiddling with the latch on her case.

"I don't believe her. She's putting on an act."

"Of course she is. It's all an act."

"No, curses! She's acting for me. She's hiding something. Her interest is too intense. Her effort is too concentrated. Something's not right."

"You wanted her to comply, and that's what she's doing. You should be proud of your accomplishment!"

Gothel sticks a finger in her ear and wiggles it around. She rubs her nose. She scratches her face. "Something's wrong, I tell you. She's hiding her light. It hasn't been put out; it's been put under."

"I'm sure she's perfectly spellable," says Cantata, opening the case.

"She's happy," growls the witch, biting her nails. "Happy. It's not right."

"Oh, for heaven's sake, Gothel. What's gotten into you? The plan is underway. We've had a stroke of good luck this morning. Don't go all doubty and uncertain on me. You're not the only one with an investment in this project. We've got to go forward with absolute conviction. Your daughter is about to make you powerful and rich."

"Yes, of course," Gothel says, blinking into space.

"Everything will go according to plan. The king's son will ride into the forest, and he will find her because you will leave earlier than usual, and we all know she sings after you're gone. He'll beg her to come out of the tower, but she'll tell him that her mother won't allow her to leave until she has a marriage proposal. She'll demand to have it in writing, and she'll tell him to put the letter under the thorn bush. You have to tell her that. Make sure she knows. Oh, and look here, Cousin!"

Cantata snaps the case open and lifts a wand from its blue velvet bed. It isn't long and thin like her other instruments. It has more heft. "I've been working on it for some time." She moves her hand over the tip of the wand, and it bursts into a blinding commotion of light that blasts Gothel right off her chair, and sends her scuttling underneath it.

"You might have warned me! Turn the wretched thing off!" she shrieks.

"Powerful, eh?" Cantata shoves the wand through the curtains, making a huge rent in the lace. It goes out in the sunlight, leaving a momentary pocket of darkness and acrid smoke. "Ha! Made you blink!" she snorts triumphantly to the sun.

She ponders her wand. "I'm having a brain wave. If there's any light left in your girl, you can put it out with this, and polish up her little defects at the same time. Spell her thin, and she'll hate her thick waist so much she'll eat almost nothing at all."

"We haven't used a wand on her since we grew her hair," says Gothel, scrambling back onto her chair. "She's got to trust me, especially now."

"You see, that's your problem. She's not supposed to trust you; she's supposed to *respect* you. You should have put the fear of Gothel into her a long time ago. Anyway, just tell her it's spit and polish, and if you must say something nice, remind her that it's for her own good."

"Let me see that thing," says Gothel, sliding off the chair. She seizes the wand, puts her hand over it, and gets it going again. She directs it at the hole in the webby, gray curtains, and chants, "Spiders, spiders, spin the lace, spin it tight, make dark this place!"

Out of the nooks and crannies and corners of the walls, thousands of spiders appear and set to work.

Exposed

Dame Gothel tramps through the woods, hobbling as fast as she can go on her malformed legs, which entails leaping on her longer leg and dragging the shorter one behind.

It is midmorning, and the sun has still not penetrated the shroud of fog covering the forest. Had Gothel not come this way a thousand times before, she might have gotten lost, but like a little rat, she can run the path with her eyes closed.

She is not in a good mood. She doesn't want to use Cantata's powerful stick on Rapunzel, but it gives her comfort to have it in her bag. If there's any remaining light in the girl, it will surely be snuffed out. Maybe just having the wand with her will chase out what Rapunzel is hiding.

But what can she possibly be hiding? What can have gotten into her head, other than what Gothel herself has put there? Cantata's right. She worries over nothing. But what is it that is causing this infernal *doubt*?

"Something's amiss. Amiss, I say. What?!" Gothel screeches, leaping sideways, spooked by some invisible forest thing. "Light, I say. She has too much light, and she knows it. That's what she's hiding! She'll never be one of us! I will have to use force. I have every right to do so, and no one can tell me I don't."

She sniffs, and beats at the underbrush around her with her wand, using it like a scythe, cutting everything down in her path. "Let me through! Curses! I am a cousin of the queen! Maggots! How dare they call me a changeling, and put me out with the ashes and the dung. What a miserable life I have led! This is my chance—let me through, I say!"

At last, she has passed through the thicket and climbed the hill to the base of the tower. "Rapunzel, let down your hair!" she commands.

Laughter from above. The rope is thrown down. The witch climbs up, groaning all the way as the damp air has inflamed her joints. Rapunzel leans out the window with a face bright as the sun.

Oh, she has light, all right. The witch clambers through the window, leaving her bag on the sill. The girl is only partially dressed. She hasn't tied the laces on her bodice, and her hair looks rumpled. Blasted wind! It will have to be braided all over again. Wand's work …

"I don't seem to be able to get the laces tied, Mother. This new gown is not fitting me properly."

Gothel stamps over to her. "Kneel, so I can see," she commands.

THE TOWER PRINCESS

Rapunzel gets to her knees with the witch behind her, standing in the space between her calves. She pulls on the strings of the emerald corset and yanks it this way and that. The bodice doesn't fit. The cut is fine, but the figure's wrong. With aching fingers, she undoes the laces, and feels around underneath to get the shape of the girl. The breasts have grown. The waist has thickened. The womb has swelled.

"What's this?" She hammers her fingers on the girl's belly.

"It's my belly, Mother!"

"What has happened to it? Why is it so big?"

"I've hardly eaten anything ..."

"Do you think I'm a fool?" shrieks the witch. She spins Rapunzel around and grabs her hair with both her fists. "Since when am I a *fool*?!" Now her tone is cold as death. "Now I know where your light is coming from. You are *with child*!"

Rapunzel scrambles to her feet. "No!"

Gothel's tiny eyes narrow into shards of ice. "Who is he?"

"He's a prince, Mother."

"Eh? What prince?"

"The king's adopted son."

Gothel spits on the cold stone floor. "*Maggot*! He's no prince! Oh, I knew something was up! I knew it! You let him in!"

Rapunzel is backing into the window.

"You piece of rot! You're *worth nothing to me* now! You have ruined us!"

"No, Mother. He's going to marry me."

"Marry you? Ha! Not now! Nobody would marry you now, not even a stable boy. Do you think he will want your child, you ignorant slut? I should never have taken you in. I should have let your greedy mother keep you, instead of trying to give you a better life!" Gothel hobbles around the room, pulling the covers off the bed, throwing clothes into the air.

Rapunzel is horrified. "You're not my mother? You took me from my mother?"

Gothel hops down from the bed to the floor with an agility the girl has never seen before. Like a huge raptor she swoops down on her. "No, I won you, fair and square," she hisses. "You're *my* Rapunzel, you belong to nobody else but me."

Rapunzel backs into the window. "You've just been using me!"

The witch approaches, looming, growing ever larger. "And now I have no use for you," she growls. Gothel reaches behind Rapunzel and claws the bag from the sill.

It crashes to the floor, cracking open the box that holds the wand. She seizes it, and it explodes into life.

"*No!*" cries Rapunzel, holding her ears and closing her eyes. She's cornered. There's nowhere to go but backward, out of the tower window. Even there, she will find no escape. She will hang on her own rope.

"You gave me nothing! And now *nothing* will be yours. I command you to go! Go to the farthest ends of the earth! Scorch in the desert and scrounge for food. Grow old and ugly. See what it's like to be *me!*"

Gothel whacks the wand on the sill, and it cracks with the force of lightning. Rapunzel is stripped bald. She flies out the window and streaks through the air, like a comet shot to the ends of the earth.

The witch stomps to the window and hauls up the rope. The winds of her fury whip around her, hissing like snakes in a pit. She hauls a stool up to the window and climbs onto it. Crouching, she waits. When night falls, the prince comes to the foot of the tower and calls up. Gothel throws down the rope, and he climbs it, quick and nimble, eager to be with his lover. When he reaches the window, the witch's hideous face looms into view, eyes blazing, teeth bared, the space around her crawling with adders.

"So! You've come for your pretty bird, have you? Well the cat has eaten her and she will eat you too!" She claws at his face, and he rears back, losing his balance on the rope. He falls into a hedge of thorns.

"Haaaa," cries the triumphant witch.

Pain shoots through his eyes, and the light goes out of the world. He struggles to free himself from the ripping thorns. Two thick streams rush down his cheeks. Not tears on his tongue, but blood.

He staggers into the forest, wailing.

Gothel's Madness

Gothel smashes her wand into the tower wall to put it out, but she can't get the wand to turn off. It has assumed a life of its own. The room is frigid, and the walls of the tower pound with the commotion of hard, cutting light. The wand flashes like a strobe, belting out bursts of sound that resemble the word "bad, bad, bad" in a deafening monotone.

Gothel drops the wand, and the mirror cracks. Pieces shoot out into the room, each one an attack. "Ugly wretch! *Maggot!* Worthless failure! Hideous hag!" With every explosion, new attacks.

"No, no!" Gothel cries, putting her hands over her head. "Don't look at me ... Don't look at me!"

The wand whirls around on the floor. She hikes a leg up to the window to get away, but the wand flies into the air, now a cudgel. It whacks her on the legs, and she falls to the floor.

The witch staggers around the room, stumbling over objects, looking for cover. She hides in the wardrobe, but the wand comes after her. She crawls under the bed, but the wand finds her there. There is no place to hide from the wand. It flushes her out like a bird from the bushes, drives her into the center of the room, and beats the life out of her. Then, like some hungry, insatiable beast, it explodes and brings the whole tower down. Pieces of the mirror fly everywhere, and the air is full of sharp projectiles that are screaming as if the mirror itself can't bear the shattering.

Under the pile of rubble, what remains of the wand lies on the chest of the witch, flashing repeatedly like a heartbeat. At last, in the light of the sun that slips in through every crack and fissure, it weakens and sputters out.

CHAPTER SEVENTEEN

AT THE WORLD'S END

Dark Passage

The story ended, or so it seemed. I couldn't pick up anything more. I walked around for weeks in a state of dejection. I felt that I had found the whole world in the fairy tale, and then it had all gone to black. She who was the heart had been shot off to some remote place, while he who wanted to know her stumbled around in the forest, blind and unable to ever find her again. What reward did he receive for all his effort to bring her back? He'd lost everything: his position, his future, his direction, his reason for being alive—all gone from his sight.

Day after day, I went back to the story, trying to pick up from where I had left off. I tried to fire the wand of my imagination and see between the lines. But the wand had no wattage. I saw nothing. I heard nothing. Even the godmothers had vanished. The dark, starless night swallowed up all images. My earnest imagination was a weak light, a little yellow yolk, revealing nothing with no matter to settle on.

Then I realized that I was in a desert. *Her* desert. *His* darkness. It seemed to be a very valid picture of where we were in the world. Maybe

Greta and Lucy were right. Maybe we had lost our endings.

I couldn't force the story to go on, though I wanted to. I was aware of the Gothel in me, who wanted to use force to make things happen. She had pushed me a long way through life. Maybe it was all for my survival, but now I saw her clearly, and I would not put her in charge. I thought, *If the reality is that the story ends here, if happy endings really aren't possible, then I must accept that. End here.* But how could I leave the prince and princess so far apart?

Months passed. Summer ended. Fall arrived. The first winter snow flew. I kept returning to the desert, to the dark, until one day in early November, something changed.

   I hear a sound, like the ping of a bell. It's coming from inside.

"Here!" pipes a little voice.

It's Lucy, a wee spark no bigger than a firefly, flitting around in the night. She lights on my index finger, and her outline becomes distinct. She looks like some weird Tinker Bell figure, only she is an *old* fairy with big, clumpy shoes; a bald head; and a tattered tutu.

"Now you're seeing me!" she peeps, shivering with delight. "I had begun to think you never would!"

"Actually, I heard you first," I say.

"Well, isn't that just the way it goes!" she cries, fluttering this way and that. "First you feel, then you hear, and finally, you *see*! You have your fairy sight!" She claps her hands together, and then stops and looks around her. "My goodness, but it *is* dark here! And what has happened? Am I very much diminished, or have you grown?"

"I think you're diminished," I say.

"I can hardly be seen at all," she declares. "This is rather worrisome. I'm not going to go out, am I? Where is Tatatee?"

No sooner does she utter her name than Tatatee emerges at my knee. She is smaller than I remember, maybe only a foot tall. She is riding her elephant, but I have to look closely to detect him because, at first glance, he resembles a shapeless ball of moonlight.

"Well now, here we are," says Tatatee with her usual dignity. She squints in the dark and bends to touch the ground with her tiny hand. "Where are we, would you say?"

"All I can see is that we're in the dark," I venture.

"Very good observation," says Tatatee.

"Isn't it obvious that we're in the dark?" Lucy chirps.

"No," says Tatatee. "When you *see* that you're in the dark, you're not in the dark anymore. You're only in the dark when you *don't* see you're in the dark."

"Right," says Lucy. "Well put, in a nice little nutshell, which is perhaps where I should be putting myself ..."

"Say more of what you see." Tatatee looks at me with a kind of insistence that feels comforting.

In my mind's eye, I turn around to see if there's anything I can pick up. I detect a ragged line on the horizon, and the faint sparkling lights of what looks like a distant city. When I allow the details to fill in, I see that the line has a broken shape—the shape of many peaks. Towering peaks. I honestly can't tell whether the towers are flat-topped, like office towers, or pointed, like those belonging to castles in the fairy world. They're towers in both worlds. "It's a land of towers," I say.

"Towers," Tatatee repeats. "How interesting. How are they lit? Are they lit from the outside in, or from the inside out?"

"I believe they're lit from the outside in," I say. I'm not sure why that comes to me or why I feel so sure, but they do look like towers that are lit up by electric city lights. I have the impression that their interiors are unlit, like Rapunzel was unlit before the prince came in and made her aware of her situation.

"Well then," says Tatatee. "We have arrived."

Her elephant raises his trunk and screeches with joy.

"Where are we exactly?" I ask.

"We are exactly where we are," says Tatatee.

More word tricks! I become agitated and even a bit snarky. "Where is *that*? Are we Somewhere? Or Nowhere? Or Neither Here Nor There?"

"We're in the *dark*!" Tatatee exclaims with satisfaction. She hobbles up a mound of sand and looks out at the serrated line on the horizon. Then she plunks herself down on the hill, and clasps her hands on her lap as if she is prepared to sit there forever.

"We also seem to be in the desert," I say, going up to join Tatatee on the sand dune. I don't want her to get too settled. I'm not content to stay in the desert, in the dark. "I want to go on," I say. "The story isn't finished yet. The prince and the princess have been thrown far apart."

"Quite right," says Tatatee, staring ahead with her tiny, glassy eyes.

"Well, I want to find them. I'm just not sure where to look …"

"Don't look outside because it's dark out here. And it's a desert."

"Where do I look then?"

"Inside, of course."

I'm confused (again). "Haven't I been looking inside all along?"

"Yes, but it's different now," says Tatatee, pushing the sand around. "There's no story line."

She's right about that. The story of Rapunzel, as it was recorded by the Grimm brothers, doesn't give us any details about what happens after the prince is blinded and Rapunzel is exiled. We're only told that he wanders in darkness and that she lives in a desert, in poverty and misery. The story spinners dropped us here with very little thread to go on.

"What you must do now is follow your own lines," says Tatatee. "Use the wand and say what you see."

I take out my wand, and it shines a little core of golden light. "This wand isn't going to shed much light on the subject," I tell her. "It's no match for the dark ..."

"Hardly a match at all," Lucy remarks, flapping moth-like around the soft glow ball.

"How am I going to find them?"

"Perhaps you will have to find them, not by your light, but by *their* light," says Tatatee. "The way you're seeing us."

At first, I was completely baffled by what Tatatee said. I considered it for several days. The godmothers were lit up from within, by their own radiance. I wasn't exactly shedding light on them. It would be truer to say that they shed light on me. It had never been possible to put words in their mouths—what they said and how they appeared came from them, and it had to sit right with them.

Now, more than ever, I realized where fairy stories come from—they come from the power of the invisible realm to appear in the dark, and our willingness to dim the bright lights of the conscious mind and perceive them. The fairies felt closer now, and more real, maybe because I was getting used to seeing in the dark. But what did Tatatee mean when she said I would have to find Rapunzel and her prince by *their* light?

Weeks passed. Tatatee and Lucy seemed quite happy to just wait. Tatatee sat on that mound of sand like a tiny, old aboriginal woman, silent, needing nothing. In fact, she seemed to absorb the silence as if it were a medicine—a balm to the busy story that Greta had been broadcasting, and the fairies had been pouring over.

Lucy, who could never sit still, occupied herself by exploring grains of sand and looking for living creatures in the holes and crevices of the desert. From time to time, she would remark on how much activity was going on underground, though she didn't share any of her observations. Tatatee seemed to demand quiet. She didn't want Lucy blathering on. And neither of them seemed the least bit interested in what had happened to the others—to Greta, Willow, and Gangee. When I inquired after them, Tatatee simply said, "Like us, they are where they are."

There was only one thing to do. I had to find a way to *see* the story through. The challenge daunted me. How could I possibly see how Rapunzel and the prince find their way back to one another? There was a bit of a story line, but exactly how did they experience the process of coming back together? How could their happy ending be made convincing to me? Did I believe enough in happily ever afters to keep going—to keep living the story out, and making it real?

I received repeated flashes of the Garden of Eden story—the exile of the primal couple to a world of hard labor, suffering, and death. He had to go to work to try and coax (or force) some growth out of the hard, unyielding soil, and she had to suffer childbirth and all the secret pain and anguish of womanhood.

One might argue that God, like Gothel, had our best interests at heart when he set us up in the Garden of Eden. He was acting out of a strong wish to protect us from the fate of self-knowledge. Why? Why not build a world out of awareness of who we are and what we are meant to be? Why build a world made of towers, with tyrants above who keep slaves below? Why make humanity leave their own natures in a bid for stardom? What is better than the treasure we find in our own hearts?

The godmothers' message was that we're headed the wrong way—we're going outward without going inward; we're going up without going down. The tree will topple without its roots; the tower will come down.

The tower *had* come down. The two lovers had been torn apart and flung to opposite ends of the universe.

Surely, I didn't have the eyes to see in this profound darkness. The golden wand had served me. It had helped me to reveal what I saw between the lines, but now, with no story line, it was only me and my weak heart.

I almost gave up the project. Life poured back in. I prepared a synopsis of the fairy book for my publisher and sent sample pages, hoping to have the sort of recognition that would keep my courage from flagging. But I received no response whatsoever. As if the pages had been fairies themselves, they flitted in and out of the publisher's offices, neither seen nor heard. I was confounded. Disheartened. Dismayed. Instead, the publisher wanted to revive an earlier work, writings about career transition, mythological work employed for the specific purpose of helping people through job changes—good, solid, useful stuff, but nothing to do with fairies. Nothing to do with the problem of reviving the heart of the world.

I wondered how long Tatatee and Lucy would hang out on the dark side of the daylit world, staring at the serrated horizon line. How long before the golden line faded? How long before the fairies retreated, and gathered again on the dark side of the moon to hear Lucy say, "Well, we tried"?

Meanwhile, we had been having trouble at the farm. Since the fall of the year before, our land had become overrun by dirt bikes. Ian had been trying for months to get the neighbors to understand that they were shattering the peace of our little community. In spite of Ian's efforts, our neighbors' dirt bikes had buzzed and shrieked all through the summer, making it impossible to go out in the backyard and enjoy wind and birdsong. Our connection to the land had been broken, and everywhere it seemed that people had become oblivious to the dangerous increase of noise and light in the world.

We began to lose hope that the farm would ever be our home. Perhaps, we thought, we should sell it and settle in the city—say goodbye to the land, to the fairies. All around me, it seemed that the war against the heart was winning. A dark brand of reality was taking over, bent on splitting the very atoms of our humanity, pitting men against women, rich against poor, white against black, citizen against immigrant ... The noise had become seriously calamitous.

I couldn't go it alone anymore, but also I didn't want to pack it in. The manuscript stayed on my desk—pages from far away, chattering, their tiny voices overwhelmed by the more insistent concerns of the day. I understood that the call was to go into the dark and go deeper, somehow, into the fairy world. I didn't know how, but what was really holding me back was the unbearable isolation. I was too alone. My deep feeling of not belonging in this world, of not being able to share my inner experiences with anyone else, was just too hard to bear. I realized that if I were to go back in, I would have to find someone in this world who could join me in that place.

Then one winter day, a little voice said, "Annie. Go and find Annie." Annie was a novelist, and a counselor with a background in Jungian psychology. Annie would know what I was doing. "Go to her," that little voice said. "Show her where you are." So I did.

I went to visit Annie. In her early fifties, Annie was blonde, radiant, and ever youthful, although she had survived lymphatic cancer and other devastating heartbreaks. Annie, with her bright eyes and her wide, warm smile, had fairies all around her. I knew, the moment I passed her the manuscript, that she would understand what I was trying to do, and she did. She read it with interest and amazement, and when she got to the end of Dame Gothel, when she came here, to the deserted, dark edge of the world, she said, "Go on."

"Annie, will you come with me?" I asked.

"Yes," she said. "Absolutely. Send me the pages as you go."

She gave me a lifeline. I went back into the dark—into Somewhere, Nowhere, Neither Here Nor There … and *Where We Are.*

  I walk up the mound and sit beside Tatatee. She stands up and calls for her elephant: "Yoo-hoo!"

  In her call, I hear the voice of my grandmother May, who died in the mid-1990s.

  "Yoo-hoo! Michelle!"

  The elephant has been nosing around in the sand, using his trunk to divine water or buried treasure. He answers with a little screech and lopes toward us. *Such a heavy animal, so light on his feet,* I think to myself. At the base of the dune, he kneels before Her Tininess. She reaches into a saddlebag, and produces a pen-sized wand that grows in her hand to a length of about eight inches. She passes her hand over it as Dame Gothel did, and it sparkles into life. I recognize it as the same wand that Lucy first used to grant my wishes—a miniature version of Cantata's wands.

"Here is another one of your gifts," she says. "You are ready to use it now. As you know, the golden wand breaks spells, while the silver wand casts spells. I need not tell you that it is not meant to be used on others, only on yourself. Transform yourself." She hands me the wand, her tiny eyes dancing in the silver light. "Are you beginning to see the possibilities?"

"I can turn myself into ... anything?"

"Precisely. Now, let us see both your wands, dear."

I take out the golden wand and hold it in my left hand, while the silver wand glitters in my right. I find myself lit by two kinds of light. The sparkling silver light draws one's attention to it. Its glamour is exciting, spellbinding, and brilliant. On the other hand (quite literally!), the golden light glows warmly, peacefully, not drawing attention to itself but lighting up the dark and hidden places.

"Now, as you can see," says Tatatee, "you have two wands. Properly speaking, the wands are meant to work together. To begin with, as you know, you are everything in the story. It is your mirror, and there is nothing in it, not even one of us—that is, not one of your own. The question is, who do you wish to know? The silver wand will turn you into anyone or anything, but the golden wand will take you where your heart wants to go."

"How will I know where my heart wants to go?"

"You will feel a pull to something that wants to be seen. You may not want to go there. It might be a difficult place, and possibly not very spectacular. The silver wand will have other ideas, but if you want to see what the story is telling you, then you must allow the golden wand to guide you. Then use the silver wand to change your shape."

"So what you're saying is, I can change my shape for the purpose of revealing what my heart wants to see ..."

"There you have it."

"Who will you become, then?" Lucy asks, landing on Tatatee's red kerchief.

"I'm not sure ..."

"She will go where her heart takes her," says Tatatee decisively. "There are no lines to follow. But do not dally. Those who spend too long becoming sticks and stones are bound to lose their way."

"Where will you be?" I ask, casting about for reassurance.

"Here," says Tatatee. "We are always Here."

Sitting there with a wand in each hand, I begin to feel the pull to different characters ...

Rapunzel, hurtling through the air, confused, scrambled, sent to the ends of the earth by the curse of her mother's fury ...

The prince, feeling his way through the forest, tormented by hunger, insects, and loss ...

The tower in ruins, relieved to have toppled after all the tension of holding itself upright ...

Where is Rapunzel?

That is the cry of my heart.

The Serpent Speaks

I begin to morph into something. It's not Rapunzel. I'm feeling the sand underneath me, all the way down my body. I'm entirely in contact with the ground. Am I the sand? No,

I'm surfing the sand. I dart and glide over the surface, but I also know the undersurface. I know where to find the hollows, the burrows, and the springs. I slide over the desert hills, throwing myself before me, sidewinding with the ease of water. I am the essence of grace. I am the snake.

I feel the thud of a large body hitting the ground. I freeze. A human has landed beside me. She has dropped from the sky. Barren hills with lone scrub rise in the distance, but here there is no protection from the fierce midday sun. Already, it's burning through her skin and drilling a hole into her bald head. She looks around in terror, covering her eyes to protect them from the blinding light and the grit of windblown sand. She gets to her feet and stumbles in one direction and then the other, but she doesn't know where to go from here.

She's wearing nothing but a shift. She will be roasted quickly. She starts digging a hole in the sand, using her hands. The derisive wind laughs at her, repeatedly filling the hole. But she's determined. She digs like a badger, until the hole is big enough to crouch in. She piles the cooler layers of sand over her body and the lower half of her face. She has made her own grave.

After the sun goes down, when the air cools, she sits up and begins to wail. Crying is unwise. She will lose what little water her body holds. There's a scent in the air. A small group of humans lives nearby in the hills to the west. They will have water. I can take her there. It seems like a preposterous idea. Who will follow a snake? Humans have a deadly fear of them. I know that.

I stay where I am, where she can't see me. The moon rises full, drawing the underworld creatures to the surface. After a long time, she exhausts herself. By the light of the moon, I see her face, round and sweet with fine, delicate skin. The face of the moon herself. She shudders. She seems to accept that it is over—that she will die by her sandy grave.

How will I make my presence known without frightening her? I can't move slowly. I have a flinging motion that usually works in my favor, because it causes other creatures to fear that they're under attack. I think long and hard about how to approach, and quite frankly, I'm tempted to stay hidden. Stay out of it. But it is conceivable that I'm her only salvation because I'm the one who knows the way to water. Who else even knows where she is? I'm filled with a sense of ... well, I won't say importance, but I will say destiny.

I slither down the ridge as slowly as I can, and wave by wave, I make my signature on the side of the hill under the light of the moon.

She notices me, and watches me with wonder. She doesn't experience any fear at all, to my surprise. Maybe she's not familiar with snakes. I'm able to get closer, and soon I am within arm's reach. She extends a gentle, white hand and touches me, sending shivers of contact up and down my spine.

"Hello, friend," she says.

I stay where I am, and I allow her to touch me again. Her fingers settle lightly on my spine, and they have a relaxing effect. There's no fear in her touch—none at all, only fascination. She is sensitive. She can read me. Humans have a remarkable capacity to read creatures, though most have long forgotten they have the gift. She might understand after all. I feel certain of it. I swing myself up the hill and come back several times until she sees what I'm showing her. She gets to her feet and follows me, shivering in the cool night. I lead her to the humans, who are gathered around a fire. She stumbles toward them, poor little ghost, shaking with fear and weakness.

I feel a tug—the spell's hold loosens, like a dream letting go in the morning. I wouldn't mind staying a while longer in my snakeskin. Here's a whole new way of seeing—a wild new world to explore. But the story has its own momentum and direction, and I have to follow it.

Lucy Goes to Find Greta

On her hill in the desert, Tatatee has made a little campfire, and a few weak stars have appeared out of the mist of the sky. She stands in the firelight, warming herself. She and Lucy have seen the scene; they've been where I've been. I don't know exactly how they've seen it, but when I think about it, Lucy might have been the sun, and Tatatee might have been the moon, or even Rapunzel herself.

Lucy sits cross-legged, staring into the fire pit while perched on the head of the little elephant who is on his knees, resting. "How extraordinary," she says. "Rapunzel has landed at the end of her mother's fury. That's where we are, at the *end of fury*! Somebody has got to tell Greta."

"Where is Greta?" I ask.

"Out of earshot—a long way away," says Tatatee.

"Right where we left her, I suspect," says Lucy.

"Why didn't she come with us?"

"Because she is too heavy," says Lucy. "She's packing too much weight."

"So she can't hear the story?"

"No," says Tatatee, shaking her head.

I can't let the story get beyond Greta. She is our storyteller, our ancestral recorder, the one who can connect this little story to the big picture. We can't just cut ourselves off from her, and leave her sightless and deaf in the tower world. We need Greta with us!

"Lucy, dear," says Tatatee, "can you keep your link-up with

us while you go and find Greta?"

Lucy adjusts her antennae. "I believe so. These things have finally started to work!"

"How will you find your way?" I ask.

"The same way a bee finds her way to the flower, I expect—by way of attraction."

"Well, make a beeline for Greta, then," says Tatatee. "And tell her what we have seen."

Lucy shoots off into the headwinds, and takes me with her on the ride. To get to Greta, she's got to battle the winds of fury that carried Rapunzel to the ends of the earth. The winds afford no easy entry, but Lucy, being clever and sharp-sighted, finds the air pockets and darts through the front like a bee through a honeycomb.

She soon lands in the field where Greta had been broadcasting the story to the fairies. Hurricane winds have loosened trees from their roots and flattened the surrounding forests, scattering the fairies to the four corners of the earth. But they haven't moved Greta. She sits on the ground, seeing nothing, like a great, passive stone.

Lucy (and I) land in her ear. "Greta!" she pipes. "Can you hear me?"

Greta is silent.

"Now, don't pretend you don't know that I'm here, Cousin. The story is continuing, and it is imperative that you come with us. Since you haven't found a way to do that, you must hear what we have heard."

We settle in the cave of Greta's ear canal, as Lucy tells her where Rapunzel has been found, which is to say, at the end of fury.

Greta remains silent while Lucy speaks. The only visible sign that she comprehends is that she keeps sniveling and rubbing her round nose with the back of her hand, until it shines apple red.

When she has finished delivering the information, Lucy waits for a response from Greta. She isn't patient at the best of times, and she starts shifting and scratching her tiny bottom. "Well?" she asks. "Well?" she demands, stamping her tiny, clumpy shoed foot.

Suddenly, Greta lurches up, pitching Lucy forward. She grabs a handhold to keep from tumbling out of Greta's ear into the windy night.

"You have all gone beyond me," she says. "I'm finished."

"We haven't gone beyond *you*," says Lucy. "We have gone beyond *fury*. Don't you see, Greta?"

Greta scratches her head. "No, as a matter of fact, I don't see. That's as plain as the nose that I can't see on my face."

Lucy thinks for a moment. "Perhaps you have been blinded by your fury, Greta."

"Eh?"

"Yes, and weighed down too. I know you've always been heavy, but you've become like a great stone. It's time to get past your fury."

Greta stares into space and blinks several times. "Quite right," she says at last. "There's no getting around that. But how do I get past my fury?"

"Well, perhaps you need to *see* it. What is your anger aimed at, Greta?"

"It is easy enough to answer that. Humans. How could they lose sight of their *stories*? How could they dismiss all their ancestors and wisdom keepers, and never invite us back in?! I don't see it. I'll never see it. Our uncaring children have made me blind!" she cries, as the wind whips her hair around like cotton candy.

"I daresay the wind is strong, Greta. But if you could just lighten up a bit, I'm sure …"

"What's that?"

"Drop some of that weight you're carrying. Like that book, for instance. Whatever stories you know, Greta, you know by heart. They're not in that book."

"If only I could know my heart. It's gone quite cold."

"As frozen as Kay's heart, do you suppose?"

"Oh my, my, now ... Yes, doesn't that ring true? Poor little Kay loses all his joy when he catches the splinter in his eye." Big tears spill from Greta's round, unseeing eyes. She wipes her nose with the back of her hand. "He's trapped in the frozen land of the Snow Queen. I haven't forgotten *that* story." She hauls her book off her lap, and it lands on the ground with a heavy thump. "Well, there you go, my old friend. I had hoped to be able to see well enough to read you. Anyway. A bird in the heart is worth three in the book."

"And what the dickens have you got in those pockets?" Lucy asks, peering downward from Greta's earhole.

Greta pats the breast pockets of her coat, and flaps the sides open to reveal dozens of inside pockets stuffed with lumpy things. She has pockets in her tartan skirt, pockets in her stockings, and pockets in her shoes. "Sticks and stones that break my bones," she mutters, pulling them out from her pockets. "I had hoped they would speak to me, or comfort me at least, but they've all gone silent. I suppose I don't mind letting them go."

Lucy darts out of Greta's ear and goes buzzing around her. "And what else, Cousin? What else can you let go?"

"Oh, well, my staff has been quite a heavy thing to carry along with me. That old eagle has gone as stiff as me."

"Free that old stick-in-the-mud then, for heaven's sake!"

"Oh, very well." Greta sighs and launches herself to her feet. She takes hold of her staff and grinds it into the ground. The sleeping eagle begins to stir. He shakes his feathers and pulls his feet out from the moon rock prison. Unable to believe his

good luck, he flaps his wings and launches himself into the air. Up and up he goes, flying in ever widening circles.

"He hasn't been able to see the big picture for a long time," says Greta. "Goodness knows, I had nearly forgotten about him. I had wanted him to see for me, but then, oh, what happened? I turned him to stone because ... well, I suppose because I became afraid that he would fly away and never come back."

"Greta, look ... The wind is picking you up!" Lucy shouts.

To her great surprise, Greta is scooped up by the wind and swept across the field like a big balloon, her kilt bursting into a parasol shape with her fat legs sticking out underneath.

"Oh dearie me!" she cries. "I do believe this is rather undignified, but oh, I haven't felt this way in a thousand years, I must say ..."

"Here we go!" cries Lucy, as we enter the raging wind chute and sail to the heart of darkness where fury ends.

The wind slows, and Greta floats down, and then it drops and she lands—*kerplunk*—on the desert floor. She sits straight up like a doll, with Lucy fluttering on the tip of an ear.

"Oh, my goodness me. Well, I never." Greta turns her head one way, and then the other. She stares at the ground. "Do you know, I might just be seeing something."

"What?" Lucy asks excitedly.

"I'm seeing that we're in the dark. It's different than *being* in the dark."

"That's exactly what we're seeing, Greta," says Tatatee triumphantly.

Greta touches a flushed cheek with a fat hand. "Well, I never. I never felt so *light*."

CHAPTER EIGHTEEN

THE DARK GIFT

I had finally been admitted to a pain management clinic, and had started attending the groups on a regular basis. We were learning to "manage chronic pain" through exercise, pool therapy, meditation, and guided imagery. On the first day I joined a small circle of people of all ages, who were from many different cultural backgrounds. Everybody had a story. One Italian man in his sixties had four grown children at home. They expected him to continue to work in construction and remain the family provider. "How old are your children?" one of us asked. "In their forties," he said.

We roared, "Kick them out!" He couldn't. He wouldn't.

Whatever our stories, we were all in the same situation: we were in the dark. We had inexplicable, untreatable pain, but we were willing to meet it and shed whatever light we could on it. It had not been easy for any of us to arrive at the clinic. It was the result of a long battle, many tears, and numerous failed campaigns to conquer the pain.

I felt a pang of reverence for every soul sitting around me. We were veterans suffering invisible and, all too often, discredited wounds. We had disappointed the hopes, dreams, and expectations of our loved ones. We didn't feel like heroes. We felt like failures. We endured people's judgements, scorn, and suspicion.

After telling my own story and admitting I often felt harshly judged for my "psychological weakness," as one person called it, the woman sitting beside me tapped the side of my leg with her cane. "You should get yourself one of these," she said. "Even if you don't need it, you'll get respect."

The next time the group met, we were given a presentation by a doctor and an occupational therapist. They took us through an uncomfortably long lecture on the physiology of pain and its neural pathways. When it was over, I put up my hand and I asked the kindly middle-aged doctor if he knew anything about the pathways of pleasure. He thought that was an interesting question, but he had no answers. I was left thinking, *Why do we spend so much time focusing on pain? Can't we at least balance it with an understanding of pleasure?*

My questions led me to feel that Greta was really onto something, and so were all the fairy godmothers. Not being able to see that you are in the dark is like being in pain, and stuck in a narrative that sees nothing but pain. If you can see the way you story your pain, then you can decide if it's a story you want to adhere to. You can move around a little, explore possibilities beyond the heavy burden of pain and depression. In *The Ultimate Back Book*, a doctor who was talking about non-drug alternatives to pain management called this "walking through pain." He said, "It has to do with learning how to externalize pain. You feel the pain and it hurts; the difference is that it doesn't drive you around the bend."

While I was doing the meditations in the pain management clinic, I happened upon a book called *Creative Imagery* by Dr. William Fezler. He provided over a dozen guided imageries that were specifically meant to treat pain, depression and anxiety by activating the sensual imagination. He got you tasting the colors of the sunset, peeling oranges in an orchard under the moonlight, listening to the dawn in a country house, inhaling the warmth of a fire on a snowy night. His meditations awoke all the imaginative senses, and they helped me to vividly imagine pleasurable experiences that counteracted the pain. I recorded the meditations on audio tape so that I could listen to them over and over. I felt activated, illuminated, lit up from the inside.

Soon I was consciously activating pleasure—taking pleasure *in*. I took pleasure in a soft snowfall, a fragrant bath, Ian's laughter, the company of friends. One day when I was struggling with digestive issues, feeling that I couldn't eat anything and that I was losing my 'taste for life,' I marched myself to the corner grocery store. I bought half a dozen cartons of sherbet in as many tart flavors as I could find. Cherry. Mango. Lemon. Raspberry. Lime. I tasted a spoonful of each one, letting the bright notes sit on my tongue while imagining the taste of a sunset.

Greta had given me a huge gift, and now I felt drawn to the prince. What was he finding in his blindness?

The Prince Speaks

At first, I believed that my sight would return, but it has not. The light of the world has gone out. During the day, I stumble into open fields where there are fewer biting insects, and I can feel the sun on my skin. When night falls, I find trees to climb, but the bugs defeat me. I can't rest or settle anywhere. I scrabble on, bumping into trees, falling into holes, and tripping over roots until I'm forced to get on my hands and knees, and move around like a beast. At dawn, I follow the scent of sun back to a road or a meadow. I can't get my bearings or make sense of my thoughts. My mind is full of noise. I blame myself for the whole catastrophe. We should have left sooner; we waited too long. I should never have hesitated. Why did I not get her to safety sooner, when I knew the danger she was in?

How many days have I been here? I haven't counted them. I am now lingering near a road that might be the main road to the castle. I can hear the carriages going by, and the horses' hooves clopping on the paving stones. I like the sound of their shoed feet on stone. If I could speak to one of them, I'd ask him to use his horse sense to carry me to wherever she is. But the horses are bridled and driven by stern masters. They clop by me, unspeaking.

What happened to her? Where did that old witch send her? If the horses can't tell me, the people might. But I trust people less than horses.

The road is well traveled. There must be a village around here somewhere. Farmers rattle to the market with cartloads of fruit, vegetables, and animals. Every now and then, a coach clatters by. Sometimes, though rarely, I meet someone on foot. Most people are on their way to destinations. They have business to do, and they're late, and besides, who would want to speak to me? I can't imagine what I look like, let alone how I smell.

I stop anyone who will listen to me. "Have you heard about the maiden in the tower?"

They think I'm a madman.

I try to explain. "She sang like a bird; lit up the forest with her voice. Have you heard her? She was put in a tower by a sorceress."

They push me away.

Lately, I've been getting desperate. "You must know something about her ... you must!"

"Get away from me!" they shout.

My eyes are caked in blood, wet to the touch. They must be festering. People don't want this repulsive man clinging to their sleeves. They shake me off roughly. They punch me, and kick me in the sides.

A few days ago, a man listened. I could tell he was rich. I could smell the wax on his leather satchel, the perfume on his clothes. He asked me who I was looking for. "What is her name?"

I told him. Rapunzel.

"Oh, yes. I know her," he said.

I implored him to tell me where she had gone.

He belched. "I believe I had some of her last night. Delicious. Keeps repeating on me, though. Ha ha! Come on, man, pull yourself together!" He slapped me on the back and went his way.

From time to time, people take pity on me. They give me something to eat. But they know nothing about a maiden in a tower. One morning, a man gave me a loaf of bread and some cheese. A whole loaf! He sat me down under a tree and let me take a few gulps of wine from his flask. I felt fortified.

"Tell me about this vision you have had," he said.

"She's not a vision," I told him. "She's real. More real than you and me. A sorceress named Gothel trapped her in a tower …"

"Gothel? Aren't the Gothels relations of the queen? I wouldn't be spreading rumors that the queen is connected with sorcery," the man said quietly. "So tell me, what did this maiden in your vision look like?"

I said nothing. The conversation was tiring me.

"I pity you, lad," he said finally.

"There is enough to pity here."

"You're in for worse trouble than blindness, if you keep up this mad search. There's nobody trapped in a tower in these parts, least of all by a witch, and especially not one going by the name of Gothel. Take my advice, my good fellow. Call it a dream and forget you ever had it. And find a healer to do something about those eyes."

"The sun will dry them," I said.

He got up to leave, reaching for the flask I was still holding. "What happened to your eyes?"

I didn't answer him. And I wouldn't give him back his wine

either. He left, cursing me under his breath.

I am adapting to the life of a beggar. I know what it's like to be rejected and feared. It's not all bad. Beggars and vagrants have no cares. They don't give a damn how they appear, or what others think, unless they can use the pity to get some bread.

Something is hardening in me. I'm not an uncaring person, but I have a growing distaste for humanity. There is bile in my spit.

The birds wake me, singing at dawn. I've been resting in a tree not far from the road. When my ears become attuned, something else sharpens. I see something. Not with outer eyes, but with inner eyes. A wavering blue flame dances like a serpent in the dark. She is speaking to me. She wants to give me something.

I sit up and open my hands. Something is placed there. Then the flame disappears. I press my hands together to feel what I've received, my heart pounding with the thrill of it. But I can feel nothing. The gift has no weight. It's nothing but air.

I might be angry, but I have become too numb for anger. If anything, I'm mystified. What is a gift that is nothing? An empty box? An open wound? The hollow of my eyes?

I choke back my tears. The sun has begun to rise, pale fingers of warmth on my neck. I can see it by the way I feel it, winking like a diamond through the leaves, tender as a newborn, its little fingers on my cheeks. Sweet hands caressing my face, reminding me of the love I have known. It can shine through anything, even the encrusted eyes of a blind man.

I climb down the tree and make my way to the roadside, where I stand begging. No one puts anything in my open hands. I feel only the empty space within them. Suppose I am holding a gift that I can't see? Is it possible that my blindness *is* the gift? How could this curse be a gift?

The morning sun strengthens, warming the earth and my

flesh. A lark sings in the meadow. It's the song of the mist, the newborn sun, the cheerful brook. It's a good day for singing. Before the sun has climbed to the peak of the sky, I hear the sound of coach wheels and horses' hoofs clomping down the road.

"Whoa!" shouts the driver, and the coach stops in front of me.

I hear a familiar voice. "My lord!"

It's the king's coachman, Henry. I remember him as a middle-aged man with gray eyes, a short beard, and a youthful, lusty demeanor. The ladies love him; he has never married.

I feel his strong hands on my forearms, ale and onions on his breath. And bread. I am so hungry I could eat his breath.

"Where have you been these many weeks? We had given you up for dead!"

He sees that I am limping on a blistered foot, and gives me an arm for support. He wants to get me into the carriage. "We have to get you back. What happened to your eyes?"

"It seems I've been knighted," I joke weakly.

"You'll need other eyes to see for you now, my lord," he says. "Come along."

Other eyes? "Tell me, Henry, would other eyes see better than my own?"

"Not if you had any."

My body, almost against my better judgment, goes rigid. I tell him to wait a moment. I want to stand on my own. A strange new serenity emboldens me. I tell him that I have lost what is dearest to my heart. Worse than that, I've been told by seeing people that I've lost nothing and that I'm chasing a phantom.

"It's safe to say you're hurting, m' lord."

"I am blind, Henry, but not as blind as that."

"Let me help you," he says, putting his arm under my shoulder. "We can speak about this later."

"No. Thank you for your kindness, but I seem to be the only one who is seeing today. I have not lost anything. If I love, then my love is with me, is she not? She's no farther away than my own heart! And tell me, Henry, how does the heart speak? Do you know?"

"No, my lord."

"Well, I know. It *feels*."

"Feels what, my lord?"

I stumble into the forest, leaving Henry on the roadside. In my mind's eye, I see him standing on the road, his fleecy gray hair blowing in the wind.

I move through the forest, seeking the stream. I take one step at a time—not on my hands and knees, not crawling like a beast. I stand tall, ringed in peace. My struggle against blindness has come to an end. I will no longer look outward for direction, hoping to recover my eyes so that I can find her with them. The clattering road, the rabble, and the noise of the village fall away as I move into the darkness of the wood.

She is the fragrant sun on my cheek. She is the warmth that will guide me in a thousand ways. I catch the scent of a young deer who tracks me a short distance away. I have never been more alert and alive. I follow my ears to the stream. First, I will bathe and drink. Fortify myself. Tend to my foot. After that, I will know what to do. It will come to me.

I strip and stand knee-deep in the water, steadying myself on the smooth stones. Henry arrives, breathless. I'm not surprised that he's returned. "You're not here to carry me back to the coach, are you, my good fellow?"

"I don't know what sort of journey you're on, my lord. And the king will not be pleased by my disappearance. But that's of no consequence. I'll go with you, if you'll have me. Give me time to get supplies and a horse. We'll go together."

I embrace that good man and welcome his company. But I warn him, I will be silent most of the time.

"Then I will be silent too," he says.

He leaves me sitting in the stream. I plunge my hands into the cool water and draw the cup to my eyes, lost in the wonder of my dark gift.

The Dark Gift

Squatting before the little fire the godmothers have made in the desert, Greta touches her eyes. "I see that a loss can be a gift," she declares.

"Eh?" says Tatatee, standing up on the mound of sand.

"I lost my sight," Greta says. "I have suffered it *terribly*."

"You are sounding more and more human," says Lucy, amplifying herself. She is half her usual size, and her projection has grown weaker. I can almost see through her. She catches me observing her. "We have losses too, you know, Hope. We just don't suffer them the way mortals do."

Tatatee brushes the sand off her backside, and waddles down the hill on her short legs. "Yes, but that is not the reality anymore. We are suffering losses, Lucy. The closer we get to humanity, the less we see and the more we feel. We've been away too long."

Lucy shrugs. She's sitting amid pieces—wigs and bits of clothing that she has been taking out of her open suitcase. She hasn't been able to figure out whether she should wear her tutu or something else. I think she's having an identity crisis. She sighs. "Nothing feels right anymore. Whatever happened to being able to speak clearly, say what we mean, and mean what we say? Our bright world has faded, I daresay …"

Greta winces. "I am getting those flashes again. I'm seeing Kay in the garden of roses. He's examining a red rose, and he looks quite disgusted with it. The petals are browning and will soon decay and he doesn't like that—not at all. Now he's making a face at Gerda because she's frowning. He think she's ugly. It's all because he's got a piece of the mirror in his eye. He can't stand the natural world. He wants to live in a perfect world with no bugs."

"You already told us that part of the story, Greta," says Lucy, examining skirts from her suitcase. "I daresay I could do with a few less bugs."

Tatatee clears her throat. "It is possible, Lucy dear, that if the world were free of bugs, it might also be free of you."

Lucy looks aghast, but Tatatee continues, unperturbed. "What Greta is indicating is that perhaps we went in the wrong direction. Kay doesn't like to see imperfection, so he turns away from nature, and travels into the cold region of the Snow Queen. Surely, we also ended up in the frozen outer regions of inner space. Perhaps we need to accept our losses, just as the prince has accepted his blindness."

Lucy stares at her. "You're not saying that I'm just another *bug*, are you? Surely I haven't been reduced to *that*."

"No, Lucy!" I interject. "She's saying that maybe you can't get rid of bugs! Maybe they're with you forever. Maybe we're not progressing to some perfect world like they thought in the nineteenth century. Maybe the world you're reentering is permanently different from the one you left behind."

"*Permanently*, you say?" Lucy frowns deeply. "Stuff and nonsense!"

I don't know what gets into me. Maybe it's my human experience with loss and with bugs, too, because if chronic pain isn't a hive of wasps, I don't know what is. Anyway, I'm determined not to let Lucy off the hook. "Yes, but what *if*? What if you can't recover your bright world, Lucy—at least not the way you knew it? And what if you can't get your stories back, Greta—at least not the way they were once told? Is it possible that you could accept that? Because that's what we humans have to do. We have to accept things we can't fix—losses we can't recover."

"I thought you were our *hope*," Lucy groans, giving me a stricken look.

Greta stares ahead, seeing nothing. Then she starts to shake her head, with increasing vigor, as if her neck is on a spring. "We cannot lose our stories. They're the speech of the heart. The ark of the ages! Oh, my dearie me. Just the thought of it. If I lost the stories and I could not recover them, I would fail you—all of you! The thought cannot be borne. It simply cannot be born!" Now Greta's groaning and holding her stomach, and rocking back and forth like a rubber duck in bathwater. Huge tears spill from her eyes—tears the size of plums. She makes a puddle so big that it streams down the hill and pools at its foot. Tatatee's jolly elephant slides into the wetness and rolls over on his back, wiggling happily.

When the tear storm is over, and it takes a very long time, Greta produces a handkerchief from one of her pockets and blows her nose with deafening honks.

"Now what are you seeing, Greta dear?" asks Tatatee gently. "Because you are seeing for us all."

"A big *hole* has opened up," Greta says in a husky voice. She gets to her feet, swivels around, and takes a few wobbly steps. Then she leads us down the hill and past the mud puddle, making big, round holes in the sand with her feet. She walks a few paces forward and then stops.

"Don't go any farther," she commands. "It's right here."

We look down and see that we are standing at the edge of a huge pit. It's impossible to discern the depth of it. The sand is soft and slippery, so we step back.

"Look at the size of that loss," says Lucy. "We mustn't go near it. Really, I do think the wand must be employed at this time—interference or not. It doesn't take a genius to see that that hole will suck us all in if we don't remove it."

Sure enough, the desert sand underfoot starts sliding into the hole, as if it were being sucked into a ravenous mouth. We scramble back up the mound.

"No, Lucy, you must not cover it up," says Tatatee. "This hole is what Greta is seeing. She sees what she feels, and her feeling is *real*. Leave it be."

"There's only one thing to do," says Greta, peering down into the hole and dabbing her round nose with a black and white polka-dotted handkerchief. Her nose has grown so red, it practically glows in the dark.

"What are you saying, Greta?" Lucy demands from the top of the mound.

"I cannot explain what I'm saying, but my loss is here, and I must get to the bottom of it. So here I go. Bye-bye!"

Before anyone can stop her, Greta pitches herself off the side of the chasm and goes hurtling into the cavity, her fat arms and legs spread-eagled. She falls like a stone. Not even so much as a scream comes from her, as she plummets downward.

"*No!*" Lucy shrieks. She rockets into the sky and breaks up into what looks like a thousand bees, all flying around chaotically. They gather into a cyclone and rush down the pit in one mad swarm. God knows what it would be like to be stung by a hive of Lucy bees!

I can't break the connection—she has a hold on me, and I'm struggling to get the hell away when Gangee shoots in from the stars, quite literally from out of the blue. She puts her hand into the swarm and snatches a single bee. The rest vanish. Hovering above the hole, she places the Lucy-bee gently on her lap, strokes her, and croons to her.

The crooning went on for days.

Winter dragged on. Naturally, I kept my distance from the godmothers, though I knew what Lucy was experiencing. When Greta fell into the deep hole, Lucy felt certain that the project had ended for fairies and humans. There would be no more stories, no more magic. No more Greta Greatwaite. Lucy couldn't face the loss, but I think she was even more afraid of dying. She had already become so tiny—almost inconsequential. If she had flown into the hole after Greta, she might have been altogether extinguished.

For some time, nothing more happened on the inner planes, and then one February afternoon while at the grocery store loading my basket with juice and trying to figure out how much more stuff I could safely carry home, the stasis broke. I heard Gangee sing out, "Here we go ..." and the whole kit and caboodle—Lucy, Tatatee, her elephant, and Gangee—slipped into that voracious hole and disappeared like water down a drain.

They were all gone.

Meanwhile, a book commission had come along, and I had to undertake a challenging real-world project. I felt well enough to sit up for half a day, and so I turned my attention to the book. In the back of my mind, I wondered if the godmothers would ever come back. That hole might have ended the whole business. The desert remained silent and dark, and I could only wonder, *What was the point of all of that?*

As summer approached, Ian and I resisted going to the farm. We had become the target of a great deal of anger. The previous fall, the mother of the dirt biker boys came over, and she tore a strip off us for not allowing her boys to ride their bikes on our land. She claimed they had bought their house for the express purpose of riding their bikes on our land! She didn't understand our need for peace, and if we exercised our legal rights, she warned us there would be hell to pay.

"If you think dirt bikers are trouble, you wait till you meet my biker friends," she yelled, as she stomped away from our house. Then one of her sons came tearing out on his dirt bike, ripping up the fields in plain view. We took pictures. Called the police. The boys were charged with trespassing and driving their bikes without the proper permits, but it changed nothing.

It just made those wasps angrier.

When Ian went to check on the farmhouse, he found that the house had been broken into. There wasn't much to take, but the cupboards had been ransacked and beds upturned. My gnomes were all over the floor. Nobody stole any of them! I could imagine the burglars getting freaked out when they uncovered those guys. Maybe that's when they hightailed it out of there.

Ian boarded up the broken window in the back door. The farm didn't feel like it belonged to us anymore.

Friends were constantly asking me, "Are you going to the farm? Have you been there?"

"*No*, no, no, no," I said.

The hole was sucking me in, too—a great sorrow with iron at its core. I couldn't look over the edge of that chasm without being pulled into a depression from which there was no exit. I stayed in the dark through the summer months, unwilling to see anything further with my golden wand.

After a while, it became clear to me that I had a choice. I could put my pursuit of Rapunzel on the shelf and get on with the demands of outer life. Or I could face the loss. What loss? I could hardly speak of it. It had been with me all my life. It was her, pure and simple—that lost princess, this lost heart.

Rapunzel's Darkness

I started slipping. Okay, I told myself. If you're going to slide into a depression, stay conscious as you go down. Keep your eyes open. Say what you see.

I know where she is. The scene has been flashing in the back of my mind for months. She's lying on a reed bed, in a round hut made of mud brick and wattle. She's gone through a great labor and has given birth to twins. Other women are looking after the children. She just wants to die. I see her curled up into herself, spent. She has no interest in living, not even for her children. She wants the relief that only death can provide. She doesn't have the spirit to live, no matter how much I want her to live, no matter how much hope I imagine.

She's on her way out. The heart of the world is going out.

I can't stop now …

I allow myself to slide down the banks of the depression. I let the weight of it take me deep into the dark roots of the earth. *Keep your eyes open*, I tell myself. *Stay a witness to the dark, even as you enter the dying body of Rapunzel.*

I'm bracing for the worst, so it's a surprise to find that I don't experience Rapunzel's suffering. On the contrary, I feel light, unbound by the laws of gravity. I am a boundless, aspirational energy. I leap with a mischievous delight, and the only thing that keeps me grounded is a wick that runs up my center from a pool of oil.

I can make shadows dance on the wall. With the breeze as my muse, I can stretch upward and sideways, elongate, or become still. The shadows are my cinema. They are endlessly fascinating, but I have a reason for being here, and she lies before me, curled into herself. A roughly woven gray blanket covers her bony frame. I cast my light on her pale face. She stares into the darkness, unblinking, numb. I can hardly feel her breath at all.

A brown-skinned young woman comes in. She has long black hair, and carries a bowl of water and some unleavened bread. She sets the food and the bowl on the flat wooden table where I stand. She puts her hand on Rapunzel's shoulder and speaks softly to her in a language she doesn't understand. She lowers the blanket to reveal Rapunzel's ribs and hips jutting sharply through her skin. She washes her gently, dipping the cloth in the water. She washes her face, arms, breasts, belly, groin, legs, and swollen feet. Rapunzel is unresponsive, refusing food and water.

The young woman sighs, and carries the basin away. We are left together again in the quiet room. I become still, leaning toward the girl off the top of my wick.

She blinks and looks at me. A shadow of annoyance crosses her brow. With effort, she raises her body up on an arm. She tries to blow me out.

It's a weak gust of wind, not enough to extinguish me. She groans and drops back. Then, summoning her strength, she pulls herself up on an elbow, leans closer, and blows again. That blow has more force, more annoyance to it. I hold on to my wick. Now she's getting irritated. Fighting pain and weakness, she heaves herself closer, steadies herself on her forearms, and blows again, this time with determination. I hold on. I won't go out. I won't! She can blow as hard as she wants, she can blow until she winds herself, but I won't go out.

Ha! Now she's furious! She summons all her strength and blows until she becomes dizzy. She falls back on the bed, defeated, filled with the knowing that she has no power to influence anything in the world, not even the flame of a candle. Curling into a fetal position, she whimpers pitifully.

Time passes, and no one comes. The room becomes quiet. She frowns at me. Once again, she gets up on an elbow, but this time her eyes are swimming with wonder. She wipes her nose. Her skin is glistening. I know what she's thinking.

Why won't the candle go out?

Recognition sparks in her eyes.

Maybe the flame is a friend. Maybe it's trying to tell me something. What?

Now I can speak to her. I can speak and be heard. "I am your light."

What light?

"The light that made the flowers drop and become themselves."

She adjusts her position, not taking her eyes off me.

Please say more.

"You just tried to do to me what your mother tried to do to you—blow out your light! And though you've put all your force into it, you can't blow me out because I am the light of your love."

She claps a hand to her mouth and laughs. Ha!

The bell note rings through the atmosphere. Changes everything.

Iron at the Core

Here, at the bottom of the depression that Greta opened up, there is only one story to tell. I haven't wanted to tell it. I would rather walk around it—pretend the hole isn't there or, like Lucy, wave my wand and make it disappear. But I must see it and say what I see. I must give words to my own unrecoverable loss and trust that the love-lit story will pull me through.

I came into the world with a fierce mother love. I had romantic plans for my life and fully expected to be a mother. I was raised in a chaotic family of six kids, and as the eldest sister, I cared for my younger siblings. I was always directing plays and theatrical productions to entertain the family. I assumed that my life would be like it was in childhood, full of people and music—a rowdy family gathered around a harvest table on every feast day. I loved *The Sound of Music*—I will say it unapologetically. There was something deeply compelling about Julie Andrews going off with her guitar to become governess to a captain with seven children. She left the cloister for the sake of love, and brought music and passion into a coldly regimented family. Her spiritual nature had a destiny to make music in the world, not in the convent. I wanted that kind of life—a good husband and a crowd of children who depended on my stories and songs to inspirit their lives.

But when adolescence came, I was pierced deeply. It's interesting that women refer to their periods as "the curse." Something comes in with the blood flow, with the stab of the spindle. For me, it was a pain too deep for words and too mysterious to be named. It pulled me into a whirlpool of inexpressible grief and loss. I had remembrances of times past—remote memories of wandering in exile, a mad woman, invisible and unmoored. The pain came with a conviction that rose up like a wraith in the night, to tell me that I could pursue love all I wished and yearn for it and pray for it and even give up my life for it, but I would never, ever find it in this world. It was as if the sea maid herself were rising up to say, "Look, I did everything I could. But we are not of this world, and you will never be known here. The prince has married the wrong partner, and it's over. He will never know the one who saved him from drowning because he will never know himself."

After experiencing a series of disappointing love affairs and packing up my romantic dreams, that deep conviction seemed to be affirmed. I would never find myself in this world. I could not recognize my own poetic voices, let alone make myself heard.

I sought a practical life. I focused on securing a steady income. I married and set my sights on having children, hoping that they would link me back to wonder, love, and a spiritual life. But the child never came. For the first three years of our marriage, we tried without success, and then I began to despair.

Dream Baby
This is going to be one of those days
One of those bleary, opaque days
That you see through a window of tears
I want to crawl inside a friend
But everyone's busy today
Yesterday I was so strong

I took the brunt of the hurt on
Like Joan of Arc
Let my heart be torched—
But not today.
Today, I wake up behind bars
The sky is gray
And on my tongue,
The salt taste
Of a night of crying lingers
It's a tiny torture
A dream baby
That won't come
Moon after moon
I wait for the baby
Dream, and wake
Nothing can fill the
Whole of its absence
I've done everything but
Hang out the sign
There's a vacancy here
Everyone knows it
But the gods pass me by
A vacancy here
In my womb, in my heart,
In my eyes.

I went to fertility doctors, and after six months of tests, I was put into a category of women who were diagnosed with unexplained infertility. I could have continued to search, but I was done being poked and prodded. My husband and I decided to adopt because, we reasoned, if we wanted to be parents, it didn't matter whether the child came from us or from someone else.

We sought private adoption, filled out a lengthy application for parenthood, and sent it out to a hundred obstetricians in the region. My husband had not been working full time for many months, and I was trying to support us both. I wanted to believe that things would turn around when the child came—that we would get back on track.

Then one day in November 1986, I woke up with a start, in the grip of a vision. A comet was barreling toward the planetary body of my life, and I knew with absolute certainty that if I didn't get out of the way, it would obliterate me. I had to figure out what it meant—and fast. I got up and went into my office, and I started to write my way to some kind of understanding. I cancelled all my appointments for the day, which included a couple of business meetings and a fitness class I was supposed to teach. After several pages of brutally honest writing, I realized that I was desperately unhappy. I had to face the hard truth that my dream baby could not be, because my dream marriage was not real. We were in no way equipped to have a child.

It was Wednesday. All day long, I drove around town, waiting for my husband to get home. When he came into the house, I poured him a glass of wine, and we sat in the living room while the sun set. I told him that I couldn't maintain the charade anymore. Our marriage had to end. He knew it, too. The evidence was sitting right in front of us. We each had a stack of applications to mail out and I had mailed mine weeks before, but his pile was still sitting on top of the bookcase.

Ironically, we had planned to attend a wedding out of town that weekend. At first I said I'd go, but as the weekend approached, I started to come apart. My perfect facade was developing cracks everywhere. On Thursday night, I threw a few clothes into a bag, ran down the stairs to the car, and drove to my aunt's house. She took me in, while my husband went to the wedding on his own. During that whirlwind weekend, with the help of my aunt, I found an apartment and moved out. On Sunday night, my husband returned to a half-empty house. He later told me that when he came in, he ran around looking to see what I had taken, and then the phone rang. It was an obstetrician. A baby had been found for us.

When my husband told me about the call, I was bewildered. I was precipitously driven out of our marriage as if it had not been my destiny to receive that child. Was I meant to have a child? Maybe not. Maybe it wasn't in the stars.

I was left with a great hole of grief. Yet, somewhere in the hole there was a light, a knowledge that said, "Don't force the matter. Make room in your heart for the vacancy, for the child that may never be born."

My friends didn't understand. After I met Ian, they said, "Why don't you try again?" But Ian, whom I deeply loved, didn't want to father a child. Psychics who tuned into my hole of grief assured me I would be a mother one day. One friend offered herself as a surrogate. Everybody wanted me to fill the void, while I bore it, and in so doing, I suffered the accusation that I was acting like a victim. If you want a child, go get one. I couldn't find anyone to affirm my truth, which was that I yearned for a child who would never arrive because the child wasn't meant to arrive. I was meant to hold the empty space and the mystery.

One day, I sat with my mother in the back garden of her house. Stretched out on lawn chairs, we looked out over the fields beyond the fence, and drank in the heat of the summer sun. We were both in bare feet, wiggling our toes in the sun. My mother asked me how I felt about the fact that a close friend, who had been trying to conceive for years, had finally become pregnant through in vitro fertilization. I tried to hide my grief. I didn't want my mother to see it. I didn't want her to pity me. I said I was happy for my friend, which was true, but not wholly true.

My mother stared at her toes for a few moments, and then she sighed. "I don't know what I would do if I didn't have children. I don't think I could grow old without them. I don't think I could bear the loneliness."

I got up from the chair, drifted into the house, and shut myself in the bathroom. I sat on the toilet and wept silently, so I wouldn't be heard, so no one could see my pain. My mother's own mother couldn't bear children for thirteen years, and none of my grandmother's sisters bore children, either. I knew how my mother saw the childless woman—the specter was mine too.

She came to life in a novel I had once read called *Judith Hearne*. Judith had no children and no friends. At Christmas, she would be invited for dinner by dutiful family members who dreaded having her around. She would sit on the sofa alone, staring at the buttons on her shoes. She called them her "shoe eyes," and they were her only company.

The tragic specter of the "barren woman" is with me, here in the abyss. She is the curse of the women in my family. It seems that I am meant to embrace her; go beyond where my mother could go; find a way to heal those old feminine wounds. But the word *barren*, oh it is so cruel! For generations, we have condemned childless women. We've banished them. We've burned them as witches and reviled them as spinsters.

Spinsters!

Gangee takes shape before me. She has been crooning to me all this time. "Now you see that you are one of us," she says, tucking me into the folds of her starry cloak.

CHAPTER NINETEEN

THE RISE OF THE PRINCESS

Rapunzel Speaks

A bolt of sunlight streams in through the open door ... a tiny old woman sits by my bed. She has nut-brown skin and is cloaked in indigo cloth. Her cheeks are crinkled, and she has no teeth. I watch her hands busily weaving reeds. She rocks back and forth in little motions, and sings in a thin, sweet voice. She isn't like Dame Gothel at all. There is no ferocity in her, no madness around her, only a quiet knowing.

When she comes to the end of her song, she rises, leaves the hut, and comes back in with a younger woman. They show me my babies, slowly unwrapping them as if they are the most priceless treasures. The old woman holds a girl, and the young woman holds a boy. I don't have the strength to do anything but pet them. The women carry them out to be nursed by someone else, perhaps by a goat.

I drift in and out, floating on the lingering song of the old woman. It has no beginning and no end. From time to time, the girl comes in to wash and feed me. I keep thinking there must be some reason for all this attention and care. What do these people want from me? I will have to get to my feet soon enough. But my limbs are weak and I'm afraid to stand and walk into the light. The dark hut comforts me. I feel safe here. My heart thumps like a wild thing every time I think about going outside into the sunlight. Who am I? What story will I tell? I am nothing but a pale ghost, torn from her roots. The women seem to understand my terror. They ask nothing of me.

One day, supported by the younger woman, I stand on my legs and shuffle to the door. I can see nothing in the blinding, wide open space. I am not able to take in the light—it makes me sick to my stomach. My head spins and my helper leads me back inside. The old weaving woman, who never leaves me, nods and smiles as if to say, "That's good. Small steps are good enough."

Meanwhile, the women care for the babies. They take them for feedings, clean them, play with them, rock them, and sing to them. I look on, powerless to help. I don't have the faintest idea how to be a mother. Watching the old woman cradle the babies opens the gulf between us.

Memories well up from long ago.

I can't imagine my mother rocking me. Gothel raised things to be strong, so they would stand up to the fierce climate of the world. Did she sing to me? Never. If she did, the refrain would be harsh: "Do what you're told, or you will become as vile and as ugly as me."

I remember her bottles. She had shelves in her kitchen, built to the ceiling and crammed with glass jars containing liquids, oils, and powders. Many of their contents were brightly colored, and to me they looked delicious. Dame Gothel busied herself mixing liquids and powders and cooking them in a cauldron that hung in the kitchen hearth. She stood on a stool and worked at a high table with her back to me. She never played with me. I can't imagine how my mother would play! She was far too self-absorbed—all wrapped up in her schemes and stratagems.

She did give me a box of dolls once, I remember. There were six of them, and they all looked the same. They weren't baby dolls. They had perfect painted faces and full figures, and they came with a large assortment of fashionable clothes. There were no males, of course. I hadn't learned yet what a male was. I had never gone beyond those strange, retreating garden walls. I had grown to think that the walls disliked me, the sun hated me, the birds feared me, and the flowers would rather die than be touched by me. I was tormented by feelings that my mother would never allow me to admit—feelings with no names. My Night lover taught me their names: loneliness, sadness, despair, resentment, and bewilderment. We went over and over them, and re-enacted them in games.

When I was a child, expressions of feeling—even affectionate ones—offended my mother. They displayed weakness, indicating spoilage. Her disapproval terrified me. She was quite prepared to put me out on the street if I became too troublesome.

I remember one day in particular, when I was around seven. It was an uncommonly warm spring day. Blue sky and birdsong had given me courage, and the jars on her work table looked so pretty. I was dazzled by their colors—the twilight blues, cherry reds, saffron yellows, and peppermint greens. I wanted to get closer to them—taste them, touch them, smell them....

"Can I climb up, Mother, just this time?" I asked.

She was standing on her stool, stirring something in a pewter bowl.

"I suppose. But don't touch anything." She peered into her recipe book.

Excited, I dragged a small stepladder over to the table and

climbed up. I perched myself on the edge of the table and arranged my skirts neatly around me so as not to upset her. I clasped my hands together so that I would not be tempted to touch the jars beside me. The one closest to me was filled with a lime green liquid. I peered into the paint-pot pool. The liquid was foul and acrid; it got up my nose and burned.

"Ow," I said, rubbing my nose.

She ignored me while I sneezed a few times. I needed to blow my burning nose, but I didn't want to leave the table. So I just sat there, trying to sniff quietly.

Finally, I said, "What are you doing, Mother?"

"Mixing potions, if you must know."

"What are they for?"

"They keep people from becoming old and ugly like me."

"Oh."

My poor mother was very ugly and also very old. I wondered why her potions hadn't worked on her, but I was afraid to ask. She wasn't beneath whacking me hard across the face, if she didn't like what came out of my mouth. I studied her face. The awful stuff was getting up her nose too. A stream of snot was making its way down from her long nose, over bumpy skin, and to the edge of her festering, purple lip. She would soon need to use one of those handkerchiefs that she had stuffed in her pockets. Now I knew why she constantly sniveled!

"Get down," she commanded.

So I did.

My mother would later explain why her potions didn't work on her. She had been cursed with too many feelings. The force of those feelings had carved lines into her skin. They had twisted her spine and made her so misshapen that even her strongest medicines and spells were useless. She was evidence of spoilage—of what would happen to me if I were to let my feelings out. They had to be repressed, denied, and altogether dismissed. We had to remake ourselves in the image of what pleased others, especially those in power. If I didn't change my nature, I would end up rejected like her. That was my mother's song, and it was as pungent and bitter as the liquid in her jars.

One of the babies is crying. The old desert woman puts her reed weaving down and leans over the soft nest of wool blankets that has been made for the babies in their hammock. She wiggles her fingers over the baby's face, chattering softly. The baby stops crying, fascinated by the fingers. Then the old crone gathers her up and cradles her, absorbed in the baby. She falls asleep in her arms.

Now it is me who is crying. The old woman puts the baby down and puts her old brown hand on my chest. I feel as if she is drawing up all the poison from my wounded heart. It doesn't matter to her that I am unfit to be a mother or that I shed so many tears. Tears don't offend her. She understands that they are necessary—that they water me like a little tree.

As the children begin to toddle and walk, I too begin to stand on my weak legs. I resolve to make the long, terrifying journey out into the world. It isn't to make myself useful, though I am prepared to serve these good people any way I can. Nor am I venturing out so that I can be found by him. I have lost all hope that my love will find me. I stand for my own reasons. The desert is calling me. I don't know why.

Little by little, I step out into that dry, glaring wilderness. The people here live a simple life, relying on a nearby well and giving thanks for everything the desert provides. They live without wands or potions, the way they have lived since the beginning of time.

Rising Up

I rise from the depths of the hole, floating on the waves of Gangee's twinkling cloak. When we surface, I step onto dry, sandy ground while she continues to sail up into the starry sky. I notice that she's drawing threads from the deep earth and twisting them round her spindle. They are so delicate they can barely be seen, but every now and then, a ray of starlight catches the edge of a line. Beaming, she settles above me like a bird in the nest of some invisible tree.

The night sky is spangled in stars—diamonds, emeralds, and sapphires. Jewels above, jewels below. What is it the indigenous people say? "Beauty above, beauty below, beauty all around me. The path is beautiful. Ho."

The quiet in the desert is amazing. Tatatee's statement, "The ultimate frontier is a settlement," rings through me. I feel strangely settled. For once in my life, I have no anxiety about how I've failed or wasted time or disappointed expectations. I see that I made a powerful choice by allowing the emptiness, and not trying to fill the void or get rid of it. Of course, I continue to feel the vacancy in my life. Every time a new child is born in the family, I celebrate and grieve simultaneously. But out of the void, new possibilities have become apparent to me like the threads that Gangee is drawing up out of the abyss. I have woven a life together out of material I never would have discovered had it not been for the hole in my heart.

Gangee puts her monocle to her eye and creaks, "Oh my, now look at what is coming up!"

I gaze into the chasm and see a light way down below, at its very core. A single white star begins to circle, spiraling around the perimeter of the hole in ascending rings. As the light comes closer, I can see a figure carrying it, with others following, holding their own lights. They're glowing like colored gems on a string. As they come into view, I recognize Greta as the leader, holding a luminous white star in the cup of her hands. She's wearing a hooded, purple robe and smiling happily, her round nose and fat, red cheeks aglow. When she steps out of the hole, she holds her star lamp up to my face.

"I can only see you a little by this light, but I do see you, and oh, my dearie, look at you." A big tear spills from her glistening eyes. She wipes it with the back of a hand and carries on over to the fire that is crackling on top of the dune.

Others come up behind her, hidden in colorful, ghostly robes. They walk past me, up to the fire. First, a tall, sapphire figure, then a smaller figure in emerald, then a wee moving lump of gold, proceeded by a smaller mound of amber. When they have all gathered round the fire and I have joined them, the figure in sapphire doffs her robe.

It's Lucy, of course, and she tosses her robe into the air. It shimmers, fizzes, and goes out with a pop. "Well, here I am again!" she declares. "I thought at first I was a goner, but now I am not certain that I *can* go out!"

She looks at me with her buggy, watery eyes, and I wonder what she has been through down in the hole. She seems to have become saddened, or sobered. Maybe she's seen how much trouble she's been or that, for all her powers, she can't change her nature. Maybe all of the above.

Her clothes have changed. She's lost her tutu and now wears a long, leafy skirt that drops in sheaves to her shins. Her feet are bare, speckled, and rather (dare I say it) webby.

She notes my interest, sticks out a foot, and grins sheepishly. "I seem to have lost my tap shoes, by golly. I've lost my clout!" She flaps the webby toes up and down in an attempt to point them. "They're not very becoming, I daresay, but then I suppose, the point is that I'm *unbecoming!*" She laughs heartily, kicking her legs to express the kick she's getting out of everything.

Then the small figure in gold stirs, and Tatatee shakes herself out of her robe like a bird shaking its feathers to the wind. The robe goes out with many small crackles and pops.

"Yoo-hoo, you too," she toots, addressing the amber figure. Her happy little elephant shakes himself out of his amber covering.

"Well now," says Tatatee with satisfaction. "The revelation is almost, but not quite, complete. Let us now see you, lovely *you*." She tugs on the sleeve of the figure in the emerald cloak, and the cloak dissolves into the thin desert air with no sound at all, just as if it were a cloud. It's Willow! But not the pale, timid, ghostly white lady she was. Willow looks exactly like the princess I saw in my vision, wearing a blue riding jacket and a shining cream skirt.

She smiles at me so tenderly I want to weep. I can hardly absorb the love that radiates from her. I certainly don't feel that I deserve this affection. I was, after all, the one to dematerialize her. In any case, she is here, standing in front of me: all present, ever present, and real.

"I'm sorry, Willow. I am so sorry."

"You didn't drive me out of the world, Hope," she says sweetly. "Quite the contrary. You have made it clear that the light of love cannot be put out. We can only forget. And when we remember, we bring ourselves back to life!"

Tatatee steps forward. "What impresses us, dear Hope, is your *stamina*."

"Yes," says Willow. "You have stamina."

Stamina. What does the word actually mean? I am compelled to look it up.

Stamina. Consisting of threads, the warp of cloth. The threads spun by the fates. Native or original elements and constitution of a thing. Vigor of bodily constitution; power of sustaining fatigue or privation, of recovering from illness, and of resistance to debilitating influences. Staying power.

"So, you must continue your story," says Willow, smiling at me with shining eyes.

Rapunzel Speaks

As I gain strength, I move outward, little by little. It isn't easy. I feel safe in the dark hut. The people outside meet under a common shelter, where the food is prepared and cooked, but when I am in the hut, no one comes in uninvited.

Only a scattering of people remain here—most have left the village because the well is nearly dry. We are less than two dozen women and girls, with a few men, mostly boys and old ones. The husbands have gone away in search of new settlements.

The well is half a day's walk from here. Every morning the women make the trek, bearing their clay vessels on their heads. I have been preparing to take my turn. One needs a strong neck, strong arms, and a strong back. I am not yet strong enough. Even the old ones carry water. How I admire them!

I get up before dawn and go out to watch the women leave. They tell me it is not difficult to go to the well. But returning is agony. Each pot of water has the weight of a five-year-old child. If anyone weakens, the whole line must slow down and endure the scorching sun. I watch them go, carrying their vessels with dignity like queens, their colorful robes flapping in the wind.

There is little for the old men and the boys to do at camp. The women dig, gather, carry, weave, grind, wash, and prepare meals. The men swap stories or barter with the occasional traveler, while the children run around, making a game of everything. The women have no time for amusement, so they amuse themselves with everything. They sing to keep up their spirits.

They have weaving songs, grinding songs, milking songs, and trekking songs. Songs are their comfort. Here we are, cradled in song.

Now the water level in the well has dropped dangerously low, and what water we can get must be rationed. The burden of the vessels grows as their weight lightens, and the water is brown and murky. No one admits their fear, but it is everywhere—in the masked expressions of the women when water is mentioned, and in the tears they blink back when the children whine.

I have been in the desert for three years. My little ones are running around my feet. My daughter is like her father, quiet and dark skinned with searching eyes and a gentle, enchanting presence. My son is like me, fair and playful with thick copper hair that he wants to wear long.

I haven't met the husbands. They were gone a full year before I arrived. Now, more than ever, the women place their hopes in the return of their men. "Come back and bring us to water," they chant. "Come back with your water bags full."

They are not receiving any news of their men, and they have begun to lament and curse them. "Where are you when your children are dying?! Come back, you brutes!"

I do not sing for my husband to return. I have no hope that he will find me. If there is any hope, the desert holds it, and the desert is like my mother: governed by the winds of fury. I have never had a mother! And now that I am a mother, how am I to find her in me?

From time to time, despair takes me over. The madness usually comes at the end of a day, at sundown, just before the snakes and scorpions reclaim the dry land. I am drawn to a particular place a short distance away from the camp. There is no distinguishing the place, except for a small shrub and a shallow depression in the earth.

Here, the sand feels strangely soft. There's some sort of tenderness here. Here, I feel that I am touched by the desert, and the desert is touched by me. I have the odd thought that if I were to bury my mother, I would bury her here where the earth is tender enough to receive her.

More and more, I am thinking of her. I did love her. I loved her because she was so pitiful and because I knew her. I knew her desperate scrabble to get something for herself. I knew the loathing she had for the withered, fierce little burrowing creature she'd become. I knew her neglect, her constant busyness, her anxiety, her plotting and planning, her potions and brews. I knew her secrecy, the way she scurried from the sun to the shade. I knew her pain in the curses she uttered when she crawled up my hair.

Though I was no more to her than a means to an end, she doted on me. She could not hope to be loved—it was not possible, though it was her most fervent, secret wish. It never seemed fair to me that the sun would create her, only to expose her to such pain and humiliation. The cruelty of making my mother so deformed was greater than anything she could do out of the hurt inflicted on her by her ugliness. To accept the sun is to accept the shadows it makes. That is hard.

We are the same now, my mother and I. We are both uprooted and outcast. And here is the root of the sorrow, the soft spot in the earth. Here is where the tears spring up.

"Do I mean nothing to you?" I cry, hammering on the tender breast of the earth. "Are you so hard-hearted?" For a moment, it seems that I might break through—that the desert might let me in, here where the ground is soft.

"My tears are here," I say suddenly. "The water is here. It is here." *What am I saying?*

I go looking for a digging tool and come back with a spade. The sun slides under a wandering cloud. As the air cools, a strange spell comes over me. I have no fear of snakes and scorpions. I assume they are with me, on my side, urging me on: "Dig, dig!" I'm doing it for water—I'm doing it for us all.

I don't get too far before an old man approaches, leaning heavily on his walking stick. "What are you doing, my daughter?"

"The water is here," I grunt, digging in a daze.

"How do you know?"

"This is where my grief is buried."

The old man nods. Perhaps he understands because he is so ancient, or desperate, or because he is in the proximity of his own burial place. He leaves me and goes to speak to several strong boys. They find digging sticks and trowels, and we dig all through the night while the old man looks on, smoking his pipe.

The hole deepens and widens as a dozen boys drive their tools into the ground. It becomes so deep that we need a team to draw up the buckets of earth we've dug. Disgruntlement grows as morning approaches and hopes flag. The old man keeps casting his eyes about, trying to imagine where else the water might be. I begin to feel ashamed. The boys make jokes, digging into my humiliation, jabbing into that soft earth. Just before dawn, they come to a layer of hard clay. The boys give up and haul one another up to the surface. Only one boy remains. He lays his hand tenderly on the smooth surface and puts his cheek to the ground. The clay is damp and cool.

"I can hear it," he says. "The water is here."

Is it possible?

Three boys slide back into the hole. The old man brings a chisel and rolls it down to us. The boys drive through the hard crust, and right away, they hit a spring. Water shoots into the air, high as a date palm. Whooping and laughing, we widen the hole to make room for the fountain of life.

What can I say, about what water is to those who thirst? We wake every day thinking we must have dreamed the well. We stay close to it, fearing that the parched desert will become jealous and swallow it up. The children splash in the pool, laughing. Desert flowers are blooming. Reeds, date palms, and acacias are popping up around the shore. We watch frogs and fish wriggle out of their ancient burial places—hundreds of fish, blind fish, delicious fish, more than we can eat. Birds arrive from every direction—geese and cranes, wrens and finches. People are flocking to the water, coming with their goods and stories. Husbands are returning, and families are coming together again.

I have no hope that my husband will return, but I am singing. I am singing to my children, singing with the crickets and the frogs, singing with the water. The people have given me a new name—or rather, a medley of names: Well Woman, Washer Woman, Water Woman. I have never known such happiness. Even in my loss, or perhaps because of it, I have found my roots.

Henry Speaks

It's slow going following a blind man, but he's taken the lead. Even if he gave it to me, I would have no idea where to lead him, except back to the castle.

He's feeling his way. He might not have eyes, but his other senses have sharpened. He can pick up the scent of any animal, the movement of a spider, any change in the atmosphere. He has become a still point around which everything is moving.

He doesn't want me telling him anything. When he reaches the edge of a cliff, I say nothing. When he comes to a river or stumbles over a felled tree, I say nothing. I will help him if he asks, but I resist doing anything that will interfere with his mission or draw him back into the world he's leaving. I don't tell him the king is dying. I push away all bothersome self-doubts and thoughts of obligation. I just tend to the supplies, prepare the meals, and try to make him comfortable.

We hardly ever speak. I speak to the horse at times; she's a good old mare. I am generally invisible, and yet, in that invisibility, I'm acutely aware. I've entered his world. I move at his pace. I hear what he hears. Mad as it seems, we're both relying on horse sense.

Now we have come to the edge of the forest where the desert begins. Nobody has claimed this land. People call it the World's End. There's nothing here but a desolate shape-shifting ocean of sand. People have tried to cross it, but they've never returned. Legend has it that the desert wind is the fury of Old Mother Earth, who is taking the land back from Her conquerors.

We stand on a cliff edge, exposed to the vast, wind-sculpted sea. Grit scours our cheeks and drills into our teeth. The wind is full of shrieking voices—voices of lament.

"We can't go on," I tell him. "This is the World's End."

"Then we have arrived," he says, dropping down on all fours and feeling the ground.

"We'll run out of water in a day. The horse can't walk in the sand." I can think of a thousand reasons why we can't go on. It's madness to consider it.

"Find a way, Henry."

He feels the slope of the cliff. Sand and scree roll under his fingertips. He tilts his head upward in my direction, and his expression radiates gladness. His scabbed eyes are unaffected by the stinging sand. "She's here," he says, sliding his palm along the slope of the cliff as if it were the thigh of a woman.

I have gone as far as I can go. I can't follow him into the desert, and neither can the horse. I give him all the water I have.

I hand him a cloth to cover his head and a shirt that will cover his arms. He won't take the dagger. Doesn't need it, he says.

With nothing but a flask of water strapped to his back, he carries on down the cliffside, feeling his way like a tarantula, using his hands, feet, elbows, knees, and cheeks. When he gets to the bottom of the canyon, the wind captures him, sweeps him into her wild cloak, and carries him away.

The King Speaks

I have no fight left in me. I hover above myself, halfway out. Death is not so bad. Life has become tiresome, and the burden of a misguided man is too heavy to bear.

It is quiet in here, except for my wheezing. I am aware that there is something I need to see before I can let go. Some secret wants to be known. It bothers me, beating its wings on my chest. It wants me to surrender my mind. It won't come into view until I do. I have never been one to surrender anything, least of all, my mind.

Someone has come in—a chambermaid, skittering around, noisily trying to make herself invisible. She draws the bed curtain. Light splashes on my white sheets. Ugh. I see myself as anyone would see me. A pale corpse. A white, shrunken post.

She tries to feed me clear soup. I swat the spoon. I don't want the broth. I can't swallow it.

"Pull the curtain," I say.

Now she's adjusting the sheets.

Don't bother me! Take the soup away! Leave me in peace!

My wish is granted. There is that fluttering sensation again. What is it? It tells me I am not alone. Something is going into the grave with me. A dream. What dream? Think, man! The dream of the ages, born long before you. Oh, I see what it is.

The dream of perpetual youth.

A butterfly, the color of the sky, hovers over me where I lie. Shall we go to the grave together, my dream of perpetual youth? She flaps over my belly, chest, throat, nose …. She wants me to say goodbye—goodbye to the dream. Why? Why does it have to die? Wasn't it a good dream? Doesn't everyone want perpetual youth, a life without pain and suffering?

"Do you know what you have lost chasing me?" she demands.

I pursued her all my life, only to die chastised.

"Do you know what you have crushed in your campaign against mortality?"

Mortality. Ugh. I hate mortal weakness. I've never been able to tolerate simpering, whining, fawning, failing things. My breath is foul. She flutters over my face. What is she saying now? I'm too weak to care.

"Fly on!" I say.

She won't. She'll do what she wants. I never did have her in my grasp. How strange that she is with me, here in my grave. *Why are you still with me, my beautiful dream? Why won't you fly away?*

The Prince Speaks

I failed her. I will never find her.

I should not have found her in the first place! I should not have desired her! It was my desire that undid us, and now the sun is undoing me. It is my fault. I was not worthy!

There is no end to the fury of old mother desert. She will survive us all. When all her lands have been conquered, divided, and wasted, she will still be here, hiding her water, cursing us!

My own sweet mother, is that you? I don't need my eyes to see you! I have never forgotten what you said about my uncle, when I was just a small boy. He had taken your land and killed your husband … he had taken everything, and you were holding me, holding me for dear life. I hated him. I wanted to kill him! But you said, "Don't be angry with your uncle. Pity him."

"Pity him, why?"

"Because he cannot imagine how we have suffered him, and if he cannot imagine how we have suffered him, how can he possibly imagine how he is loved?"

I didn't understand. I cried, "Surely you don't love him, mother, surely?"

What did you mean? Why did you have to die? I can't blame you, mother. You died of a broken heart. But then I went to him, and I suffered him, alright! I suffered his two despicable sons. I suffered all their abuses and lies. But there comes a time when suffering liars makes you a liar, too. And now what am I? Nothing!

Take me, old mother desert! I will cling no more to your prickly shores. Show me how you suffer us!

She swipes me with her stiff broom of sand. I am her rootless scrub—let her burn me, and tumble me whither she will.

She whisks me into the setting sun, over the barren moonscape, cracked flats, and salt pans … driving me to the ends of the earth, sweeping me out of the world with her broom. Where will it end? Where will her fury end?

I am raked over the side of an arroyo. I roll down over sharp rocks and drop into a cool place. The sun ducks behind a cloud. Relief at last. Oh, merciful cloud!

She is quiet now, satisfied. She has cleaned her house. She puts her broom away, takes up her knitting, and sits by the fire of the sun. She puts me out of her mind. Or does she? I listen keenly. What is she thinking, sitting there? I hear her panting, her heart heaving.

A splash of water on my bare boiled arms. On my bare boiled feet.

Gothel Speaks

Cantata bursts through the front door, uninvited. She stomps into the living room and confronts me. "What have you done, Gothel? I demand to know!"

I do believe she's out of sorts. Everything about her is out of sorts, from the muddle of her hair down to the torn stockings on her bandy legs. She hasn't dyed her hair for weeks and she's got her arms crossed over her saggy breasts. I must say I do enjoy the sight of her haggy bagginess. Her ugliness is the best thing that's happened to me all day.

"I haven't been able to get my wands to work. What's going on?" she demands.

"I don't know what you're talking about."

That weird white cat's outside again. It just jumped up to the window. The thing won't leave me alone. It woke me up under the rubble. Didn't ask me, crazy darn cat; yowled until I had no choice but to roll over and crawl to the light.

Rats to cats. I can't kill it. I can't change it into anything either, not even a rat. What's it doing in my garden? I'm not your rat! Get out of my garden, rodent! How to get rid of the cat? I've been working on that problem for a while now. When I go out, it rubs itself against my leg. The other day I went into the garden to check on all the (mostly dead) flowers, and the cat was there.

"You better not be spraying on my flowers," I told it, "or I'll kick you to the moon." I couldn't smell any piss. It wasn't hungry. The beastly thing was just there. *Oh, screw the flowers,* I thought. *Let them die.* I went into the house.

I haven't been able to keep my beauties upright. The power is leaving me.

"Are you listening to me?" Cantata whines. "What did you do to my wands?"

"Since when do I have any power over your wands?" I said. "I'm no match for your sticks."

"Ever since you sent that girl away, they won't work. I can't get the spells to hold. Everything I've made is falling apart like your flowers." She stomps to the window in a snit and kicks the table leg, misses, and slams her shin. My nice iron plate goes clanking to the floor.

"Cursed table!"

"Oh, give it a rest, Cantata. I'm sick and tired."

"What's the matter with you?"

"You name it. Everything."

The cat meows at the window, and Cantata jumps. "What's that cat doing here?"

"Leave the cat alone. She's my problem to fix. She found me in the rubble and showed me out. I didn't see you mounting any sort of rescue operation."

"Where did it come from?"

"How should I know? I never saw her before, and now she's the only thing I see."

"Well, we've got to get rid of it."

"Good luck to you. Now get out. I've had enough of you. Leave me be to sit on my chair and chew my nails and figure out my next plan, which won't involve you."

"I want that cat," she says, leaning over the table.

Look at that. She's trying to slide the window up. I could tell her it's stuck, but why spoil the fun? "Have it your way."

Now she's wrenched her back. She bangs on the window with her fist, and the cat disappears—just like that. *Poof!* What magic is at work I don't know, and I don't care, but I do enjoy watching it elude that baggy old hag.

"Don't you dare give me whatever that *cat* has given you!" she says, all bent over with her hand on her back.

Off she goes, limping out. I hear the door slam. I can see her from the window, tottering down the garden path to avoid the cat. When she gets through the gate, she runs wee, wee, wee, all the way home.

The cat jumps back on the windowsill and stares at me with her adoring green eyes.

The days slide by. I give in to the cat. She can have her rat.

"Come in, kitty," I say one morning, opening the front door. She slinks around my legs, eats on my table, and sleeps in my bed. I'm getting weaker by the day. I can't come up with a plan because nothing will stick in my head. I lose interest in an idea before it's hatched. Leave the scheming to younger wizards and such. I don't know what's wrong, only that I don't have my old spunk. I stay in bed all day with the cat lying on my chest and kneading my sweater. She has her rat.

Meanwhile, Cantata is shriveling and looks more and more her real age, which is, in fact, at least a hundred years older than me. She can't fight Mother Nature with her spells anymore. Her own garden has died, and she has to do all her seamstress work by hand. She shuffles over with her long face, wearing rags the color of dried blood. She croaks at me in my bed, all sick smiles, yellow teeth, and rotten-eggy breath.

"Look, you've got to kill that cat because she's giving you something, and I'm sure I've got it too," she squawks.

"Thanks for asking after me."

I have no intention of killing the furball that purrs on my chest. I can't keep anything down anymore, not even water. I'm fine with that. It doesn't matter that my mother put me out because she couldn't stand the sight of me. I would have put me out, too. *Right, kitty?*

"I'm telling you, that cat's got some kind of disease," says Cantata. "We've got to find out what it is."

I stroke the cat. Damn, that woman's ugly.

"This house creeps me out," she says finally. "I'm leaving."

"Toodle-oo." And off she goes again.

"I know what you're killing me with," I say to the cat. "But I don't mind. You just keep giving it to me, and who knows, maybe I'll change. Rat-a-tat-tat. Rat into cat. I'll be a friend to you."

CHAPTER TWENTY
SETTLEMENT

Reunion

I'm seeing things. It's all rushing in …

I see the prince in the canal, feeling his way along a dry riverbed. Water from the sobbing sky is splashing on his arms and feet. The earth is waking up underneath him, rolling like a woman in her bed, stirring before dawn. He hears a rumble and clambers up the riverbank, his ragged shirt ripping on the camel thorn. At the top, the atmosphere has changed. The air is green, infused with vegetation.

Children's faraway laughter rings in his ears and a song flowers in the watery air. He stumbles in the direction of the voice he knows so well. He would know it anywhere. Even if he were dreaming, he would know it to be real.

She's washing her clothes in the spring, singing a washing song, sung to the beat of cloth on stone. She looks up, and sees a specter appear on the rise.

The figure wobbles in the heat waves, feeling the air with its ragged arms. She puts the washing down and approaches the hill. A returning husband, she thinks.

Coming closer, she sees that he is blind. His fingers are like antennae, sensing the water, the grasses, the advance of acacias, and the whole improbable hive of life in the desert.

Now she knows who he is. But what has happened to his eyes? He has embraced the night entirely! She reaches for him, holds his face in the cup of her palms, and kisses the poor, scarred eyes. Her tears fall on the sealed lids.

A crack in the shutters. Light slashes in, sharp as swords. He blinks. Light strikes again. He covers his eyes, crying out in pain and laughter. She leads him down the hill and they crouch in the cool shadows of a slender olive tree. She is holding him in the sweet flow of her voice. Color and form, long forgotten, seep in. He traces the contours of her face, her generous lips, high cheekbones, and weeping eyes. He pulls off her scarf to free her thick, untethered hair.

The giggles of children trickle in. A small pair, still new to running, throw themselves into the lap of their mother. She rests her hands on their heads. He catches flashes of her freckled hands, her muscled arms, her breasts loose under the soft shift.

She's telling the children their father has returned. He laughs softly and puts his hands together in prayer, aware of his monstrous filth.

The sinking sun dips under a cloud and casts a fan of rays into the sky. Little by little, the world is coming into view. It will take years for him to integrate what he is seeing with his new eyes.

A flock of cranes lands on the water. Beyond it, where the sun has crowned, his mother's castle can be seen on the distant mountainside, its golden towers and parapets gleaming.

For days I kept getting flashes of that fabled castle on the mountainside. I imagined all sorts of things.

I saw Rapunzel and the prince and the children making their way to the mountains. I saw people streaming to that glorious place. I imag-

ined a big wedding being prepared, heralds carrying the news to all four corners of the earth.

Invitations fly out to all the villages. They sail through the air like leaves from a magical tree, each one intent on reaching its destination.

A flock of invitations lands in the village where the story began. A letter settles on the doorstep of the house where Rapunzel was born. Rapunzel's mother comes out the door. She is wearing a simple blue dress and she looks aged. With difficulty, she stoops to pick the letter up. She reads it, clasps it to her breast and cries out with joy.

She turns and goes into the house. She greets her husband who is standing in the landing. His beard has gone white but his blue eyes are brimming with kindness. She presents him with the letter. He reads it and drops his head on her shoulder.

Her fading copper hair streams down the back of her lavender dress, like the departing rays of the sun. How beautiful they both are. Time has washed and softened them.

"Shall we go to the wedding, Jacob?"

"There are no directions, Kate."

"Perhaps because we are there already," she says, twining her arms around him.

I imagined all that, but I could not imagine myself in that castle on the mountainside. I had gone as far as I could go in the story. My feet were pinned to the ground. The sun set and the godmothers disappeared into a starless night. Everything went into stasis and I stopped getting flashes of the wedding.

Summer came to an end. Dismayed by the noise of the dirt bikers, and now the target of their hate, we put the farm up for sale. In the fall, we didn't go out to the country. We stayed in the city, cooped up in our apartment. Boxes of books and office supplies were stacked against the walls in our cramped living room, because we had shuttered both of our businesses. I continued to have limited ability to change my environment, and now we had nowhere to be but in an apartment that increasingly felt more like a storage closet than a home.

Winter arrived. Our little gray gambrel house in the country stood alone under a blanket of snow. It didn't feel like ours anymore. It waited for someone to come along and fall in love with its humble beauty. But no one fell in love, perhaps because it stood there, shuddering; abandoned.

When summer came round again and the house hadn't sold, we decided to try a new agent. We went to the farmhouse to meet with the man. He strode in through the back door in a three-piece suit, all business and high performance. He was followed by a dark-haired woman dolled up in high heels, a tight skirt, and a white blouse with a plunging neckline. They sat across from us at the dining room table. He presented us with a clear plastic folder containing house price comparisons and property values. Then he showed us the bottom line, a bargain basement price. He could pretty much guarantee selling the house in ninety days.

We drove back to the city with sinking hearts. What to do now? Shouldn't we just cut our losses and sell? It seemed like the reasonable thing to do. But it didn't feel right. The house was too precious, the land was too precious. We didn't want to treat it like some cheap tawdry thing, so we stuck to our original price.

I stayed away from the farm that summer. I didn't want to face the loss. I didn't want to be reminded of how much I would miss the birdsong, the trees, the gardens, the meadows and hills.

Meanwhile, I kept coming back to the rise in the fairy tale and gazing at the castle shining on the mountainside. Slowly, over months, the picture I imagined changed. Stars began to wink in, on the cloak of the sky. I continued to feel this sense of people and birds flocking to the castle, but I couldn't get any closer. Instead of landing me in happiness, the story had amplified my feelings of loss and disappointment. Is this where all my efforts had led me? To sorrow? Was Lucy right to think we had lost our happy endings?

What did it mean for the prince to be returning to his mother's land? What did it mean to me? In the Grimms' story, the family returns to the kingdom of the prince, but in my reading of the story, the land belongs to his mother. I felt that it would take him years to see with his new eyes, to integrate the new light. I would have to be patient. It might take me a lifetime to understand the ending of the fairy tale. It may never stop sparking wonder, I told myself. You can't expect to know a happy ever after overnight.

Then one night, I had a dream. The United Nations had created a prize similar to the Nobel Peace Prize, only it was called the Noble Peace Prize. Nobody in the world was considered successful until they had won the Noble Peace Prize. No matter how high they had climbed in society—no matter who they were—nobody was somebody until they had won this prize. Anyone could win it, from any rank of society, but to do so they had to come to a settlement. They had to settle scores, settle differences, settle with their pasts, settle with their situations. Those who were given the Noble Prize were said to have attained their full humanity, and when they returned to their communities, they were considered to be leaders, whatever they did.

The dream burrowed into me. One bright sunny August morning, when Ian was packing to go to check on the house, I thought, "What a dishonor you're doing to the land, Michelle, by not going to say goodbye. Face the loss. Settle with it. Go."

So we went to the farm. The moment we drove into the driveway, I started to cry. We went into the house, unpacked the groceries, and carried our bags upstairs to the bedroom. Then I went outside. I walked around the gardens. The grass had been maintained by a lawn-cutting company, and it grew thickly, gleaming green. The gardens looked happy, if a bit weedy, but the flowers didn't care. Birds came and went, flocks of goldfinches lit up the trees with their sweet chirps and bursts of melody. The hummingbird swooped in several times, buzzing past our ears, bullying for nectar. Nothing had changed. I lost time wandering around the gardens, kneeling here and there, remembering times I had spent in various parts of the garden, listening to the song of the jack pines, inhaling the sweet air from the hammock that we hung between the Manitoba maples. I went out to the fire pit and watched the setting sun turn the hills to gold. Still the tears came, freely.

That night I lay in bed and watched the full moon rise through the eastern window. It lit up the room like a lamp. I drifted in and out of dreams, waking every few minutes to wonder where the moon was as it rose to the top of the sky and then reappeared through the western window, where it slowly sank.

After the moon set, I got up and put my clothes on. I wanted to see the dawn. I went out the back door, through the gardens, and across the road. I walked through the field where the soybeans grew, thick and thirsty, dripping in dew. I followed the short path through a grove of cedars and wild apple trees, and came to the pond. Standing on a mound of earth overlooking the water, I watched the sun rise. It painted the sky in shades of mango and lavender and cast a pink light on the spring. The flush of warm air made the water mist. A kingfisher arrived, lighting on the barren elm tree that stood by the pond. The tree had died when we dug the spring, and it had remained to mark its own grave.

As I watched the kingfisher dive, a tightness in my heart let go. I loosened my hold on the land. I had no claim to it. I had no claim to any place on earth, not even my own body. Everything came and went. I could only be present to the coming and going, the gifts and the losses. In that openhearted state, I felt truly real. I wasn't imposing my preferences on life. I was taking it straight up, unfiltered by what I wanted or refused. Settling. That's where the story of Rapunzel ends, I realized. In contentment.

Motherland

For the last time, I have come to the hill in the fairy tale. I am ready to say goodbye to the bright world I imagined. As soon as I arrive, the sky starts popping with stars that are shooting in from all directions. Two bright lights drop from the heavens and plop at my feet. It's Tatatee and her elephant! He's looking very regal in a purple headdress that tinkles with golden coins, and Tatatee is dressed in her familiar red bandana and turned-up jeans. Before I can greet them, a big gauzy star floats in and Lucy pops out of a glistening bubble, formally attired in a high-collared green cape, purple wig and leafy skirt. Then Greta arrives, sailing down on the back of an eagle. When she dismounts, he soars into the sky and remains there, flying in rings. Everyone is speaking at once, gushing about the upcoming festivities. They aren't really paying any attention to me.

"What's all the excitement about?" I ask.

My question puts a stopper in their mouths. "The *wedding*,

of course!" Lucy exclaims. She gives me a bit of a worried look, as if to say, "Are you sick or something?"

"It is a tremendous event!" Greta booms. "The moon has found the sun—the night has found the day!"

"Yes, but I don't know what that *means*." I figure I might as well be honest about the final "happy ever after" scene. I don't want to leave myself (and you, my dear reader) running around wildly catching clues. I want something concrete.

Greta steps forward. "You don't know what the wedding means, after coming all this way?"

I have glimmerings. I've done some research on the *hieros gamos*, the sacred marriage of the god to the goddess, but to be honest, no. My heart sinks. Maybe I should know. I only have glimmerings.

"But you are coming, are you not, dearie?" says Greta. "Everybody is invited."

I can't imagine going with them, no more than I could imagine entering the kingdom of heaven.

Greta reads my thoughts. "But it is spread all over the earth!"

She peers at my foot. "Lift your foot, dearie, and set it down again."

My foot has been heavy, but now it is light. I lift it and take a step. Instantly, a white cobblestone path appears under my foot. It rushes down the sand hill, greening its borders. Grasses appear, lily of the valley, blue scilla. It races onward into the valley down to the mountain castle, as if it were late for the wedding.

"You see how the path is made?" says Greta, clapping her hands together. "With every step you take towards a settlement, you are already there."

That's what Rapunzel's mother said. Suddenly, I get it. *Happy ever after* isn't over there on the mountain side in some perfect heavenly kingdom. It's here. Christ said it, clear as day, in the *Gospel of Thomas*: "The kingdom of heaven is spread out upon the earth, but men do not see it."

And how do we enter the kingdom? By meeting our fate! *Fairies, fay, fatal*, they all come from the word *fate*. Fairy tales are fate tales, tales about what we discover when we meet our sorrows and losses. That's how the godmothers came to me in the first place! They arrived when I decided to meet my depression, and try to understand it. As long as I struggled to get rid of the pain, nothing worked. I got no help from inside or outside. I remember how hard it was to finally come around and acknowledge that I might be in pain for the rest of my life. But when I did, my quest changed. It was no longer about finding a cure—it was about finding a way to live happily within the conditions of my life. That's why Rapunzel meant so much to me. She sang from her prison tower, and she sang in the desert. She found freedom and joy within the hard conditions of her life.

It was amazing to realize, in the end, that these wildly "wishful" fantasies are in fact about embracing what is real. Happy ever after is attained in *reality*.

A star from far away moves in, increasing in size until it hovers high above us like a mother ship. As it descends, I recognize Gangee's old brown face and her starry cloak flapping softly around her like fins. She holds something in her arms, and when she settles on the ground, I recognize the little dragon from the cave, who was our host at our first meeting. He looks quite wild-eyed and frightened to be on earth.

"Do you remember our little friend?" Gangee asks. "He has wanted to be with you for a long time and now you are able to receive him."

Gangee releases him and he clambers over her robes to come to me. Poor fellow, he looks really scared. He has the vulnerability of a three-year-old child and the loving devotion of a little dog. He presses himself against my leg. I can feel a tiny pressure on the side of my right shin.

"He will walk with you from now on," says Gangee. "As you walk in an atmosphere of peace, you will discover who he is to you. He will not remain a gnonomous forever," she adds, settling back into herself. The little dragon looks up at me and grins sheepishly, as if embarrassed by his present appearance.

Gangee doesn't have to tell me that the dragon has no place else to go. It is up to me. I can create an atmosphere that will invite him to unfold himself, or I can deny him and turn him into a crippled, closed, suspicious and possibly even venomous beast. For an instant I glimpse the implications of an ever-growing and developing trust. Do we have any idea what beauty might surface in an atmosphere of mutual trust and peace?

"Indeed," says Gangee. "No one can know the possibilities of humanity, not even your godmothers. All we can tell you is that you have many gifts you have not yet received. Continue to cultivate a receptive atmosphere, and remember, the dragon depends upon your hospitality for his very life."

Gangee's voice resonates deep in the cells of my body. I am lost in the folds of it, thinking about all the gifts that have already come to me in the process of meeting my pain. Suddenly, Tatatee breaks my reverie with her thin cry.

"Look who is coming out of the dark!"

There is a commotion on the other side of the rise and Willow appears at the top of the hill, crowned in a wreath of pink roses and wearing a pearly white gossamer gown. She steps out of the night sky as if she were stepping out of a coach. Waves of sparkles ripple through the air around her, as she proceeds down the hill. Behind her, legions of sylphs draw up her long train and hold it in the air on silver threads. The air is bristling with multicolored lights as fairies excitedly zip to and fro.

Willow is followed by a crowd of little people—bearded old men, withered old crones, and caravans of gnomes. Scores of godmothers shoot in from everywhere, ladies of every shape and size, bearing their strange familiars: rocks and bushes, birds and clouds.

The fairy lights soar down the moonlit path and pop into flowers and grasses. The little people troop into the valley, disappearing into the sides of the mountain, the boles of trees, the cavities of boulders, stones and roots. They all seem to know where they are going because everywhere is home. Wherever they settle, the earth glows.

I don't have to ask the godmothers what is happening—the earth is being lit again, the stones are speaking once more, the trees and the clouds and the stars are waking to their own spirits.

It may be hard to believe that the fairies are returning. But they tell me it is a matter, not of perception, but of reception. So if a flower nods at you, or a star winks, or you meet an old woman on the street who has a message for you—let them in, the fairies say. The gifts are everywhere.

EPILOGUE

When I was little, my father used to say that he had never met anyone as fiercely determined as me. He figured that I could do pretty much anything I set my mind to. Well, that old determination did me no good when I was overwhelmed by chronic pain. My tendency to drive forward, and plow through resistance, only amplified the noise in my body. I would get so angry that I would start pulling books off bookcases or yanking bedsheets around, and I would provoke such a flare up that I'd be in bed for days after. Over and over, like a boxer in a ring, I'd get beaten down and end up 'Nowhere,' bewildered. What did I do wrong? What did I do to deserve this? My mind was seized by the constant drone of pain and all the noise of the emotions incited by it—rage, fear, anxiety, self-recrimination, and grief. As the volume of noise in my body increased, the racket muted every sweet signal of pleasure.

Intuitively I turned to fairy tales as a way of changing the channel, retuning my imagination and lightening my burdened heart. It was an act of desperation, really, but I couldn't live any more with the noise, inside and out. When I found myself "on the dark side of the moon" and got hooked up with the godmothers, I ended up getting a clear picture, if not a diagnosis, of my predicament. The 'serious effect' expressed the chaos in my system, largely created by the drivers embedded in me. Like many people in the western world, I was driven to be a star achiever in every department of life. Once I saw that 'star syndrome,' I was able to confront it and declare my overriding wish for spiritual peace.

In the 'mirror world' of the fairy tale I found my reflections. I was the princess with her bursting, broken heart, and the maiden singing robustly from her tower window. I was Dame Gothel and even Cantata, trying to force natural things into models of perfection that they themselves couldn't possibly attain. I was the dying king, surrendering to his frail mortality, and the faithful servant Henry whose love for the prince took him well beyond reason. All through the quest, I was the prince, blindly forging into the fairy tale to reunite with my own exiled self. To this day, my eyes keep opening to a way of being in the world that is radically different than what I have learned from my culture. It's a way of being here with my whole heart, and never dismissing it, no matter how difficult it is to stay true.

Somewhere in the middle of writing *The Tower Princess,* a friend called me and told me about a dream she had had the night before. She had been trying to iron the wrinkles out of a dress and was standing naked in her apartment, wondering why the iron wouldn't work. Then she looked up and a ghostly white lady came in. She went to the wall, pulled the plug, and said, "You're plugged into the wrong power source." Then she plugged the iron into another outlet.

Love is an old power, as the godmothers have taught me. It is not the brilliant genius of the mind, but a steady, constant source of warmth and illumination. It reveals us, burning away whatever is not true. It draws us out of our high towers, down to our humble roots, and back to the common ground of all living beings. On that ground, we are all spirits—human and non-human—living in a form, wearing a body mask. Every living being thrives on the recognition and appreciation of their spirits. I am left feeling that we have hardly begun to experience the reverberations of this very practical, spiritual love. Even now as I'm writing, the neighbor's black cat Molly has just left my room. She came in for a visit, purring so loudly that I still have the motor of her purr in my belly. She has left it in the space of the room. It is a lingering imprint of our mutual appreciation.

As a white woman of mixed European descent, I spent many years searching for a spirituality that would root me in indigenous wisdom, and I found it in the fairy tale. Our ancestral mothers, who carefully spun the thread and the patterns of the old tales, must have known their radical, restorative power. We have almost lost sight of the stories because, like the fairies themselves, they disappear in the blinding light of day. But they still hold their magic, and, like the shirts that broke the spell cast upon the swan brothers, they can still find us in our isolation, wrap us in their magic, and carry us home.

April, 2021

ACKNOWLEDGEMENTS

Over the years, this book has had many friends and supporters who have encouraged me to keep believing in it. Special mention goes to Annie Jacobsen, Anna Simon and Jean Sheppard who have been rooting for the fairy godmothers since they first made their appearance. I am grateful to my mentors in the storytelling community, and to all those invisible authors of the fairy tales who continue to whisper to us through the stories. I feel the presence of ancestral mothers between the lines, and many loving aunties. Finally, I want to thank my partner Ian, who has cherished me from the get-go, and has taught me the wisdom of love through daily example.

ABOUT THE AUTHOR

Michelle Tocher has been writing, telling stories, and speaking about the healing power of fairy tales for more than two decades. She is the author of several celebrated books, including *How to Ride a Dragon*, and *Brave Work*. She is also a guide into the wisdom of fairy tales who offers an entry through her website, **www.wonderlit.com**.

To find out more about her talks and books, visit:
www.michelletocher.com

www.ingramcontent.com/pod-product-compliance
Lightning Source LLC
Chambersburg PA
CBHW032029290426
44110CB00012B/727